THE
HALF-WAY HOUSE
OF FICTION

THE
HALF-WAY HOUSE
OF FICTION

Don Quixote
and Arthurian Romance

Edwin Williamson

Clarendon Press · Oxford
1984

Oxford University Press, Walton Street, Oxford OX2 6DP
London Glasgow New York Toronto
Delhi Bombay Calcutta Madras Karachi
Kuala Lumpur Singapore Hong Kong Tokyo
Nairobi Dar es Salaam Cape Town
Melbourne Auckland

and associated companies in
Beirut Berlin Ibadan Mexico City Nicosia

Oxford is a trade mark of Oxford University Press

© Edwin Williamson 1984

Published in the United States by
Oxford University Press, New York

British Library Cataloguing in Publication Data
Williamson, Edwin
The half-way house of fiction.
1. Cervantes Saavedra, Miguel de Don Quixote
I. Title
863'.3   PQ6352

ISBN 0-19-815784-3

Library of Congress Cataloging in Publication Data
Williamson, Edwin.
The half-way house of fiction

Revision of thesis (doctoral)—University of
Edinburgh, 1980.
Bibliography: p.
Includes index.
1. Cervantes Saavedra, Miguel de, 1547–1616. Don
Quixote. 2. Arthurian romances—History and criticism.
3. Literature, Comparative. I. Title.
PQ6353.W5 1983   863'.3   83–17300
ISBN 0-19-815784-3

Printed in Great Britain

IN MEMORY OF MY FATHER
HENRY WILLIAMSON

AND FOR MY MOTHER
RENÉE CLAREMBAUX

PREFACE

Beyond its enduring popularity as one of the great comic novels of European literature, *Don Quixote* is of interest to students of fiction because of the special, if not unique, place it occupies in literary history. As a satire on books of chivalry it represents in many ways a watershed in the transition from medieval romance to the modern novel. Nevertheless, surprisingly little work has been done on the romance background to *Don Quixote*. Those scholars who have referred to it have done so largely in terms of individual motifs, topics, and scenes from sixteenth-century Spanish books of chivalry which Cervantes may have had in mind when writing his satire.

Cervantes himself, it would appear, took a wider and more systematic view of chivalric romance as a genre. In his prologue to Part I he declares that the *Quixote* has no other aim than to destroy 'the ill-based fabric of these books of chivalry' (p. 30).[1] I have therefore sought to elucidate the distinguishing characteristics of this 'fabric' by identifying the ideas and conventions that sustain chivalric romance and condition its portrayal of the world. To this end I have gone back to its origins in the twelfth-century romances of Chrétien de Troyes. Cervantes would not, of course, have been directly acquainted with these French romances, but without discussing Chrétien's art it is difficult to understand the underlying principles of Arthurian romance. It was, after all, Chrétien de Troyes who gave the Celtic legends of King Arthur and his knights, the story of Lancelot and Guinevere, and the quest of the Holy Grail, the distinctive narrative features that made them so lastingly popular in the Middle Ages and beyond. But although Chrétien's art is difficult and sometimes enigmatic, it shows no sign of being 'ill-based'; on the contrary, it evinces high sophistication and is capable of reflecting experience in complex and subtle ways. Cervantes satirized the sixteenth-century Spanish romances, which were the distant descendants of Chrétien's work. My intention is to study Arthurian romance on its own terms first, and then try to explain how and why the genre declines to the extent of becoming a worthy target for Cervantes's satire.

Given the enormous breadth of the field of romance in the Middle Ages and the Renaissance, any attempt to describe the process of its degeneration at first appears daunting if not impossible. This process, however, is not entirely beyond sensible discussion, for there is a verifiable line of descent linking Chrétien's work to the Spanish books of chivalry. I have kept to this line in my study, excluding other areas such as the Tristan romances or the Matters of France and Rome. Even so, the development from Chrétien to the Spanish romances is not without its nebulous patches. There are for instance the fourteenth-century Castilian Arthurian texts—surviving today largely as fragments—about which we know very little. In fact, Spanish Arthurian romance up to the sixteenth century has been called a lost genre, and it is not my purpose in this book to embark upon its discovery.[2]

I have confined myself instead to a study of *Amadis of Gaul*, and this for several reasons. In the first place, it is modelled on the French romances without being a mere translation or a straightforward imitation. As such it exhibits new forms of narrative organization and technique which serve to mark its distance from Chrétien de Troyes. Second, the extant *Amadis* published in 1508 is a re-working by Garci Rodríguez de Montalvo of a medieval text and therefore represents better than any of its successors a development from medieval to Renaissance narrative practices. Finally, the *Amadis*, according to Cervantes himself, is the best of the Spanish romances, and it is duly spared in the famous burning of Don Quixote's library.

The first romance to be consigned to the flames was the sequel to *Amadis of Gaul*, written entirely by Montalvo himself: *The Exploits of Esplandian*. I have brought the *Esplandian* into my study primarily to illustrate the characteristic weaknesses and defects of late Spanish romance, but I thought it best not to tax the reader with further examples of literary ineptitude from other books of chivalry.

My discussion of Arthurian romance is restricted in the main to the works of Chrétien de Troyes, and to Montalvo's *Amadis of Gaul* and *Esplandian*. This fairly reduced scope serves to heighten the contrast between the narrative practice of the first major writer of Arthurian romance and that of the most influential Spanish practitioner of the mode in the Renaissance.

The differences and similarities between these early and late romances will, I hope, sufficiently illustrate the genre's degeneration and provide a new context for the interpretation of *Don Quixote* itself.

Don Quixote, I will argue, is best described as a kind of half-way house between medieval romance and the modern novel. By and large when I speak of *Don Quixote*'s anticipating the novel I mean the realism of character and plot associated with the novels of the eighteenth and nineteenth centuries. But, in so doing, I am all too conscious of the modern novel as a fluid, irregular genre, admitting of many variations, resisting fixed forms, and sometimes falling outside even the broadest categories of realism. Therefore, by calling *Don Quixote* a half-way house I fully intend the allusion to Henry James's House of Fiction, the metaphor he used in the preface to *The Portrait of a Lady* to express the protean nature of the novel-form: the House of Fiction possesses many windows, each representing the unique perspective of the individual novelist as he gazes upon the human scene. Creative freedom—from prescription, theory, rules, and conventions—is the distinctive quality of the novelist. For, according to Henry James, 'a novel is in its broader definition a personal, a direct impression of life: that, to begin with, constitutes its value, which is greater or less according to the intensity of the impression. But there will be no intensity at all, and therefore no value, unless there is freedom to feel and say'.[3]

Indeed, in the name of freedom, James warns against 'clumsy separations' of novels from romances.[4] While this no doubt applies in modern writing, there remains a very real distinction between the novel and the romances of the Middle Ages and the Renaissance. It is a distinction based precisely upon the issue of the author's freedom. Medieval and Renaissance romances were not at all concerned with the individual writer's impression of life; their purpose was more consciously didactic, in the sense of seeking to interpret experience in accordance with an authoritative and universal tradition. The winning of the author's freedom 'to feel and say' beyond rules and conventions, beyond even the reader's own impression of life, was Cervantes's chief contribution to modern fiction.

This book is an abbreviated and substantially revised version of my doctoral thesis approved by the University of Edinburgh in 1980. I should like to thank the Carnegie Trust for the Universities of Scotland for financial assistance in the early years of my research. I owe a particular debt of gratitude to Professor E. C. Riley, who introduced me to the study of Cervantes, and who has always been very generous with ideas, information, and advice. I am also grateful to Professor P. E. Russell, who read the manuscript at an earlier stage and made many valuable suggestions. My thanks too are due to various colleagues for their useful comments on previous drafts of certain chapters, in particular to Professor R. B. Tate, Professor R. M. Walker, and Mr B. W. Ife. I should also like to thank Sheila Rennie who produced an immaculate typescript, and, finally, my wife Susan, whose suggestions, criticisms, and encouragement were indispensable in the writing of this book.

London, 1982

CONTENTS

ABBREVIATIONS

The following abbreviations have been used both in the Notes and in the Bibliography:

AC	*Anales Cervantinos*
BAE	*Biblioteca de Autores Españoles*
BBMP	*Boletín de la Biblioteca Menéndez y Pelayo*
BHisp	*Bulletin Hispanique*
BHS	*Bulletin of Hispanic Studies*
BJAe	*British Journal of Aesthetics*
BRAE	*Boletín de la Real Academia Española*
CL	*Comparative Literature*
ELH	*English Literary History*
FMLS	*Forum for Modern Language Studies*
HR	*Hispanic Review*
JAAC	*Journal of Aesthetics and Art Criticism*
JHP	*Journal of Hispanic Philology*
KRQ	*Kentucky Romance Quarterly*
MHRA	*Modern Humanities Research Association*
MLJ	*Modern Language Journal*
MLN	*Modern Language Notes*
MLR	*Modern Language Review*
MPh	*Modern Philology*
NRFH	*Nueva Revista de Filología Hispánica*
PMLA	*Publications of the Modern Language Association of America*
RFE	*Revista de Filología Española*
RHisp	*Revue Hispanique*
RHM	*Revista Hispánica Moderna*
RN	*Romance Notes*
RPh	*Romance Philology*
RR	*Romanic Review*
SP	*Studies in Philology*
TLS	*Times Literary Supplement*

CHAPTER ONE

Early Romance:
The Art of Chrétien de Troyes

(i) *The Ideological Background*

Although the origins of the Matter of Britain remain lodged in the obscurities of Celtic myth and folklore, Arthurian romance narrative begins with Chrétien de Troyes and Marie de France in the latter half of the twelfth century.[1] The earliest extant romance is Chrétien's *Erec et Enide*, composed around 1170.[2] Arthurian literature undoubtedly owed its prodigious popularity to Chrétien's ability to fashion aesthetically satisfying narrative forms which celebrated the values of chivalry and courtly love current in the prosperous court circles of France. These chivalric and courtly values became potent ideals throughout the later medieval period. They were the twin standards by which the nobility of various countries in successive centuries measured themselves in love and war. Even though practice hardly ever matched the ideals, the latter were acknowledged and propounded by poets and chroniclers alike. As Johan Huizinga has observed, in an age where the action of economic and social forces in the shaping of events was ignored or misunderstood, the laws of chivalry were useful means of making sense of history in however restricted or simplified a manner.[3] Heroes could be praised, enemies condemned, and both natural and military disasters accounted for by referring to the moral scheme of chivalry. However, more often than not, chroniclers paid lip-service to the ideals of chivalry before proceeding to relate in the main body of their narrative incidents of appalling cruelty and treachery that flagrantly betrayed those very ideals.

This discrepancy between the recording of historical events

and the spiritual ideals of the chivalric world is of considerable significance for the understanding of Arthurian romance. It shows up a conflict between actual experience and the interpretation of history. By modern standards the interpretation of human affairs according to the criteria of chivalry would exclude far too many decisive factors to satisfy our sense of historical reality. This also applies to the account of the world given by Arthurian romance. The preternatural elements—fairies, spells, magic rings and potions—make for a remote and improbable world, which can lead one easily enough to dismiss Arthurian romance as a naïve, 'idealistic' prelude to a more 'realistic', truthful literature. The question to ask oneself is why so much 'reality' was excluded from the medieval view of the world. What prevented the medieval poet from noticing the discrepancy and adjusting his sights accordingly? The Arthurian world, which to modern eyes appears immediately restricted and implausible, held sway over people's imagination for nearly four centuries. It would be absurd to hold that this long-enduring fascination with chivalry and the Matter of Britain was due to a widespread deception perpetrated by a conspiracy of poets. Clearly we are dealing with a cultural estrangement wrought by the passing of time: we have lost that habit of mind which could relate experience to ideal realities without being unsettled by a sense of irony. Chrétien's romances will appear to be just a series of loosely connected adventures with no overall meaning or coherence of design unless an attempt is made to understand the author's motivation, the literary conventions he observes, and the ideas on which his view of the world rests.

The fundamental premise upon which medieval culture is based is that the universe has been created by a benevolent deity. From this follows the conviction that the universe must conform to a perfect design and an intelligible structure. If the latter is not immediately obvious it is because man's imperfections prevent him from perceiving it directly; to this extent the order of the universe is hidden from man. This idea divides the world into the visible and the invisible, the phenomenal surface and a subjacent order of reality. According to Marc Bloch:

In the eyes of all who were capable of reflection, the material world was scarcely more than a sort of mask behind which took place all the really important things; it seemed to them also a language, intended to express by signs a more profound reality. Since a tissue of appearances can offer but little interest in itself, the result of this view was that observation was generally neglected in favour of interpretation.[4]

This Platonist attitude to the world held sway throughout the medieval period even though it was modified and transformed by the revival of Aristotle in the thirteenth century. However, in Chrétien de Troyes's own century, there was a particularly strong renewal of interest in Platonism in the form of the rationalism of the school of Chartres with its predilection for the *Timaeus* and the neo-Platonism of pseudo-Dionysius.[5] The masters of the school of Chartres were interested in observing nature, its laws and cycles, the harmonious order of natural things which reflected the omnipotence of God. This new fascination with the world of nature was to meet opposition from the abbeys of Cîteaux and St. Victor where the traditional attitude of the Fathers tended to prevail. According to this view, the world symbolized spiritual realities: man's condition, as Augustine had taught, was rooted in the events of sacred history, in the facts of original sin and redemption; it was impossible to arrive at any knowledge of his nature or destiny through the contemplation of the natural order.[6] Nevertheless, the optimistic rationalism of Chartres led to criticism of the marvels and fantasies which had fascinated men of earlier periods. Attempts were made to distinguish between preternatural or miraculous occurrences where natural laws are suspended by the will of God, and the supernatural order of grace, properly speaking, which does not necessarily intrude into the normal operations of nature.

These two divergent attitudes to the world of nature were not always clearly distinct, but they reflected a tension which exists in Christian thought. The predominance of one or other of the two attitudes to nature was often due to a matter of personal emphasis in an age of great intellectual ferment and varied philosophical influences. However, in spite of these differences and antagonisms, the philosophical themes of Augustine's Platonism constituted the common property of theologians in the century. M.-D. Chenu summarizes these themes as follows:

All things comprised an order . . . the key to this order was at once the distinction and the intimate relationship between the intelligible and the sense-perceptible worlds into which the universe was divided. True reality belonged to the intelligible world, which alone was unchanging and which alone, therefore, was true. . . . God, author of this universe and this order, was the source of all reality and of all truth; as such he was transcendent, and it was his very transcendence which underlay his omnipresence. Man was composed of a body and a soul, and through these he entered into the two worlds. . . . Man's dualism had implications for the ways and means by which he knew; the soul had two faces, one turned towards the intelligible world, the other toward the sense-perceptible world.[7]

Symbolism was the means by which man could discover and articulate the relationship between the intelligible and the sense-perceptible worlds. The symbol was an instrument of cognition which was clearly distinguishable from reason for it expressed a reality which was not accessible to reason at all; it revealed the presence of God in the physical universe. The basic principle in this process of symbolic revelation was what Michel Foucault calls 'resemblance': 'It was resemblance that largely guided exegesis and the interpretation of texts, it was resemblance that organized the play of symbols, made possible knowledge of things visible and invisible, and controlled the art of representing them.'[8] For example, the walnut was considered to hold the cure for ailments of the head because of certain physical signs of affinity with it: the furry skin covering the shell resembles the scalp, therefore this part of the walnut was thought to contain a cure for wounds of the pericraneum; the kernel of the nut resembles the brain, thus it signifies its virtue as a cure for internal head troubles.[9] The invisible qualities of the walnut are indicated to man by the particular material shape given to it by God. Like every other created object, the walnut has been assigned a specific place and value in the order of the world.

Likewise, in human history there was to be found evidence of God's will in the underlying meaning of events. If the symbols of nature were fixed and determined, existing as they did in an already created world, the symbols of history, corresponding to the sphere of man's free will and the operation of divine grace, participated in the developing plan of salvation.[10] Natural symbols were susceptible of investigation, but a true appreciation of the symbolic character of history was dependent on faith, free will, and the refinement of spiritual insight.

The paramount vehicle of the sacred symbolism of history was the Bible, where historical events were narrated on a literal, denotative level, but possessed other figurative levels which conveyed their spiritual character. According to the tradition of Patristic exegesis, the Scriptures could be read on four levels: (1) the *literal*; (2) the *allegorical*, concealed beneath the literal, where the secular events, when related to subsequent events, evinced a sacred meaning; for example, the conquest of Canaan foreshadowed the entry into the Promised Land, the city of Jerusalem prefigured the Church founded by Christ; (3) the *moral*, which was that sense of the literal that served as a guide for the conduct of one's life; (4) the *anagogic*, which referred to the sacred truths pertaining to the eternal life, such as the release of the soul from sin to grace, or the redemption of man's fallen state through the sacrifice of Calvary.[11] Figurative language in the Bible enjoyed a precise, denotative status; unlike tropes in secular discourse, the symbols and allegories of Scripture were not arbitrary or conventional embellishments of language, they actually *referred* to things, even though these things might normally remain unperceived by the senses. Figuration, however, in no way diminished the concrete reality of the historical events themselves. It was through the inspired and authoritative interpretation of these events that their ulterior meaning came to be revealed. The symbolic mode, then, did not detract from the immediacy and concreteness of man's experience of either nature or history. It sought rather to penetrate beyond these primary perceptions in order to grasp their spiritual significance without thereby invalidating either reality.[12]

The philosophical idealism which flowered in the twelfth century had its social and political counterparts in the new idealisms of chivalry and courtly love disseminated principally through the works of vernacular poets and romance writers. In that century, the aristocratic classes began to refine the barbarism of their forebears by cultivating the values of prowess, loyalty, trustworthiness, generosity, courtesy and, especially, a disinterested love of glory as a sole motive for taking up arms. These chivalric values soon fell under two powerful influences.

The Church attempted to give a more religious orientation to chivalry by adapting its ideals to Christian morality and by harmonizing the quest for glory with the Christian's search for salvation. More decisively, chivalry was to become closely interwoven with ideas of courtly love which owed their first appearance in France to the troubadours of the South. For these poets love was 'the emotion produced by unrestrained adoration of a lady'.[13] Love improved men's natures and enhanced the chivalric virtues, and it was doubtful whether a man who did not adore a lady could be accounted a proper knight. As Sydney Painter observed, 'by developing this idea that a noble could not be a perfect knight unless he loved a lady the troubadours laid the foundation of courtly chivalry'.[14] In northern France the ideology of *courtoisie* was closely associated with the Platonism of the school of Chartres. *Courtoisie* became a philosophical as well as a social ideal, corresponding to the kind of wisdom or *sapientia* allegorized in the poetry of the schools.[15]

In the case of the early writers of romance, the values of courtly chivalry were incorporated in the creation of a poetic world set in an ideal mythical past represented by the Celtic legends of Arthur and Tristan that came to be known as the Matter of Britain. Exactly how this Matter of Britain arrived in the courts of France is not altogether clear. Frappier sees two basic lines of transmission.[16] The *Historia regum Britanniae* by Geoffrey of Monmouth which appeared in 1136 was very widely believed to be true history although it is now known to be fictitious. There were several translations of this history into the vernacular, of which the most popular was the *Roman de Brut* by the Norman clerk Wace which appeared in 1155 and was probably dedicated to Eleanor of Aquitaine, the mother of Chrétien's patroness Marie de Champagne. However, as Frappier notes, neither the *Historia regum Britanniae* nor the *Roman de Brut* can fully account for the particular subjects and adventures treated by the romance writers of the latter part of the twelfth century. The function of these chronicles was rather to confer upon the Matter of Britain the authority and prestige of true history: King Arthur could rank alongside Charlemagne or Alexander in poems and romances as an indisputably historical personage.

The other line of transmission must be sought in the popular stories and songs drawn from Celtic folklore disseminated in France in the late eleventh century by Breton troubadours after the Norman Conquest of England. Marie de France, Chrétien de Troyes, Thomas d'Angleterre, and Béroul, who each composed a version of the Tristan legend, all refer to these *contes d'aventures* or *lais* sung by troubadours on their harps. In Frappier's view, this attests to the considerable development of the Matter of Britain in France outside the more learned tradition represented by the *Historia regum Britanniae* and the *Roman de Brut*. In the hands of educated writers like Chrétien and Marie de France these stories were transformed into lengthier and more sophisticated narratives, the first Arthurian romances. Chrétien's fusion of the Breton legends of Arthur with the value-system of courtly chivalry and the neo-Platonist mentality of twelfth-century France produced, in the words of W. P. Ker, a 'revolution from which all later forms and constitutions of romance and novel are in some degree or other derived. It was this revolution . . . that finally put an end to the old local and provincial restrictions of narrative'.[17]

(ii) *Courtly Chivalry in Chrétien's Romances*

The life of the hero in Chrétien de Troyes's romances is directed towards two supreme goals: the winning of renown through feats of arms, and submission to the demands of courtly love. Since these goals are often in conflict, the central concern of the romances is the striking of a lasting balance between the public duties of the knight and his private obligations to his lady.

The public sphere is dominated by Arthur, the king, whose duty it is to see that the values of chivalry are maintained: 'I am King, and must keep my word and must not permit any baseness, falsity, or arrogance. I must maintain truth and righteousness. It is the business of a loyal king to support the law, truth, faith, and justice' (*Erec et Enide*, p. 24; 1749-55).[18] The knights at Arthur's court assist the king in this task. But, at the same time, it is incumbent on the individual knight to increase his honour by embarking on adventures or by defending the weak and innocent against evil. Glory and renown are the fruit of a knight's feats of valour, they are the public reflection of an abundance of honour. The pre-eminent proving-ground of chivalry, as Cligés informs his uncle King Alis, is the court of Arthur:

> I am not brave and wise enough, nor would it be seemly for me to join myself with you or any one else in the duty of governing this empire; I am too young and inexperienced. They put gold to the test when they wish to learn if it is fine. And so it is my wish, in brief, to try to prove myself, wherever I can find the test. In Britain, if I am brave, I can apply myself to the whetstone and to the real true test, whereby my prowess shall be proved.   (*Cligés*, p. 146; 4197-210)

At King Arthur's court, the highest knightly virtues are embodied in Gauvain. It is against his standard that Chrétien's heroes—Cligés, Yvain, Lancelot, and Perceval—are measured. On the other hand, there are negative qualities attendant on too obsessive a pursuit of renown. These defects are represented by the seneschal Kay, who is portrayed in the romances as a proud, vainglorious braggart, excessively touchy about his honour, and given to sarcasm at the expense of his fellow knights.

Knights can safeguard themselves against such moral blemishes by love-service to a beautiful lady, for amorous feelings, since they require selflessness, courtesy, humility, and loyalty, are spiritually ennobling. Chrétien, however, accords to love the status of a whimsical demiurge liable to strike quite suddenly and take hold of a knight's heart. Once smitten, the knight must obey the will of love as diligently as he must defend his honour. There is, therefore, a negative aspect to love: it can imperil chivalric honour by absorbing the knight so deeply in his amorous devotion that his public duties are neglected. Chrétien is not afraid to show his love-stricken heroes in a ridiculous light: Alexandre, for example, lies awake all night kissing a shirt which has a strand of Soredamors' golden hair woven into it (*Cligés*, p.112; 1615-23), Yvain is so terrified of his lady that her maid has to lead him to her by the hand (*Yvain*, p. 205; 1945-66), Lancelot becomes entranced by thoughts of Guinevere and allows himself to be thrown from his horse into a river (*Lancelot*, pp. 279-80; 710-71). Love can make fools of heroes and even compromise their honour just as the relentless pursuit of glory can turn them into insufferable bullies like Kay. However, the achievement of the courtly ideal of harmonizing the rival claims of love and glory is no easy matter. Chrétien describes with relish all sorts of delicate quandaries and subtle moral conflicts suffered by his knights as they strive through a variety of pitfalls, errors, and trials towards the realization of the courtly ideal.

The principal instruments of an education in courtly chivalry are solemn pledges and the recourse to arms. Both are means of ensuring that outward action conforms to hidden motives. Vows and pledges commit a man to his word, fasten his will to a declared course of action, and allow no latitude for deception or changes of heart. But if a knight should renege on his promise or betray his pledge, truth can still be established by resorting to combat. In the form of a judicial duel or an adventure, combat establishes truth objectively because its outcome is held to accord with the will of God. The areas of human life that are clarified by pledges and combat are precisely those where appearances are most susceptible to deception: the identity or moral character of a person, his intentions, the veracity of his statements, the justice of his demands. In the romance world, no less than in the real world, identities can be misleading, words unreliable, and justice capable of perversion, but unlike a character in a modern novel, a knight can apply the instruments of chivalry to right these abuses or to dispel doubts.

Courtly chivalry is, therefore, a system designed to maintain an order of absolute standards and ideals which is perennially under threat but which can be re-affirmed through the Providence of God and the active vigilance of his knights. The threat to chivalric order can come in three forms. It can emanate from an external source in the shape of a wicked baron, an evil giant, or some other demonic creature. Secondly, it can arise from an internal flaw in the character or behaviour of a knight, be it excessive rashness in the seeking of glory, or over-indulgence in affairs of the heart. Finally, the chivalric order is at risk from the mere passage of time whose indifferent flow may sweep away the standards by which men should live and submerge the eternal verities beneath a bewildering surface of false appearances. In order to stem the tide of time, knights must repeatedly impose established customs and priorities on the present moment. As King Arthur declares to his knights: 'You, too, would doubtless regret to see me strive to introduce other customs and other laws than those my royal sire observed. Regardless of consequences, I am bound to keep and maintain the institution of my father Pendragon' (*Erec et Enide*, p. 24; 1763-70). The seemingly gratuitous and compulsive nature of chivalric adventuring derives its more profound logic from this imperative need to defend the order of chivalry from the encroachments of time.

Chrétien's romances are, not surprisingly, set in a frame of nostalgic didacticism. The romance of *Yvain* begins with an evocation of Arthur's court where the knights converse with their ladies after a feast:

Some told stories; others spoke of love, of the trials and sorrows, as well as of the great blessings, which often fall to the members of its order, which was rich and flourishing in those days of old. But now its followers are few, having deserted it almost to a man, so that love is much abased. For lovers used to deserve to be considered courteous, brave, generous, and honourable. But now love is a laughing-stock, for those who have no intelligence of it assert that they love, and in that they lie. Thus they utter a mockery and lie by boasting where they have no right. But let us leave those who are still alive, to speak of those of former time.   (*Yvain*, p. 180; 12-30)

The present, a time of lies and treacherous appearances, must look back to a past age when the truth of men's words and actions was tested in adventure, and ancient custom nobly upheld.

The hunt of the White Stag in *Erec et Enide* provides an example of the chivalric world's reliance on adventure and custom as bulwarks against the ignorance fostered by time. King Arthur announces to his knights that he wishes to hunt the White Stag 'in order to observe worthily the ancient custom' (*Erec et Enide*, p. 1; 38). The arbitrarily proclaimed adventure in itself threatens to provoke a crisis, for whoever kills the White Stag is entitled to kiss the most beautiful damsel in the Court, but since each knight covets this honour for his own lady, the result is likely to sow discord in the fellowship of knighthood. In the event, it is Enide, an unknown and poorly dressed maiden recently arrived at Court, who is kissed by Arthur after he kills the White Stag. The justice of Arthur's choice is unanimously acclaimed by the assembled knights. Thus the enaction of an adventure which seemed pointlessly to threaten chivalric order is seen to possess the underlying purpose of revealing the hidden qualities of Enide, the maiden who will eventually inspire Erec to realize the courtly ideal. Custom and adventure do not merely sustain the order of chivalry, they plunge it into a crisis from which emerges a higher knowledge that will enhance and reinforce it. Without experience of adventure, a knight is unable to see beyond the surface of things. The young Perceval's failure to ask the Fisher-King to explain the significance of the Grail is an instance of chivalric immaturity; he observes the purely formal rule that a knight should not talk too much because he does not yet recognize the transcendent importance of the Grail vision (*Perceval*, pp. 92-4; 3118-290).[19] Adventure refines a knight's insight, it affords him the privilege of piercing the veil of appearances that masks the intangible truths of the spirit.

(iii) *Appearances and Reality in the Romances*

It is the continual interplay between the visible and the invisible, external events and hidden meanings, appearances and essences, that betrays the pervasive, and indeed determining, influence of medieval Platonism on Chrétien's romances.[20] It shows itself in all aspects of his work, major and minor, as a deep-rooted habit of mind.

Let us take *Cligés* as an example. The whole object of the romance is to resolve a conflict created by the alienation of social facts from moral and spiritual realities. When he takes Fenice for his wife, King Alis breaks a solemn pledge to his brother that he will never marry. He thereby jeopardizes the succession of his nephew Cligés to the throne of Constantinople. To make matters worse, Cligés and Fenice are already in love with each other, so Alis's treachery puts the entire constitution of the public world at variance with the rightful order of things.[21] The healing of this breach is the task Chrétien sets himself. He employs two strategies: Alis is prevented from consummating his marriage with Fenice, while the legitimate heir Cligés proves his moral and spiritual superiority over Alis by winning chivalric glory at King Arthur's court. The narrative ideas and devices that Chrétien invents to fulfil his purpose are based, both in conception and execution, on a Platonist distinction between sense-perception and essential truth.

Chrétien's first strategy relies upon magic. Fenice is saved for Cligés by the administration of a philtre to her husband Alis which creates the illusion that he can possess her when in fact he is fast asleep. Chrétien savours the irony as he gloats wickedly over the strange plight of a man who has become the helpless slave to a counterfeit sensuality:

And he sleeps and dreams and believes he is awake, and that with much effort he is trying to flatter the maid. And she shows great fear and defends her maidenhood; and he entreats her and very gently calls her his sweet love. He believes he holds her; he holds no part of her. But with nothing he is very happy. He embraces nothing, and kisses nothing, he holds nothing, and clasps nothing, he sees nothing, speaks with nothing, disputes with nothing, struggles with nothing. Well indeed was that poison prepared which so works in him and masters him. For nothing does he strive with such effort, for he imagines, and esteems himself thereby, that, in truth, he has taken the fortress. Thus he imagines it, thus he believes it. It is of nothing that he wearies, from nothing that he desists.[22]   (*Cligés*, 3309-28)

Damnation to a hell of pure sensation, utterly divorced from true knowledge of reality, is for a Platonist a cruel fate indeed, even though a modern empiricist might not, in the circumstances, be much troubled by the difference.[23]

Chrétien's second strategy also evinces a Platonist cast of mind. Cligés participates anonymously in a great tournament at Arthur's court. Each day he wears a suit of armour of a different colour and defeats various adversaries. It finally dawns on the other knights that behind the changing appearances—green, vermilion, white—it is the same knight who is winning these splendid victories. When Gauvain, the flower of chivalry, is unable to defeat the newcomer, Arthur calls a halt to the duel and Cligés reveals his true identity to the Court (*Cligés*, pp. 151-6; 4583-965). By devising this curious play of appearances, Chrétien expresses with force and economy Cligés' achievement of public renown to match his essential worth.

Even the famous puns and conceits in *Cligés* are inspired by a sense of the difference between appearance and reality. Chrétien impishly plays on the words *l'amor* (love), *la mer* (the sea) and *amer* (bitter) when, during a sea-voyage, the sickly pallor of Alexandre and Soredamors, caused in reality by the bitter pangs of their undeclared love, is mistaken by the Queen for sea-sickness: 'I think she would have divined the cause had the sea not thrown her off her guard, but the sea deceives and tricks her, so that she does not discover love because of the sea; and it is from love that comes the bitter pain that distresses them' (*Cligés*, p. 98; 539-44). Not without a characteristic touch of humour, the sea becomes an image of the unreliable, shifting surface of the material world which traduces the signs of a genuine movement of the spirit.

Similarly, in another well-known passage, Chrétien fashions a conceit from the near-homonyms *cuer* and *cors* (the old French forms for heart and body, respectively). Cligés, now reunited with Fenice, tells her that while his body may have been at Arthur's court in Britain, his heart had remained with her at Constantinople: 'In Britain my body was without my heart, as a piece of bark without the wood. Since leaving Germany I have not known what became of my heart except that it came here after you. My heart was here, and my body was there' (*Cligés*, p. 158; 5120-5). What might appear to be little more than a preciosity in the conventional rhetoric of courtly love, actually distils the essence of the entire romance—the severance and eventual renewal of the bond between the outward aspect of things and their intrinsic character.

(iv) *Marvels: Magical and Miraculous*

This Platonist division of reality into temporal and spiritual implies the existence of a supernatural realm in which reside the principles of good and evil. Good seeks a concordance between the temporal and the spiritual life, while the forces of evil strive to disconnect one from the other in order to sow confusion in the natural world. The presence of a supernatural dimension to ordinary experience is signalled by marvellous happenings in the romances.

These marvels are largely drawn from the store of folklore-motifs in the Breton sources, but the mythic material has been selectively rationalized and transformed by Chrétien. The *lais* of Marie de France, for instance, with their talking animals and metamorphosed human beings, remain closer to legend. In Chrétien, there are a good many marvels, ranging from magic rings, potions, and philtres to magical castles and kingdoms, but they are carefully graded in character and intensity, and subordinated to an overarching moral design.[24]

Jean Fourquet has observed that the episodes in which the mythic features have been least rationalized, such as the Joy of the Court adventure in *Erec et Enide* (pp. 74-83; 5689-6358), the *Pesme Avanture* in *Yvain* (pp. 246-55; 5101-768), or the Land of Gorre episode in *Lancelot* (pp. 296-301; 2014-425), are usually manifestations of mysterious evil laws which the hero overcomes.[25] In the Joy of the Court adventure, for example, Erec comes across a garden surrounded by a magic wall of air wherein the knight Mabonagrain is held in thrall to a beautiful lady reclining on a silver couch. Mabonagrain is obliged to do battle with every knight who chances to pass that way, and will only be released from his spell when he is finally defeated. His enslavement, due to a promise rashly made to his mistress, represents a strange perversion of love-service, recalling Erec's own excessive devotion to Enide earlier in the romance. Although the nature and source of these magical powers are not explained, the episode is integrated into the moral structure of the narrative, and can be read as a warning against the dangers of spiritual subservience inherent in courtly love-service.[26]

By contrast, there exist marvellous elements in the romances which betoken the power of good. In *Yvain*, for example, there is the ointment which restores the hero to sanity, or the magic ring which makes him invisible to his enemies. Both phenomena are providential and regenerative. The difference between the malignant marvellous and the beneficent, however, is that the former produces a dead-end—Mabonagrain is a prisoner in his beautiful garden, the three hundred damsels in the castle of Pesme Avanture live in servitude, and any knight who enters the Land of Gorre cannot return—whereas the latter is a means to an end. As in the case of the philtre administered to King Alis on behalf of Cligés and Fenice, benign marvels liberate their beneficiaries from intolerable restrictions in order that they may proceed towards the fulfilment of the courtly ideal. A distinction may be drawn between the 'magical', representing the obscure, enslaving forces of evil, and the 'miraculous', which demonstrates how the laws of nature are occasionally suspended by the will of God in order to guide the hero towards his destiny.[27]

The problem of how far Chrétien and his audience literally believed in the marvels of romance is probably insoluble. However, the distinction between the 'magical' and the 'miraculous' would conform with contemporary attitudes and beliefs. Even in the the aristocratic court-circles of twelfth-century France, a belief in miracles and the powers of Satan would not have been considered far-fetched. Chrétien, moreover, sets his romances in the remote past and in distant Britain where many strange things must have seemed possible. But whatever the degree of credibility they would have commanded, the marvellous elements are major factors both in the structural development of the narrative and in the elaboration of its symbolic meaning. It remains to discuss, therefore, how these marvels work in the romances, how they are, in effect, related to the more realistic elements, and to Chrétien's comic irony.

(v) *Symbolism and Irony*: Matiere, Conjointure, Sen

In the preambles to *Erec et Enide* and *Lancelot* Chrétien refers to the nature of his poetic activity. In *Erec* he states that one should 'strive to speak well and teach the right'. To this end he will fashion a very beautiful structure (*une molt bele conjointure*) from a tale of adventure 'whereby it may be proved and known that he is not wise who does not make liberal use of his knowledge so long as God may give him grace' (p. 1; 9-18). In *Lancelot* (p. 270; 26-9) he says that he has received his material (*matiere*) from his patroness Marie de Champagne and he will apply his effort and skill to invest it with meaning (*sen*).[28] Poetic creation is conceived, not as the invention of fiction, but as a re-working or interpretation of material which has been derived from other sources. It is the grace of God that bestows upon the poet the knowledge and skill to give meaning to this material by ordering it into a fitting structure. Since Chrétien claims to be doing no more than unravelling the significance of subject-matter taken from his sources, questions about the ontological status of the romance are superfluous; it is unnecessary to ask whether King Arthur and his knights actually lived because they are assumed to exist prior to the composition of the romance itself in a general tradition of legends and historical tales. Unlike later writers of romances and novels, Chrétien does not feel compelled to prove in the process of telling his story that it has the status of true history.

Chrétien's romances are thus organized on two closely related levels. In the first instance, there is the level of historical action, comprising the various incidents and adventures taken from the sources, but there is a second-order level of meaning to which the surface action symbolically refers. This is the level of the *sen*, and it possesses its own logic of development which corresponds to the spiritual significance that underlies the hero's career. The existence of this symbolic significance is not made explicit, it is suggested by the marvellous elements which, although manifest on the level of action, are not entirely bound to it. Acting as hinges between the two levels of the narrative, these marvels often exhibit a curious ambivalence which, as we shall presently see, Chrétien sometimes exploits to comic and ironic effect in order to create a double perspective—temporal and spiritual—on events in his romances. The double perspective affords Chrétien the creative freedom to indulge in irony, since it enables him to point to an underlying meaning which might elude either the characters or the reader at a particular juncture in the development of the story. Chrétien's irony, however, is *positive* because the hidden meaning it reveals, corresponding as it does to the designs of divine Providence which covertly animates the action, is always more beneficent than either the reader or the characters have been led to expect.[29]

The connections between Chrétien's positive irony and the marvellous symbols can be illustrated by his treatment of the lion in *Yvain*. When Yvain goes mad with despair over his broken promise to his wife Laudine, he is restored to his senses by a magic ointment. He then comes across a lion which is being attacked by a serpent.[30] Using the criterion that poisonous creatures are evil, Yvain kills the serpent first. He now expects the lion to turn on him but instead it bows and genuflects before him as a sign of gratitude. This in itself is an example of positive irony. Yvain's expectation of danger is suddenly contradicted by the animal's unwonted benevolence; a surprising reversal which, as with all irony, the observer appreciates with a smile.

The lion then follows Yvain devotedly and comes to his rescue whenever he is on the point of being defeated by adversaries. Yvain's lion, however, always remains ambivalent. In many ways it is a perfectly ordinary lion, hunting prey and scaring people with its ferocity, but it occasionally behaves in a fashion which belies its animal nature: not only does it bow before Yvain and accompany him loyally, on one occasion it even attempts to run itself through on Yvain's sword. Given these sometimes comical fluctuations between animal and human behaviour, what symbolic value, if any, can be attributed to the lion? Julian Harris has suggested that it is a Christ-symbol because lions were identified as such in medieval Bestiaries, but Peter Haidu has argued that the lion's comical oscillations between the animal and the human preclude solemn religious interpretations of its significance and might indicate, furthermore, that Chrétien's intentions were ironically to undermine serious symbolic readings in favour of a surreptitious realism.[31] But even though the lion may not be a fixed symbol this is no evidence of a lack of serious symbolic purpose in the romance. Beyond the lion's obviously providential role in Yvain's life, its various interventions create symbolic meanings in context.

When the lion bows before Yvain, for example (p. 224; 3388-97), its surprising behaviour serves to re-establish the knight in the spiritual hierarchy of the world because the lion's obeisance measures the distance Yvain has now put between himself and the animal state into which he had been recently plunged by his madness. This impression is reinforced when Yvain cooks the deer which the lion kills for him (p. 225; 3459-61), whereas his earlier practice while insane had been to hunt prey himself and eat it raw (p. 217; 2828). The lion's homage is also reminiscent of Yvain's original genuflection before Laudine when he first pledged his love (p. 205; 1974-5). But, curiously enough, at this point in the narrative, Yvain cannot recall that pledge because the madness has effaced all memory of his earlier experience. The connection, therefore, between the bowing lion and the bowing chivalric lover is apparent only to the reader. The lion's non-animal behaviour becomes here a signal to the reader that Yvain's renewal of his chivalric activity is also a step towards reconciliation with his wife, even though at this stage the knight himself has absolutely no memory of her.

Again, the lion's puzzling suicide-attempt acquires symbolic significance when read in context. Yvain returns by chance to Laudine's magic spring, the sight of which reawakens his memory of the broken promise and causes him such grief that he nearly loses his wits again and falls into a swoon. Believing its master to be dead, the lion takes his sword between its teeth, rests it against a tree, and throws itself upon it (p. 225; 3500-13). The effect is plainly comical. However, the very disproportion between its animal nature and its human reaction suggests that the lion has not been conceived in purely naturalistic terms. It is as if Chrétien were resorting to comic irony in order to accentuate the distinction between the lion's animal and human attributes. And yet, the lion's ambiguous behaviour is reminiscent of Yvain's own recent fluctuation between human and animal conditions, and in this sense, its attempted suicide assumes a specific significance. Bearing in mind that the lion's appearance in the romance coincides with the renewal of Yvain's chivalric commitments, its attempted suicide is, for the reader, a symbolic recall to the danger that Yvain's revived memory of Laudine's wrath might plunge him once again into an animal state of madness and despair, a form of moral suicide that would extinguish the knight's burgeoning spiritual life. Yet even on this symbolic reading the suicidal lion retains its full comic value because it is used to ridicule the spiritual absurdity of Yvain's short-sighted amorous despair. Chrétien uses the lion, quite startlingly here, as an instrument of parody, but it is parody aimed not at undermining the lion as symbol, but at the *potential* consequences of Yvain's recovery of his memory.

Although Yvain's lion functions primarily as an embodiment of Providence, Chrétien's actual handling of it converts it into a versatile and flexible vehicle of symbolic meaning. As we have seen, it can measure Yvain's progress by recalling earlier incidents, it conveys information to the reader which is unavailable to the characters, and it can even represent the potential moral dangers that attend the hero's actions. Moreover, the ironic oscillations between the lion's natural and marvellous behaviour indicate that Yvain is operating on a plane which can no longer be confined to the normal experience of the temporal world. There are new and unsuspected stirrings in the romance, as of a spiritual reality slowly being roused from its quiescence.

Symbolic values in Chrétien's romances are not, as in allegory, determined solely by reference to a traditional system of meaning which exists outside the narrative, they are created internally by virtue of their place and function in the unfolding of the story.[32] This contextual production of symbolic meaning is what Chrétien, I believe, means by the *conjointure*: no symbol is entirely fixed, nor is it decipherable by isolating it from the movement of the narrative, it is a grasp of the structure as a whole that reveals the underlying symbolic *sen*.

(vi) *The Logic of the Narrative*

Chrétien's art is, above all, an art of structural arrangement. He presides over his material with a God-like freedom to control and manipulate the action. In a sense, the real protagonist of these romances is the author himself, who in the guise of Providence orders the narrative in surprising and ironically unexpected ways. The characters are, in fact, secondary, their motives being conventional, their behaviour guided by well-established rules of conduct, and their feelings expressed in impersonal forms of rhetoric. The primacy of the author over his characters can, of course, be accounted for by Chrétien's portrayal of man's place in the world. For all their derring-do, Chrétien's heroes are not masters of their own destiny, they do not create meaning in their life. Instead they are subsumed in a larger, spiritual order which is regulated by the benevolence of grace and Providence. The logic of the narrative, in consequence, is based not on psychological motive, as in the modern novel, but on the workings of this supra-human order. Thus, although many crucial events in these romances might appear implausible or arbitrary to a modern reader, they find their justification in the freedom Chrétien enjoys to represent the interventions of Providence in the affairs of men. Chrétien, of course, exploits this creative freedom by contriving to remain several jumps ahead of his audience. He delights in setting up quandaries and impasses for his characters which he then lingers over in rhetorical musings on the ironies of love and honour before proceeding to resolve the difficulties with great ingenuity and even, on occasions, an element of impudence.

The logic of Chrétien's narrative art can be illustrated by his resolution of *Yvain*. The equilibrium between love and honour enshrined in Yvain's marriage to Laudine is shattered when Yvain breaks his promise to return to his wife's side within a year after an absence spent in pursuit of chivalric adventures.[33] Laudine's decision to reject Yvain is absolute and irrevocable, and Yvain reacts to the news by going mad.[34] This situation creates what would appear to be an insuperable impasse in the romance: the irreversibility of Laudine's decision precludes the possibility of reconciliation, and yet, without the love of his lady, Yvain could not begin to function as a knight and would be condemned to remain in his alienated condition. The narrative deadlock is caused by the theoretical interdependence of chivalric glory and courtly love; neither spouse can assume the initiative towards reconciliation without debasing one or other of the two absolute ideals. Since a resolution of the impasse lies beyond the powers of either knight or lady, it can only be brought about by an agency whose authority surpasses the limits of human endeavour. Chrétien is now able to assume direct control of the narrative, and even though his interventions might appear to flout psychological plausibility, they nevertheless conform to a logic determined by the possibilities and constraints of the chivalric system.

The first step towards resolution is the providential healing of Yvain's madness by a magic ointment. Yet after he is restored to his senses Yvain is unable to recall the past. This loss of memory is no incidental detail, it is a prerequisite for the eventual denouement because it enables Yvain to embark on chivalric action without being crippled by the knowledge of his former disloyalty. As Z.P. Zaddy has rightly observed, Yvain's blank memory precludes a psychological explanation of his subsequent adventures as a process of conscious expiation.[35] With no recollection of the past, Yvain is free to pursue chivalric glory with the disinterestedness which is the hallmark of true chivalry. But equally, Yvain's amnesia, because it circumvents the question of conscious expiation, prevents Laudine becoming the final arbiter of his destiny. Were Laudine to be the sole source of Yvain's forgiveness, the object of the romance would amount to little more than the settling of a lovers' quarrel. If this were to be the case, at what point would Laudine decide that Yvain had repaid his moral debt to her? In a world of ideal values sustained by the divine will, there exists a higher standard by which Yvain's rehabilitation can be measured. If reconciliation depended simply on Laudine's change of heart, the absolute purity of the courtly ideal would be compromised by the mediocre relativism of a sentimental accommodation.[36] The device of Yvain's blank memory is, then, designed to reinstate the quest for chivalric renown as an ideal in its own right, and not as a mere instrument of reconciliation with Laudine; it thereby preserves the notion of the courtly ideal as an equilibrium between love and glory.[37]

The twofold nature of Yvain's destiny is represented structurally by the interweaving of otherwise unconnected episodes. We have here the origins of *entrelacement*, which was to become the standard structural technique of medieval romance.[38] As in other Chrétien romances, it is used to counterpoint some duality which must be integrated in the denouement of the narrative. The adventures which follow upon the restoration of Yvain's sanity, namely his defeat of Count Aliers and his rescue of the lion, symbolize the resumption of his quest for public glory. This quest is, however, interrupted by a revival of the problem of private honour in the episode where he collapses once again after coming across his wife's maidservant Lunete, who has been imprisoned for having advised her mistress to marry Yvain in the first place. The glory-seeking is only now consciously intertwined with hopes of reunion. Under the pseudonym of the Knight with the Lion, Yvain defeats the three knights who had advised Laudine to punish Lunete.[39] But after this victory he refuses to seek a reconciliation by disclosing his identity to Laudine, instead he rides off to seek more adventures.

The pursuit of chivalric glory culminates, after further

adventures, in a spectacular duel with Gauvain at King Arthur's court. Having disguised their identities, the two knights fail to recognize each other and, although in reality the best of friends, they engage unwittingly in a fight to the death. Once again Chrétien has contrived an ironic situation where appearances dangerously belie the truth. But the irony is resolved positively: the knights turn out to be so evenly matched that they agree to suspend hostilities and reveal themselves. Yvain is shown at last to have attained the summit of prowess by having fought Gauvain to a draw at King Arthur's court.

One element of the hero's twofold destiny has been realized, but Yvain has still to be restored to his wife's affections. There being nothing he can do now by way of chivalric action to change his lady's heart, he resolves to go to her magic spring and, as a form of desperate supplication, provoke the violent storms that are unleashed when it is attacked. Laudine is greatly distressed by these assaults on the spring, so she accepts Lunete's advice that its defence should be entrusted to the mysterious Knight with the Lion who had earlier killed the three wicked advisers. Lunete, however, makes her mistress swear a solemn oath that she will do her best to restore the Knight with the Lion to the favour of his lady. Little does Laudine realize, of course, that she is in effect committing herself to forgiving Yvain.

It might appear peculiar that Lunete should tell 'little white lies' to Laudine, as one critic has put it, at the very climax of the romance.[40] But Chrétien observes that it is done without malice, in a most courtly manner (*molt cortoisement*, 6625). In fact, Lunete's deception is called a 'game of truth' (*geu de la verté*, 6624). Jean Frappier has inferred from the context that this *geu de la verté* was a society game practised in contemporary court-circles.[41] While this may be so, such an inference encourages perhaps a trivialization of Lunete's strategem which would overlook both the originality of Chrétien's imagination and the deeper narrative justification for the truth-game.

Lunete's ruse might be taken as the epitome of positive irony, the hallmark of Chrétien's narrative art. Although it involves a form of deception, the purpose of the game is to benefit Laudine *in spite of* herself, by making her appreciate that the admirable Knight with the Lion is, ironically, the husband she abominates. Because Laudine had set her mind so adamantly against Yvain, Lunete is obliged to manœuvre her into a position from which she can *objectively* appreciate Yvain's deserts. This Lunete achieves by playing off two axiomatic conventions of the chivalric system: the inviolability of oaths, and the reliance on combat as a measure of personal worth.[42] Laudine is thereby entrapped within this double commitment to respect the truth; any objection will have been disarmed when the identity of the Knight with the Lion is revealed. A persistence in refusing Yvain would now appear, even in Laudine's own eyes, to be a form of perverse self-indulgence, a moral error.

The economy of this denouement reveals the structural control Chrétien has achieved over his material. He draws out a thread left loose at a much earlier point, namely, the significance of the Knight with the Lion's defeat of Lunete's three false accusers, and now uses it to sew up the whole. At the same time, the truth-game conforms perfectly with the symbolic logic (the *sen*) of the romance. Having reached the peak of chivalric glory in his duel with Gauvain, there was absolutely nothing Yvain could actively do to effect a reunion with his wife. On the other hand, Laudine could not be made to relax the courtly principles on which she had based her categorical rejection of Yvain. With Lunete's providential trick Chrétien wittily resolves the deadlock without diminishing the absolute value of either ideal. The game of truth is proof, therefore, that the lightest touches of Chrétien's narrative artistry are profoundly motivated by the ideology of courtly chivalry.

(vii) *The Platonist Element in Romance as a Genre*

Love and adventure are the two major concerns of romance. Of the two, adventure is intrinsically more important because love in romance is always conceived as a form of adventure: the wished-for union of the sexes is never less than a hazardous, accident-strewn enterprise. Romance action is characterized by a string of trials, a long dangerous voyage, or a quest, in which the hero has to overcome a series of obstacles in order to discover something new, to reveal an arcane truth, or to achieve some goal.

The notion of adventure involves a sense of the unknown and the unexpected; the 'adventitious' cannot be foreseen and so represents a threat to the established order of things. Through its arrangement of adventures, romance plays out a conflict between the hero and the forces which are capable of destroying him. In overcoming these dangers the hero is able to slough off inessentials and discover what is permanent and irreducible about himself; he preserves his integrity and realizes his latent powers by dominating whatever accidents and eventualities may be thrown up by Evil or Chance.

The perilous nature of these adventures ensures that the hero is a man far above the common herd; he is therefore exemplary and often aristocratic. Narrative interest lies in the manner of the hero's surmounting the obstacles in his path, in his courage and will rather than in his state of mind. Since the ability to conclude an adventure successfully is a token of the hero's worth, there is little need to delve further into his consciousness or psychology. Adventures define characters, sorting them out into fairly simple moral categories of good and evil, courageous and cowardly, upright and base.

This defining virtue of adventures makes them the principal source of meaning. As the characters are judged by their performance, their adventures acquire symbolic value. Different adventures may signify different levels of attainment and their often discontinuous arrangement in the narrative gradually reveals an underlying design that informs the outward behaviour of the characters with symbolic significance. In his organization of the narrative the romance author is able to play God or Providence; he structures the characters' experience through coincidences, reversals, sudden discoveries, *deus ex machina* devices and other procedures which need not be psychologically plausible nor represent time and space in a verisimilar way.[43] It is the order of the narrative that counts, and by understanding that order the hero fulfils himself and realizes his quest.

Adventure, then, even in its most elementary form, is important because it postulates problems of identity and destiny.[44] It is no accidental detail that in three out of five

Chrétien romances the hero's identity is either hidden or unknown for about half the duration of the narrative. The reader does not learn Lancelot's name until line 3660; Perceval is utterly anonymous, ignorant even of his own name, until line 3561; Yvain loses all sense of self during his period of madness in the wilderness and thereafter calls himself The Knight with the Lion, a surrogate identity which he only finally discards when Laudine agrees to forgive him. The hero's achievement of a stable identity amounts to the fulfilment of his destiny.

Romance recounts the vicissitudes of exceptional men confronting the evils of non-being, striving to exist on a plane beyond temporal contingency. Erich Auerbach has observed that:

Except feats of arms and love, nothing can occur in the courtly world—and even these two are of a special sort: they are not occurrences or emotions which can be absent for a time; they are permanently connected with the person of the perfect knight, they are part of his definition, so that he cannot for one moment be without adventure in arms, nor for one moment without amorous entanglement. If he could, he would lose himself and no longer be a knight.[45]

This heightened state of vigilance accounts for the intensity and remoteness of the romance world. It is a world which 'is sustained by its own inherent, often obsessive laws'.[46] By means of these laws the hero comes to appreciate and understand his destiny; they enshrine objective standards of absolute truth which, if adhered to, will lead the hero, via the shedding of false, distorting illusions about himself and the world, to the realization of the essence of his experience.

Romance is therefore expressed on two levels, representing everyday mutable experience on the one hand and the unchanging world of ideals on the other.[47] It can acknowledge the contradictions and perplexities of temporal experience, but in contrast to the modern novel, these existential difficulties are perceived to be susceptible of solution when properly related to another, transcendent order of reality. Through the mediation of symbols and marvels, romance creates a mysterious traffic between the material world and the spiritual; its heroes operate on that elusive borderline between two worlds, attempting to cross from one to the other through a prolonged inward trial symbolized often by the traversing of perilous regions like a forest, a wilderness, or the sea.

In the twelfth century Chrétien de Troyes used the marvels of Celtic myth as symbolic pointers to the world that transcends nature. The fairy Other World of Celtic mythology thus came to function poetically as the spiritual realm of Christian Platonism, with the code of courtly chivalry serving as the ethical system that guides the hero in his passage from temporal experience to true knowledge.[48] A form of attenuated Platonism is, after all, inherent in the ideology of courtly chivalry: both sexual love and military glory are so highly prized precisely because they are deemed to be outward signs of metaphysical realities.[49] In *Cligés*, Arthurian chivalry is represented as the means of spiritual refinement for the rulers of an otherwise barbarous and unjust Oriental empire. In other romances of Chrétien, however, a more sustained analogy is drawn between the knight's struggle to realize the ideal of courtly chivalry and a process of spiritual perfection. The analogy is given structural expression in both *Erec et Enide* and *Yvain*, where the narrative is divided into two major sections: the first gives an account of the hero's achievement of the requisite courtly harmony between love and glory, whereas in the second, this harmony is destroyed and has to be laboriously regained at a more profound and implicitly spiritual level. The analogy between temporal and spiritual knighthood is most fully developed in the *Conte du Graal*. After Perceval's triumphant reception at Arthur's court, signalling his achievement of chivalric glory, the hero's subsequent adventures are given a very explicit Christian significance, and counterpointed structurally with those of Gauvain who still performs feats of purely temporal import.

The one, glaring exception is, of course, *Lancelot*, where the motif of adultery between the Queen and the hero has been inherited, as in the case of the *Tristan* romances, from the Celtic sources. Here the adulterous passion of the courtly hero precludes the full assimilation of Celtic themes to Christian Platonism. By contrast *Erec et Enide*, *Cligés*, and *Yvain* commend marriage as the proper condition for lovers. Indeed, in *Cligés*, Chrétien refers disparagingly on several occasions to the

Tristan legend and uses magic, not as a catalyst of adultery, but as a means of preventing a similarly irrevocable fate befalling Cligés and Fenice. Just as *Cligés* can be read as an anti-*Tristan*, so can *Yvain*, composed either concurrently with or after *Lancelot*, be considered an antidote to the ruinous adultery of Lancelot and Guinevere.[50]

The romance of *Lancelot*, which Chrétien significantly left unfinished, illustrates the importance of Platonism for the stability and cogency of Chrétien's romance world. The negative ironies generated by Lancelot's adultery are as repugnant to Chrétien's interpretation of courtly chivalry as they are to Christian belief.[51] In fact, Lancelot's illicit, not to say treasonable, passion threatens to empty chivalric ideology of all meaning because it disrupts the vital correspondence between military prowess and personal honour. When Lancelot, for instance, fights Meleagant in order to defend the honour of Guinevere, who has been accused of having slept with Kay, he is upholding a casuistic version of the truth since it was he, Lancelot, who had actually spent a night with the Queen (pp. 332-3; 4971-84). The apparent cynicism of Lancelot's action gravely jeopardizes the Arthurian world's claim to derive spiritual values from armed combat. *Lancelot* shows that for Chrétien's romances to function coherently, the ironies latent in the appearance–reality dichotomy must be prevented from getting out of hand and destroying the validity, not only of the instrumental values of chivalry such as pledges and armed combat, but also of the central, organizing concepts of honour, loyalty, and the spiritually ennobling effects of love.

Lancelot remains a puzzle to critics. Most would agree with Jean Frappier that it constitutes an anomaly among Chrétien's romances, possibly the result of an uncongenial request by his patroness Marie de Champagne to re-work the Celtic legend.[52] Most recently, *Lancelot* has been interpreted as a manifestation of the medieval notion of the world upside-down, a deliberate inversion of Christian values designed to alert the audience to the spiritual perils attendant upon the pursuit of an exclusively temporal form of chivalry.[53]

Indeed, the story of Lancelot and Guinevere fascinated and troubled the medieval imagination. With the Grail-Quest, it came to form the core of the Arthurian tradition. In the thirteenth century whole cycles of romances appeared based around the story, as if in an effort to contain its powerfully subversive, pagan ironies within an orthodox Christian explanation of the world.[54]

CHAPTER TWO

Late Romance:
Amadis of Gaul and *Esplandian*

(i) *Allegory and History in French Prose Romances*

The romances of the thirteenth century, although composed
not long after Chrétien's time, are quite different in form and
spirit. To begin with they are far longer and involve many more
central characters on a much broader canvas. Eugène Vinaver
attributes this largely to the revival of the chronicle material of
Geoffrey of Monmouth's *Historia regum Britanniae* dealing with
the earlier history of Arthur's kingdom.[1] But even though these
writers had the same ultimate purpose as Chrétien, which was
to elucidate the spiritual significance of the Matter of Britain,
they evolved different narrative methods which reflect new
concerns.

These developments in Arthurian romance may be partly
explained by a change of milieu from the courtly, aristocratic
circles of Chrétien to the religious atmosphere of the
monastery, where an interest in orthodoxy and didactic clarity
led to a further Christianization of the mythic elements of
romance in order to render the stories more accessible to a
wider audience outside the aristocracy. Chrétien had sought to
create a poetic analogy between courtly chivalry and Christian
Platonism by using the marvels of myth as symbolic hinges
between two orders of reality, but now the link was forged
directly in historical time. For instance, the mysterious Grail,
originally a Celtic mythic motif, becomes the vessel of the Last
Supper in which Joseph of Arimathea collected Christ's blood
after the Crucifixion.

This historical connection between the life of Christ and
King Arthur's court is first made in Robert de Boron's trilogy of

verse romances where the pre-history of Arthur's kingdom is related using material from Geoffrey of Monmouth's chronicle.[2] Only the *Joseph* and part of the *Merlin* are extant. In the former is told the story of Joseph of Arimathea's salvaging the Holy Grail, and its subsequent tortuous journey to Britain. The second romance introduces Merlin, mage and enchanter, who knows the past and can see into the future. Possessing the secret of Joseph and the Holy Grail, Merlin becomes the magical protector of the Kings of Britain. The third part of the trilogy, surviving only in a *remaniement* known as the Didot *Perceval*, relates how Perceval completed the adventure of the Grail and how Arthur's kingdom was destroyed through Mordred's betrayal.

Already in Robert de Boron's trilogy one finds the new thirteenth-century interest in chronicling the total history of the Arthurian world instead of relating the story of a single knight. Arthurian romance is beginning to change from the symbolic ordering of individual experience to the portrayal of a microcosm of history where Christian truths can be shown to operate in the unfolding of a collective destiny over a large span of time. Thus in the next series of romances, the Vulgate Cycle, the major heterodox element in Chrétien's civilized world of courtly chivalry—Lancelot's adulterous love of Guinevere—is fitted into the picture of Christian history. Where Chrétien had attempted to harmonize earthly and spiritual chivalry, the clerical writers of the Vulgate Cycle created a conflict between the two and bypassed the conceptual and moral difficulties inherent in the pagan legend of Lancelot's adultery. Under this new dispensation courtly love is profane and must be renounced in favour of the search for union with God. By combining the theme of Lancelot's love affair with the story of the Grail, the Vulgate authors strove to organize the Matter of Britain into an orthodox pattern of Christian experience of sin, punishment, repentance, atonement, and salvation.

Nevertheless, contradictions between the ideals of courtly chivalry and Christian doctrine survive in the Vulgate Cycle. Although the three principal Vulgate romances, consisting of the *Lancelot*, the *Queste del Saint Graal* and the *Mort Artu* (collectively known as the Prose *Lancelot*) are linked by a network of analogies and forecasts, the allurements of courtly chivalry have not been decisively renounced.[3] The first part of the Prose *Lancelot* trilogy is modelled on Chrétien's *Chevalier de la Charrette* and retains much of the twelfth-century idealization of courtly love: Lancelot and Guinevere's passion is still an ennobling experience, and Lancelot is an admirable and honourable knight. It is in the *Queste del Saint Graal*, believed to have been written by a monk of the flourishing Cistercian order, that courtly love has become unambiguously sinful. The trappings of the Arthurian world are preserved—there are knights errant who embark on adventure and fall in love with ladies—but the marvels derived from the Celtic legends are converted into the familiar currency of the Christian symbolic tradition.[4] The Grail is by now established as a symbol of grace, and its first appearance at Camelot is reminiscent of Pentecost. The Siege Perilous and the sword in the stone symbolize the coming of the new Messiah. Even the adventures of individual knights become spiritual journeys whose significance is revealed in visions, or interpreted by hermits. In this religious scheme of things Lancelot, spiritually blinded by concupiscence, is unable to discover the Holy Grail, which is revealed instead to the ascetic Galahad.

When one turns from the *Queste* to the *Mort Artu* the religious allegory yields to what Frappier called a 'climate of Greek tragedy'.[5] Here is described Lancelot's relapse into sin with Guinevere, the treachery of Arthur's bastard son Mordred, the mortal enmity between Gawain and Lancelot, Arthur's final battle at Salisbury Plain, his death, and the destruction of the kingdom of Logres. Such calamities, of course, spell the utter dissolution of the Arthurian romance world as it might have been conceived by Chrétien de Troyes.

All the most fundamental premisses of romance seem to be systematically destroyed. In the first place, God has withdrawn his protection from Arthur's court after the quest for the Holy Grail has ended, and this removes the linchpin of the whole romance system. Second, the beneficent agency of Providence, which played such an important part in guiding the steps of Chrétien's heroes, is here replaced by the vagaries of the Wheel of Fortune which swings against Arthur who, it is said, has risen too high in success and fame. Third, there is a conflict between two loyalties, Lancelot's love of Guinevere and his obligations to Arthur and Gawain. Now in Chrétien, as we have seen, this is precisely the sort of conflict that the whole romance was designed to resolve, but here in the *Mort Artu* it proves to be insoluble and the processes of romance are rendered ineffective. Finally, Arthur is killed by his own son Mordred whom he had fathered in incest. Such a sin would have been inconceivable in Chrétien, where Arthur was a pillar of moral authority, and where the faults of the knights were infractions of a subtle code rather than such heinous carnal extravagances as incest.

The process of rationalizing Celtic myth into a Christian structure and presenting it as true history is completed in the Post-Vulgate Cycle, known as the *Roman du Graal* or the 'Pseudo-Robert de Boron' cycle, and consisting of a revision of the Vulgate romances combined with material from the First Version of the Prose *Tristan*. The *Roman du Graal* has not been preserved in its entirety but, as Fanni Bogdanow has demonstrated, it constituted a 'new Arthuriad', a well-knit, unified account of the rise and fall of the kingdom of Logres.[6] It is significant that the story of Lancelot's adultery is vastly reduced in importance: there is no branch which corresponds to the actual *Lancelot* of the Vulgate Cycle. This is further evidence of doctrinal consolidation in so far as it extinguishes the light-hearted spirit of courtly love that survived from the twelfth century in the Vulgate *Lancelot*. Now the Lancelot story is cut down to size and treated with due moral consistency. Thus in the *Roman du Graal* the miscellany of Breton *contes* that made up the Matter of Britain is at last welded into a coherent whole and transformed into an awesome mirror of history under the aspect of a Christian God.

This long and elaborate evolution of Arthurian romance in the early thirteenth century was undertaken in a constructive spirit, responding as it did to a desire to eliminate inconsistencies, resolve contradictions, and fill gaps in earlier material. Vinaver has given an excellent example of this process of elaboration at work in the Grail stories after Chrétien's *Perceval*.[7] There are three motifs in Chrétien's unfinished original—the wounded king, a miraculous weapon, and a land laid waste—which are not linked in a coherent sequence. Perceval sees an old man in the castle and is later informed that it is the Fisher-King who has been wounded in battle. The reader is subsequently told that Perceval's failure to ask the question expected of him has prolonged the king's agony and inflicted untold misery upon his land. The Wasteland theme proper only occurs in connection with one of Gawain's adventures when an anonymous character predicts that the kingdom of Logres will be laid waste by a mysterious lance. Chrétien's text does not in any way associate this lance with the one Perceval saw in the Grail castle.

However, in the First Continuation of Chrétien's unfinished version, the new author connects the Wasteland and the maimed King by having Gawain find a weapon lying broken upon the body of a dead man. When he asks the right question, as Perceval signally failed to do earlier, the land regains part of its fertility. These three motifs recur in the Vulgate *Queste del Saint Graal*, with a significant variant: the wounding of the king by the magic weapon does not cause the blight of the land, but Perceval's sister promises Galahad that the king will be cured when he should come to him. Thus a fourth motif is introduced—that of the curing of the maimed King by Galahad. It is in the Post-Vulgate *Suite du Merlin* that the four motifs are finally woven into a single causal pattern: the weapon, the wounding, the blighted land, and the blight removed by the healing of the wound.

The causal sequence marks an interesting development from Chrétien's symbolism. In the First Continuation, the *Queste*, and the *Suite du Merlin*, the key emphasis is on healing and restoration, which depend on a specific action by one of the characters. In other words, the incidents of the story respond to the actions of the knights, whereas in Chrétien's romances incidents were by no means connected as directly and causally as this on the surface of the narrative but only at the secondary level of symbolic meaning. The causal sequence therefore makes it easier for the reader to perceive moral significance in the shape of the action, an immediacy of signification that involves a crucial shift in focus away from Chrétien's underlying symbolic *sen* to the historical surface of the narrative. Symbolic meaning and historical experience thus become more closely identified with one another, evincing a tendency for narrative incident to be seen as an externalization of a character's moral life, and the story interpreted in consequence as an allegory rather than a history.

The greater ideological clarity that allegory aims at requires a structural technique that would bring out the overall moral design of the action. In the Vulgate cycle the technique employed has been called *entrelacement*: episodes are interrupted by others which are in turn interrupted to resume earlier ones so as to link the separate themes and actions into a vast interlocking web which fits into a detailed time-scheme of days and hours.[8] This technique, which is embryonic in Chrétien, is used systematically in the *Lancelot*, the first of the Prose *Lancelot* trilogy and by far the longest. The enormous expansion of historical material from the *Historia regum Britanniae* in terms of different adventures and characters would naturally have made the elaboration of a consistent and compact symbolic sense, as in Chrétien's romances, difficult if not impossible, but *entrelacement* provides a way of combining history with allegorical purpose. In spite of many faults such as Loomis has observed—the otiose episodes, the needless repetitions and disgressions, the many unintegrated themes and actions—the technique of interweaving does succeed in providing romance with a supple free-ranging structure which endows the action with meaning.[9]

This movement away from what Robert Guiette called Chrétien's 'liberté de symbole' to allegory proper is another aspect of the monastic writers' attempt to render Arthurian romance more intelligible to a general audience.[10] Chrétien's symbols, such as the magic spring, the lion, or the Grail vessel, were imprecise and therefore mysterious, their significance could not be reduced to a single pattern of meaning. But the authors of the Vulgate and Post-Vulgate romances begin to dispel the mysteriousness in order to achieve a greater clarity, a more acceptable rational outline of the previously enigmatic forms of the pagan myths.

Allegory admits of a greater certainty of interpretation, it is exact and logical, and is therefore an instrument of didacticism and ideological explanation.[11] The figures in allegory are correspondingly clearer than in symbolism because they represent well-defined concepts or refer to a system of meaning which is antecedent and external to the text itself, in this case the Christian doctrine of grace and salvation. Allegorical meaning is not immanent, it is not created in context as are the symbols in Chrétien's romances; instead, the reader grasps the figurative meaning by referring the incidents and adventures to an established body of knowledge. From Chrétien's aesthetic of symbolic discovery one passes in the thirteenth-century prose romances to an aesthetic of allegorical recognition, where the initially bizarre surface of the action is like a veil which is periodically folded back to reveal an arrangement of familiar Christian verities.[12]

Paradoxically, the evolving allegorical relationship between the Matter of Britain and Christian knowledge opens the door to fantasy. It is as if the possibility of relating the narrative to an ulterior Christian meaning had released the author from the constraints of probability and enabled him to indulge himself in such marvels as floating stones, airborne sacred vessels, cloud-wrapped knights transported over long distances, colour-changing trees, and similar extravagant inventions. Allegory leads to an increase in fantasy through a species of alibi: the author's freedom to invent new marvels or to manipulate the action can always be justified as furthering didactic ends.

The fact that allegorical marvels distance the narrative from historical verisimilitude is not in itself objectionable. However, a contradiction is inherent in these romances because of their concomitant claim to historical authenticity. The Vulgate *Queste*, for instance, is brought to an end as follows:

When they had dined King Arthur summoned his clerks who were keeping a record of all the adventures undergone by the knights of his household. When Bors had related to them the adventures of the Holy Grail as witnessed by himself, they were written down and the record kept in the library at Salisbury, whence Master Walter Map extracted them in order to make his book of the Holy Grail for love of his lord King Henry who had the story translated from Latin into French.[13]

With this claim to an eyewitness source, the romance rests on an ambiguity. On the one hand, it pretends to the status of a chronicle, deriving its authority from an accurate report of the events as they actually happened, while on the other, it seeks to justify itself as an allegory where the narrative surface is a mere shell that holds a more substantial kernel of religious truth. Each criterion of truth is legitimate in itself but it is only when a text founds its claim on both criteria at one and the same time that difficulties may arise. If the *Queste* is true history, what is one to make of the floating stones and other marvels? And if it is an allegory, why claim that such extraordinary events actually occurred?[14]

The supreme, indisputable authority of Scripture allows figurative and historical meanings to coexist without risk of contradiction. Similarly, the oral narrator of epic derives a special authority from the power of the human voice and does not, in consequence, need to prove the veracity of his words.[15] With Chrétien de Troyes, as we have seen, there is no great concern to authenticate the story on the grounds of its historical truth; confidence in his artistic skill and in the grace of God are sufficient to secure the authority of his imagination. But the pretence to historicity in the prose romances of the thirteenth-century reflects the beginnings of a growing preoccupation with the question of truth in narrative. The *Mort Artu*, which concludes the whole of the Vulgate cycle, ends with the following observations:

At this point Master Walter Map will end the story of Lancelot, because he has brought everything to a proper conclusion according to the way it happened; and he finishes his book here so completely that no one can afterwards add anything to the story that is not complete falsehood.[16]

This desire to establish exclusive rights to the Arthurian world follows logically from the process of assimilating the Matter of Britain to a Christian order of things. The author of the *Mort Artu* seeks to safeguard the orthodox Christian interpretation of Arthurian history by foreclosing the possibility of a subsequent revival of the profane attractions of courtly chivalry. Like fantasy, the pretence to historical truth emerges as a product of ideological rationalization. But the resultant contradiction between allegorical marvels and historical veracity will progressively deepen in so far as the didactic alibi tempts romance authors to greater imaginative extravagance while the tokens of historicity become correspondingly more elaborate.

In this contradiction between allegory and history, fuelled by the didactic alibi, one finds the mechanism of degeneration which will eventually deprive Arthurian romance of aesthetic coherence and make it ripe for Cervantes's satire. For the didactic alibi increases the author's creative freedom at the cost of diminishing the authority of his imagination. In the climate of growing religious and political stringency of sixteenth-century Spain, the degeneration of romance accelerates as the narrative imagination loses confidence in its own authority and cleaves ever more desperately to justifications based on doctrinal rectitude or historical veracity. For more detailed illustration of this phenomenon we shall proceed to *Amadis of Gaul*, the first of the Spanish sub-Arthurian romances of chivalry, whose eponymous hero was to become the acknowledged mentor of Don Quixote.

(ii) *The Structure of* Amadis of Gaul

Arthurian literature was introduced into Spain in the late twelfth century, partly as a result of a series of marriages between the house of Castile and the Anglo-Norman royalty of England, but also through the influence of courtly love introduced by the troubadour circles in Catalonia which had considerable contact with Provence.[17] Arthurian stories took much longer to spread to a wider non-courtly public and it was only in the fourteenth century that translations from the Arthurian texts began to be made into the Iberian languages. There have survived in whole or in part a number of redactions and translations from the Post-Vulgate *Roman du Graal* but Spanish versions of the Prose *Lancelot* trilogy exist only in fragmentary redactions. There are also fragments of Spanish copies of the French Prose *Tristan* and a single imprint of the Tristan story, the *Tristán de Leonís*.[18]

These translations and copies greatly influenced the composition of indigenous romances of chivalry in the peninsula. *Amadis of Gaul* is unmistakably modelled on the French romances, most particularly on the Post-Vulgate romances, from where it takes the figure of a knight who secretly falls in love with a royal lady, a great king whose knights are dedicated to chivalry, an evil enchanter Arcalaus derived from Merlin, and a good fairy Urganda the Unknown descended from either Morgan La Fay or the Lady of the Lake.[19] However, Bohigas

Balaguer has shown that the core of the plot of *Amadis* can be traced back to that of the Vulgate *Lancelot*: an unknown youth is accepted at the court of the king whom he serves loyally, but falls in love with his daughter or wife; there are two main vicissitudes in the course of the love affair: the knight rescues his lady from an abduction by an evil opponent, and the lady becomes jealous after a false report and rejects the knight who loses or comes close to losing his senses and lives in solitude.[20] The knight, moreover, conquers a marvellous abode—the Joyeuse Garde or Firm Island—to which he takes his lady in time of peril. Beyond the Vulgate *Lancelot*, R.J. Michels has detected the surviving influence of Chrétien's *Chevalier de la Charrette* both in the wording of Amadis's dedication to Oriana, which is modelled on Lancelot's to Guinevere, and in the sequence of Amadis's request to be knighted, the king's suggestion of a waiting period, and Oriana's effective intercession in his favour.[21] The *Amadis* thus represents the ultimate bowdlerization of the Lancelot story. Now happily rid of the offending adultery, its plot can be re-formulated and its themes revived so that a new public may savour once again the stirring adventures of knights errant and the captivating manners of courtly love.

The dating of the original version of the *Amadis* presents enormous problems since it is well established that the version published in 1508 by Garci Ordóñez de Montalvo, who in subsequent editions appears under his correct name Garci Rodríguez de Montalvo, was very much re-worked from an earlier version or versions, of which there are vestiges in the extant Montalvo text. Attempts to reconstruct and date some of these earlier versions have produced limited results.[22] It is best to take the broad details of E.B. Place's hypothesis:

(i) The original version X, dating probably from the latter half of the fourteenth century but possibly earlier (Sir Henry Thomas does not discount the possibility that the original story could have been written by the Portuguese Joham de Lobeira in the last half of the thirteenth century). According to Place, X would be the prototype of the extant Books I and II.

(ii) Y3, an addition by someone else to X, or a re-working of the earlier version. Rodríguez-Moñino has shown that the extant Book III is a much reduced version of Y3. This could be the earlier version which according to Lida de Malkiel ended with a tragic duel between Amadis and Esplandian.

(iii) Montalvo's extant Books I-IV of which II and IV would be a re-working of Y3 with I and II largely intact, at least in outline. Place shows that the language of IV reveals archaisms and occidentalisms which indicate that Montalvo was not inventing his own Book IV but re-working the considerable material left over from Y3.

(iv) Montalvo's Book V, *The Exploits of Esplandian*, which he conceived and wrote himself but many of whose episodes are modelled on Y3. The fatal duel which formed the denouement of Y3 would, according to Place, correspond to Chapters 28 and 29 of the *Esplandian*, although such an outcome is averted.

In short, the extant books of the *Amadis* are the last version of a series covering a period of nearly a century and a half. Montalvo re-worked a previous version Y3, which was itself a revision and expansion of X, excising passages of which he did not approve and re-organizing it into four parts to which he added a fifth, the *Esplandian*, largely of his own invention in order to improve upon and supersede the profane values of worldly chivalry and courtly love in his original.[23] Once again we encounter a Christianizing process even in the Spanish heir to the already-purified French romances of the thirteenth century. But what is of particular interest is that thanks to Montalvo's intrusions into the *Amadis*, and his composition of the *Esplandian*, one can observe the operation of the didactic alibi, and the resultant aggravation of the contradiction between fantasy and historicity. Taken together, the *Amadis* and its sequel span the distance that exists between the French post-Vulgate cycle and the Spanish sub-Arthurian genre of romance that became the butt of Cervantes's satire.

Presumably because of the successive revisions, the *Amadis* we possess lacks an easily discernible structure. Scholars mark certain points in the narrative which they surmise to be relics of previous endings that have been opened out by different authors. Thomas, for example, sees a natural ending in Chapter 10 when Amadis discovers his true identity. He also believes that after the rescue of Oriana and Lisuarte, and their reunion with Amadis and the other characters, another 'opportunity of ending the story is avoided'.[24] This too is the opinion of Grace Williams and of Armando Durán, who consider the grand reunion in Chapter 30 as a natural culmination of a series of partial reunions between the characters orchestrated through a technique of interlacing.[25] Durán sees in this evolution through postponement a deliberate compositional principle in the work by which the author delays the denouement indefinitely, and which leads to a progressive expansion of the story. But for Menéndez y Pelayo the amplification of the narrative produced a decline into formlessness inasmuch as the coherence of the first book, where there exist few authorial interpolations, is lost in the later books as the pace and variety of the incidents give way to lengthier and more numerous discourses by Montalvo.[26]

The *Amadis*, I will argue, observes a coherent structural principle which is eventually overwhelmed by the sheer scale of the action. The narrative is initially organized as a series of cyclical crises where the rotation of each cycle encompasses a successively wider field, but the compass of the last cycle becomes so vast that the author himself appears to lose sight of its cause. The characteristic movement of a cycle is initiated by a crisis which disrupts the life of the hero or the kingdom. This is usually followed by a prophecy about the significance of the crisis and a heavily-veiled foretelling of its resolution. After various adventures, the crisis is settled through the efforts of the hero. Finally, another prophecy confirms the earlier one and looks ahead to the next crisis.

The first crisis concerns the identity of Amadis who is the natural son of King Perion of Gaul and Elisena, daughter of the King of Brittany. Conceived during a secret tryst, Amadis is born without his father Perion's knowledge some time after the latter had left to pursue his adventures as a knight errant. Elisena puts the baby in an ark together with a parchment and a ring given her by Perion, and delivers him to the waters of a river. The box is found by the Scots nobleman Gandales who adopts and raises the infant. Since Amadis's name is not known he is called the Child of the Sea. While he grows up in the court of King Languines of Scotland, the prophetess Urganda the Unknown and a hermit foretell the child's glorious future.

Urganda exhorts Gandales to 'believe firmly that all will happen as I tell you' (I.2.43).[27]

The Child of the Sea soon falls in love with Oriana, the daughter of Lisuarte, King of Great Britain, and we learn that this love is reciprocated although each is too shy to tell the other. However, Oriana persuades her father to knight the Child of the Sea, who then leaves the court and completes several resounding adventures. Eventually he defeats King Abies of Ireland who was at war with his unknown father, King Perion of Gaul. When the Child of the Sea goes to Perion's court he gives his ring to a damsel who had lost hers, but Perion sees this ring, which he had originally given to his wife Elisena after the secret tryst during which Amadis was conceived. He now suspects Elisena of having an affair with the Child of the Sea and, seizing his sword, makes for the Queen's chamber to demand an explanation. The secret of the illegitimate baby and the ring emerges, and Amadis comes into his own. Internecine destruction is averted, the crisis overcome. At this point Urganda sends her emissary, the maiden of Denmark, to remind King Perion of an early prophecy that Ireland would lose the flower of its knights when Perion rediscovered his lost son, thus giving significance to Amadis's otherwise unconnected defeat of King Abies of Ireland.

The second cycle consists of a double crisis: one in the world of love, when Oriana is captured by the evil enchanter Arcalaus, and the other in the world of public affairs, when King Lisuarte is captured by Barsinan, a kinsman of Arcalaus. Amadis defeats Arcalaus, rescues Oriana, and later plays a decisive role both in rescuing Lisuarte and in winning the battle against Barsinan. At the end of this cycle Amadis is declared the best knight in the world by way of fulfilment of Urganda's prophecy.

Amadis's reward for rescuing Oriana is his night of love with her in the forest. This event, rather paradoxically, triggers the third cycle. Amadis leaves the court with his brother Galaor and the knight Agrajes, and decides to fulfil a promise he had made to the beautiful Briolanja that he would avenge her and help win back her lost kingdom. When Amadis sends a dwarf Durin back to the court to collect a sword Briolanja had previously given him, the dwarf is led to believe that Amadis loves Briolanja, which suspicion he inadvertently discloses to Oriana. At the start of the second book, Amadis reaches the Firm Island where he successfully completes a test that proves that he is the world's most loyal lover, but, immediately after this, he receives a letter from Oriana rebuking him for his alleged infidelity with Briolanja. Amadis, like Yvain and Lancelot before him, is driven by despair to abandon his friends and retire to the wilderness, feeling himself to be spiritually dead. A hermit he meets gives him the surrogate identity of Beltenebros.

In spite of his predicament, Amadis has a dream which the hermit interprets as an augury of better times ahead. His morale is restored and, under the identity of Beltenebros, he wins many famous victories, meets Oriana secretly, and successfully completes with her a test of the loyalty of their love. In a final battle he comes to the aid of the beleaguered Lisuarte by revealing his true identity to the troops, thereby spurring them on to victory. Urganda then appears at the court, confirms the loyalty of the lovers, and interprets the battle so as to show that, since Beltenebros dealt the crucial blows, the victory is entirely owed to him. She now prophesies future developments in an involved allegorical dream which foreshadows the next cycle, caused by Amadis's unjust banishment from the court by Lisuarte who has been misled by a group of envious knights.

The cause of this fourth cycle is clearer than some of the earlier ones, and it provides a ready key to the others. The new crisis entails a misunderstanding, a failure to read certain signs correctly. Amadis is banished because the envy he inspires in some quarters provokes two knights to give mendacious advice to Lisuarte about a conspiracy against him planned by Amadis. Lisuarte's readiness to believe a lie represents a failure of proper insight and wisdom, a form of culpable folly on his part. He accepts these accusations without seeking further signs that might reveal the truth, and so things become blurred and confused, and a crisis ensues. But what actually gives rise to this act of folly is the envy of Amadis's enemies. In other words, the crisis has the specific sin of envy at its root, and it is this sin which puts the signs of truth in disarray. This fourth crisis therefore has a double cause, the external cause of the advisers' envy and the internal cause of Lisuarte's lack of insight.

The earlier crises also have a specific sin as their primary cause, and a consequent misapprehension of truth that creates confusion. The first crisis was provoked by the secrecy of Perion's pre-marital knowledge of Elisena which later led him to misread the real significance of the Child of the Sea's ring. Similarly, Amadis's night with Oriana explains the dwarf's misconstruction of Amadis's wish to retrieve Briolanja's sword, since he had no means of knowing about Amadis's secret commitment to Oriana. In both cases it is secrecy which directly leads to someone mistaking appearances, misreading the true reality of things. Now this secrecy is necessary because, as the author explains in the case of Perion and Elisena, sexual intercourse outside wedlock was punishable by death (I.1.33). But the question then arises as to why these worthy knights, Perion and Amadis, should commit such a heinous sin. The answer given by the author is unsatisfactory but, as will emerge later, rather revealing: it is God Himself who permits such sin to occur in the furtherance of his own inscrutable purpose ('that all-powerful Lord through whose permission all of this came to pass'). This has to serve the author as an explanation for a flagrant inconsistency in the portrayal of his characters: Amadis, an otherwise unimpeachable hero, commits a grave sin when he fulfils his love as reward for his earlier prowess. Quite clearly, the Christianizing instincts of the author led him to try to reconcile the inherited profanity of love in Arthurian romance with the need to adhere to the Church's moral precepts by presenting the sin as a structural cause of the crisis while ascribing the contradiction rather neatly to the unknowable ways of the Almighty.

This crisis-pattern is not dissimilar from those in Chrétien's romances. There are, however, certain important differences that indicate the cultural and intellectual distance that exists between them. In Chrétien's romances the crisis was provoked by a moral failing, but this was not so much the commission of a definite sin as the result of a lack of moral balance, an indulgence of the heart over the head, the sort of failure of judgement that Chrétien termed folly as opposed to good sense. The hero's actions were dependent on contingent circumstances or on limited, subjective perspectives, his motives conditioned by a complex of moral and cultural factors which brought the story to an impasse. In Chrétien's poetic world the crisis is essentially internal to the life of the hero, and it is presented in terms of a dilemma between the rival claims of love and honour. By contrast, the crises in the *Amadis* are incontrovertible violations of the laws of the Church; there is little interest in the personal, interior quest for virtue but rather, as in the Vulgate and Post-Vulgate romances, an emphasis on a public ethic of sin, punishment and reward administered by the direct interventions of God and his delegates. The world of *Amadis* is, as a result, less troubled by spiritual paradoxes and moral dilemmas than Chrétien's.

Nevertheless, in these early books, Amadis's world is still divided, in the medieval Platonist manner, into a visible, temporal realm and an invisible, transcendent realm; the connections between the two, as in the French romances, are mediated by signs. But whereas in Chrétien the signs were not always immediately identifiable, in the *Amadis* they possess a lapidary clarity which makes them so recognizable that they can by disregarded only at one's spiritual peril. For the author in the *Amadis* there would appear to be no inherent problems in the world, no blurred edges, unless the signs are culpably misinterpreted or ignored through sin. The features of good and evil are severely etched on the surface of persons and things. For example, in Book II Chapter 61, Queen Madasima is said to be beautiful but she refuses to marry her defender and champion Ardan Canileo because he is ugly. Amadis sees this as sufficient reason to defend Madasima and relegate Ardan to the category of the morally inferior.

This mechanical interpretation of signs is evident in the application and observance of the chivalric code. Armed combat in Chrétien was a subtle cognitive medium, but in *Amadis of Gaul* it is applied as a virtually automatic decoder of identities, motives and spiritual states. In Book I Chapter 26, Amadis is in hot pursuit of a wicked knight when he is stopped by another knight who challenges him to reveal the motive for his haste; Amadis says he is too pressed to explain, so the knight engages him in battle; Amadis unhorses and badly wounds his adversary and then rides off on his original mission. A similar incident occurs to Galaor in Chapter 36 when he too is chasing Lisuarte's captors and is halted by a knight who claims that Galaor must be fleeing from some crime and should therefore declare the reason for his haste or engage in combat. Again in Chapter 17, Amadis is challenged by the squire of an unknown knight: 'Sir knight, you do not pass any further unless you concede that the lady love of that knight lying under the pine is more beautiful than yours.' Amadis replies: 'If it is God's will... I shall never concede such a great falsehood unless by force you make me say it or you take my life' (I.17.195). Combat in the above examples is considered an adequate means of establishing someone's real motives or even an aesthetic quality. On another occasion it is used to determine an abstract, conceptual truth. In Book II Chapter 46, p. 379, Amadis, who has received Oriana's rebukes for his alleged lack of fidelity, is broken-hearted and curses Love for not repaying his loyal service; out of the blue a strange knight appears singing the praises of Love, who has made him fall for the peerless Oriana. Amadis is persuaded by his squire to challenge the knight's assertions about Love: 'Now come and defend its rights, and let us see whether it won more in you than it lost in me' (p. 449). Amadis duly defeats the boastful knight and so the results of the duel register beyond dispute the truth of Amadis's claim that Love is ungrateful and inconstant.

The chivalric code in *Amadis of Gaul* has become an unfailing guide to objective truth, a dependable turnstile between the material world and the world beyond the senses. Its mechanistic character is best exemplified by the truth-revealing tests which appear in the narrative, namely the Arch of Loyal Lovers and the Forbidden Chamber (II.44.430-1). The former is used to test the fidelity of lovers and the latter to reveal the most excellent knight and the fairest lady in the world. The Arch and the Chamber function as machines which calibrate, with a nicety not given to human faculties, the quality of the characters' inner life or intangibles about the relative beauty and fidelity of ladies, by producing signs issued by authoritative powers from the other world. Such tests do exist in Chrétien's romances but they do not have this automatic character, the hero has usually to enter into arduous and uncertain battle against a powerful adversary. By contrast,

Amadis is passively processed through halls and chambers until the verdict is given. The world of the *Amadis* is one of incontrovertible certainties and ready meanings; the order of things has been set out and it is periodically checked by a supervisory deity.

Hence the importance of prophecies and dreams in the structure of the narrative. Since the initially dense and enigmatic language of the prophecies is clarified for the reader as the action unfolds, the impression is created that all eventualities have been foreseen if not actually predetermined by the Almighty. The romance is as much an account of the intervention of supernatural forces in the world as it is an alleged record of historical events. As the narrator says of Amadis when he is in the depths of despair: 'We shall relate in what form when most without hope, when he had already reached death's door, the Lord of the world miraculously protected him' (II.48.467). The narrative is in effect a practical demonstration of the futility of human affairs when divorced from transcendent authority: not only does the action bear out prophecies and dreams, a second prophecy retrospectively interprets what has gone before so as to impress upon the reader the efficacy of Providence. Prophecies and oracles peel away the layers of confusion thrown over the truth by sin. Just as Urganda the Unknown repeatedly exhorts the characters to 'believe firmly that all will happen as I tell you', so too does the controlled, revelatory structure of the narrative invite the reader to trust in the beneficence of God's will in the course of history.

The early *Amadis*, as it survives in the extant Books I and II, is still recognizably close to the French romances inasmuch as its structure is designed to represent the transactions between the historical world and the supernatural. Although historical action predominates, the potential anarchy of adventures is harnessed by the cyclical patterns which are explained, as in the Post-Vulgate Cycle, by prophecies, dreams and oracular devices. However, the fourth cycle, initiated in Book II Chapter 62 when Lisuarte falls out with Amadis after heeding false advice, is the last crisis in the romance with any sort of organic necessity or internal moral causation; from this point on, the decline into formlessness begins.

This fourth crisis-cycle encompasses the vast field of the whole of Books III and IV, whereas the previous three cycles, although of increasingly wider range, were contained in Books I and II. Since no order or stability can come to the chivalric world until the breach between Amadis and Lisuarte is healed, all else remains incidental to that basic conflict. The adventures that follow seem therefore to be increasingly arbitrary and unmotivated. For example, Amadis's decision to embark on a five-year long quest for adventure in Germany, Bohemia, and Constantinople in Book III has no direct or even symbolic connection with Lisuarte or Oriana, nor is it motivated by any sense of chivalric mission as in the French romances. Subsequent crises are caused by equally arbitrary external factors—either by the attacks of evil forces such as King Aravigo or Arcalaus the Enchanter, or else by Amadis's response to requests for help from beleaguered kings and princes in struggles against rivals. Because the characters' moral natures are now taken for granted, their objectives become predominantly political and territorial rather than spiritual. For instance, the immediate result of Lisuarte's change of heart is his refusal of Amadis's request that he should allow Queen Madasima to marry Galvanes Lackland with the island of Mongaza as dowry, thus provoking a great battle for the territory. Again, Amadis takes possession of the Firm Island which he won in Book II and where he retires at strategic points in the narrative. More generally, the hero's theatre of operations is prodigiously enlarged to include the entire surface of the known globe as he forms alliances and enmities with various kings and emperors. Lacking any inner moral necessity, the action becomes episodic and spatially diffuse; whatever sense of a qualitative, coherently sustained development the narrative may have possessed before the end of Book II is all but lost. Instead one has a purely quantitative momentum, a steady accumulation of adventures, battles, territories, and characters.[28]

Evidence of the progressive dismembering of the narrative is the fact that this cumulative growth of the action leads nowhere much after all. It contributes not a jot to the resolution of the initial Amadis–Lisuarte conflict. In Book IV, after the formation of great alliances and the amassing of huge forces,

Amadis and his father Perion prepare to attack Lisuarte and his ally the Emperor of Rome. Simultaneously, Arcalaus and King Aravigo assemble their own massive armies in order to take advantage of their enemies' internecine quarrel. Two days of fighting are followed by a truce, but before the battle is resumed the holy man Nasciano, at Oriana's instigation, informs Lisuarte that his daughter and Amadis are secretly wed, and presents him with their son Esplandian, a revelation that need not have been deferred for such a disastrously long time. Lisuarte suddenly sees sense at last and makes peace with Amadis. The resolution of the basic crisis initiated in Book II has therefore no necessary link with any of the multifarious adventures that have taken place throughout Books III and IV.

This loss of organic necessity in the narrative significantly alters and complicates the task of the author, and has important aesthetic repercussions. As the surface of the romance becomes densely peopled with secondary characters and profuse in adventures taking place over a vast geographical area, the author must intervene more directly in the narrative in order to give it shape and meaning. And yet, in this situation of unprecedented freedom of the imagination, Montalvo chooses to emulate the historian and to redouble his didactic efforts in order to justify the simple pleasure of spinning yarns about knights errant and their ladies.

Frank Pierce has noted how the *Amadis* still reveals traces of the *entrelacement* which is characteristic of the French romances.[29] It figures some twenty times in Book I, diminishing in Book II and virtually disappearing from Book III only to reappear in Book IV. Pierce suggests that this phenomenon strengthens the contention that Montalvo changed and adapted the material of Books II and III in order to expand the work into Book IV. The irregular use of *entrelacement* can be related to the appearance of prospective and retrospective devices first noted by Frida Weber de Kurlat, who demonstrated their indebtedness to the traditional narrative techniques of Spanish historiographical prose from Alfonso X onwards.[30] Moreover, Weber de Kurlat observed that the prospective and retrospective devices increase significantly in Books III and IV, that is to say, in those parts where Montalvo's revision was most concentrated. The adoption of historiographical devices is accompanied by a rise in the number of authorial asides and didactic commentaries in Books III and IV. Pierce notes five in Book I, six or so in Book II, nine in Book III, and eleven in Book IV.[31] In Book II Chapter 62, which introduces the final crisis caused by Lisuarte's quarrels with Amadis, it is significant that Montalvo should interrupt the narrative on no less than three occasions in the same chapter to comment upon Lisuarte's folly in following bad counsel, and to exhort all Christian princes to choose good advisers. Such obtrusive authorial intervention can be explained by the fact that, as I suggested above, this final crisis needlessly postpones the union of Amadis with Oriana while revealing little genuine motivation on Lisuarte's part to justify his aberrant conduct.

Interestingly, Pierce, following Vinaver, observes that the phenomenon of didactic commentary is alien to the medieval romance practice of *entrelacement*, which seeks rather to amplify and expand the narrative matter itself in order to create moral significance.[32] Montalvo's comments and authorial exclamations are themselves a sign that the narrative has begun to lose the capacity to generate for itself any ulterior moral or spiritual significance through symbolism, allegory, or structural organization. The revised *Amadis* progresses from the crisis-cycles in Books I and II to a situation in the later books where the action becomes virtually divorced from consistent symbolic or allegorical meaning. Consequently, aesthetic pleasure and moral profit no longer coincide, they begin to exist on separate levels of narration.

This dislocation of the narrative into a plane of action and a plane of didactic commentary, with the occasional bout of semi-allegorical fantasy, further compromises the status of fiction. It is evidence of the growing incapacity of the author to justify the freedom of his imagination. Unable to find much intrinsic worth in the fictional narrative itself, Montalvo strives to establish some validity for it by claiming an equivalence with history, or attaching to it orthodox Christian doctrines and *exempla*. This increasing lack of confidence in the value of imaginative fiction, which is so important for our understanding of the development of Arthurian romance, becomes much more pronounced in the *Exploits of Esplandian*, Montalvo's own attempt at the writing of a romance. Here, and in the last books of the *Amadis*, we shall see the author resorting ever more disingenuously to the didactic alibi in order to justify his fictions. The contradiction between historicity and fantasy will become correspondingly sharper, and will eventually erupt into a full-blown crisis of authority within the narrative itself.

(iii) *History and Fiction in Montalvo's Revised* Amadis *and the* Esplandian

In the general Preface to the four revised books of *Amadis of Gaul* and the fifth book *Esplandian*, Montalvo introduces the question of truth in narrative.[33] The veracity of historical writing is based on what actually occurred, on the authority of the eyewitness. But he points out that many histories have been so embellished by writers that their accuracy has been seriously compromised. Some ostensibly historical texts, he says, are not founded on the slightest shred of truth: 'There were other writers of lower quality who not only failed to base their work on fact, but on any semblance of it. These are the ones who composed the feigned histories in which marvellously unnatural things are to be found, which very rightly ought to be deemed fakes'(p. 19). Having distinguished between factual chronicles (*crónicas*) and fictions (*patrañas*), one would have expected Montalvo to be partly on the way to differentiating fiction from history, but the distinction remains confused and even further obfuscated by Montalvo's own attempts to expound the issues involved. He asks what benefit the reader derives from accounts of great military feats which are either too extraordinary to accord with everyday experience or otherwise known to be fictional. His answer is that only those which are of exemplary moral value or which illustrate truths conducive to the reader's salvation are of any worth. We have here a full and explicit acceptance of the didactic alibi. In this regard, the difference between historical and fictional discourse is ultimately denied. Since either can serve equally to promote the truths of the Faith, the problem of truth in narrative seems to be solved.

Nevertheless, when Montalvo comes to describe the nature of his enterprise, the old issues are revived once more. He writes that his faculties are not exalted enough to occupy themselves with themes that more able men have treated, so he has confined himself to correcting the first three books of the *Amadis*, translating and amending the fourth, and adding *The Exploits of Esplandian*, 'which no-one remembers having seen before'. The reason for the *Esplandian*'s obscurity hitherto, we learn, is that it has for centuries lain in a stone tomb buried under a hermitage near Constantinople whence it was brought to Spain by a Hungarian merchant and deciphered by translators before reaching the public (p. 20). Thus Montalvo abdicates responsibility for the one book of fiction he actually wrote himself and resorts to the old subterfuge of pretending that it is a historical document.[34]

One could argue that the very transparency of the subterfuge is a signal to the reader that the book is, of course, fiction. But Montalvo comes to the edge of irony without indulging in it. The ironist is always clear about his intention and detached from the object of his irony, whereas Montalvo, as we shall see, is undecided as to whether he should persist in his dissimulation of the fiction or come clean to his readers about it. The passage might well appear ironic to the modern reader who views the book from outside the aesthetic conundrum, but Montalvo's discomfort becomes evident in the tortuous closing lines of the Preface (p.20):

The said five Books, although up to now they have been considered fictions rather than chronicles, by virtue of the said emendations are augmented with moralizations and teachings of such a kind that they properly can be compared with cheap, coarse, cork salt-shakers encased and adorned with bands of silver and gold.

The central issue of the historicity of the books is neatly evaded by claiming that, although they were generally held to be fictions (*patrañas*), the emendations and added moral examples have enhanced their value.

The image of the salt-shaker, on closer inspection, turns out to be more confusing than enlightening. How precisely is the fragile, light-weight substance of the fiction reinforced by the gold bands of doctrine? Does the fictional element have any intrinsic value? If not, Montalvo should have explained why it was necessary in the first place. In any case, the image fails to clear up the outstanding question of the distinction between *patrañas* and *crónicas*; have the moral examples bestowed on these reputed *patrañas* the dignity of *crónicas*? Montalvo eschews these questions and employs a well-worn *topos* of a relativism that hardly becomes a convinced didactic writer: every reader, young or old, can find in it whatever suits him. Finally, he excuses himself for any doctrinal errors and establishes the authority of his work wholly on his faith in the teachings of the Church. Not only is the text itself unreliable, so is the author; the one unquestionable source of truth is Holy Mother Church.

Montalvo's inconclusive hedging in the Preface over the issues of historical truth and moral authority is carried over into the main body of the narrative proper. Aesthetic and moral uncertainties nag the narrator ever more insistently as the story unfolds. In the introductory subtitle to the books of the *Amadis* proper, Montalvo had claimed only to be correcting and emending the work of other authors: 'He corrected the ancient originals which were corrupt and poorly composed in the antique style through the fault of diverse poor scribes' (p. 21). Accordingly, the narration of the story was conducted impersonally, using various devices which presented the action straightforwardly, without the intervention of any identifiable narrator other than an infrequently mentioned and utterly anonymous author.

The First Book opens with a direct relation of events: 'Not many years after the passion of our Redeemer and Saviour, Jesus Christ, there was a Christian king in Little Britanny by the name of Garinter' (p. 21). Only in the second chapter does one find any acknowledged distance between the reader and the events described: 'King Perion having left Britanny as has already been related' (I.2.38). This is the first implicit mention of the existence of a narrator in the text. Later in the same chapter, there is a more precise reference: 'The author ceases to speak of this and returns to the youth that Gandales was bringing up' (p. 41). Similarly, in the following chapter, when the scene changes, the 'author' is mentioned: 'The author here tells again of King Perion' (I.3.50). Otherwise the actual unfolding of events is attributed simply to 'the History'. The narrative relations in the early *Amadis* books are therefore clear and unequivocal; these are historical events once narrated by an 'author' and now being presented to us in a written version edited and updated by Montalvo. These relations, moreover, retain vestiges of an earlier narrative situation in an oral tradition. In the early chapters of the First Book, the reader is addressed directly as if he were listening to the tale being told him by word of mouth: 'At the time that the things happened which you have heard previously . . . ' (I.3.54). Again in I.5.73: 'Don Galaor, who was being brought up by the hermit, as you have heard . . . '. And in I.9.99: 'The battle between King Abies and the Child of the Sea having been arranged, as you have heard . . . '. These conventionalized relics of an oral medium of story-telling hark back both to the recitals of Celtic folklore from which Arthurian romance sprang, and to the narrative formulae of epic story-tellers.

But even as early as I.4.63 a different narrative order can be discerned. The 'author' interrupts the narrative to apologize for the poverty of the style. This is ascribed to the youthful Amadis's amorous confusion, a state which ties the tongues of maturer men. Therefore the 'author' must be forgiven for not having recounted the episode 'in more polished words' (I.4.63). In the same passage we come across a revealing reference to the act of reading: 'and if anyone who reads these words . . . '. The true narrative situation is recognized here; we are not listening to a story-teller, we are on our own reading a book written by an author who could have chosen different words, a more elegant style to relate the same events. One's attention is drawn away from the spontaneous flow of the narrative act and deflected to the mechanics of narration. The illusion of imaginative proximity to the action is eroded slightly by this reminder of the true state of affairs: the existence of several authors who wrote words on paper which the reader now holds in his hands. The relics of oral formulae within the text highlight a contrast between the impact of vocal telling and the more complex mediations of the written word.[35]

In *Amadis of Gaul*, the differences between the two modes of narration—the sweeping confidence of an oral narrator, and the reflexive, self-conscious reportage of the written document—become starkly obvious. As the self-assurance of the narrator falters, the problems of verification and historical authenticity become more acute. In the latter books of the *Amadis*, and especially in the *Esplandian*, when Montalvo is obliged to take fuller responsibility for the composition of the narrative, the problem of verification becomes an obliquely acknowledged but none the less central concern.

To begin with, as a propagandist for the Catholic Monarchs' crusade against the Moors, Montalvo is very keen to exalt the military and religious virtues of Amadis beyond even those for which he had already been celebrated by his earlier chroniclers.[36] This ideological purpose tempts him into allegory. He introduces the Endriago, a hideous beast of unimaginable ferocity born of the incestuous union of an evil giant and his beautiful daughter. As such, the monster is an allegorical manifestation of infernal will, and Amadis engages it in battle and slays it in the likewise allegorically named Devil's Isle. What interests us for present purposes are the methods Montalvo employs to pretend that this allegorical episode is historically true and so keep the reader's incredulity at bay.

The basic principle he adopts is one of repetitious reportage. The first series of reports comes when Amadis's squire, Gandalin, relates this feat to the King of Bohemia:

And they insistently begged Gandalin to try to tell them the whole affair just as it had happened since he had seen it with his own eyes, so that they might be able to give an account of such great knightly prowess. And he told them he would gladly do so on condition that the physician administer to him an oath on the holy Gospels, so that they might believe his account and with truth put it in writing, in order that a thing so outstanding and so mighty an exploit might not be forgotten by people. Master Elisabad administered the oath in order to be more certain concerning such a great deed. And Gandalin told it all completely just as the story has related it. (III.73.177)

Nevertheless, the marvellous nature of the event is acknowledged. When the King of Bohemia and his entourage see the dead Endriago they cannot believe their eyes: 'And although they knew for certain that the Knight of the Green Sword had killed it, it seemed to them only that they had dreamed it' (p. 177).

The second series of reports begins in the following chapter when the Emperor of Constantinople receives a letter telling of the killing of the Endriago. He then asks the messenger to relate it to him by word of mouth: 'The latter told it in full as if it had all taken place in his presence' (p. 181). Although the messenger was not actually present at the killing he can relate it as accurately as if he had been there. The Emperor of Constantinople goes several steps further. He orders painters to depict the Endriago (p. 182):

And take with you master painters to paint and bring back to me an exact likeness of the Endriago, because I shall order a representation cast in metal which will include the knight who fought with him and be of their respective size and appearance. And I shall have these figures placed in the very same place where the battle took place, and on a large copper plaque I shall cause a description of the battle to be inscribed.

In the first instance, these reports convey a touching confidence in the possibility of transmitting eyewitness reports of historical events without anything being lost in the process. In fact, the act of recording it on paper, in paint, or on metal is deemed to lend the account added credibility. But secondly, Montalvo's insistence on repeated testimonies, his telling and re-telling the same incident through several mouthpieces and documents, displays a particular fascination with the certification of allegedly historical events, much as if he were rehearsing various ways of guaranteeing narrative truth. Montalvo betrays the reason for this concern when he makes Amadis say that his victory, which has astounded so many people, is alone attributable to the omnipotence of God: 'Nothing can be compared with His great power, because all is permitted and directed by His will, and to Him one must attribute all the good things that occur in this world' (p. 178). Even if the feat is so amazing that it seems more like a dream even to eyewitnesses, its apparent impossibility can be taken as a measure of the power of God, by whose leave anything can happen no matter how unbelievable.[37] God's omnipotence becomes an enabling device for the fantasy of the Endriago. Thus religious ideology is drawn upon to iron over essentially aesthetic difficulties. It is a ploy which will become increasingly frequent with Montalvo.

This radical but unresolved ambiguity towards literary invention explains Montalvo's efforts to underwrite the narrative with tokens of historical authenticity. In Book IV Chapter 97, for example, the recapitulation of the action by one character to another occurs no less than twenty-six times.[38] The primary telling is not enough to carry its own self-validating weight, so the original account is buttressed by further accounts, producing a proliferation of reports through letters, chronicles, messengers, and eyewitnesses. It is as though the author wished to reproduce the mechanics of corroboration by getting outside his original account onto a new level, which he in turn tries to supersede by yet another, in the hope of breaking out of the condition of fictionality altogether.

The wish to abolish fiction is most noticeable in the *Esplandian*. It is said to have been written 'by the hand of that great Master Elisabad who heard of and saw many splendid exploits of his, and who because of the love he bore his father [i.e. Amadis], took it upon himself to witness these great feats of arms and employ his knowledge to heal the wounded knight on many occasions' (subtitle, p. 463).[39] By contrast, when Montalvo presented the *Amadis* he claimed then only to have corrected the original manuscripts written in archaic style by different authors. Now, in the book which he has actually invented himself, he omits to record his own part in the enterprise and names instead a character from the *Amadis* as the eyewitness narrator of the new chronicle. This represents a radically new departure from the romance tradition.[40] Chrétien presented himself as the arranger and narrator of inherited stories, the anonymous thirteenth-century writers of the Vulgate Cycle hid behind the collective narrative identity of Walter Map, but here Montalvo effaces all mention of his own activity and casts a *character* from the earlier books to play the narrator. In the *Esplandian* narration has become an assumed role rather than a spontaneous act.

Although it would be tempting to see this as a stroke of genius by Montalvo who consciously invented a clever device that would subsequently assume such importance in narrative fiction, I think it would be more accurate to regard it as a fortuitous but logical development in the process of pseudo-verification. Master Elisabad is brought in as a supreme corroborative device, incorporating all the previous narrators and eyewitness reporters in a single eyewitness figure. The actual author Montalvo disappears behind the narrative persona of the scribe who had earlier registered Gandalin's oath of truthfulness before the account of Amadis's slaying of the allegorical Endriago in Book III.[41]

The device is clearly designed to enhance still further the illusion of historicity and, through that, the moral authority of the text: 'Although it is reasonable to entertain some doubts about the exploits of Amadis, one must give greater credence to those performed by this knight [i.e. Esplandian], for Master Elisabad only wrote about what he himself witnessed or what he learned from reliable sources' (18.427). The truth of the *Esplandian* is placed above that of the *Amadis* simply because the narrator was an eyewitness to the events. The fraudulence of these claims is transparent because they are so self-defeating: if Elisabad was first encountered in the *Amadis* then it seems rather contradictory to question its veracity since it might well cast doubts on the historicity of Elisabad himself, and where would that then leave the *Exploits of Esplandian?*

Montalvo's efforts to disguise the fictional status of the narrative serve only to compound the problem. The ultimate effect is one of literary *trompe l'œil* such as one encounters in the passage immediately preceding the above quotation. Here the reader witnesses the scene where Elisabad received his authorial mandate from no less a figure than King Lisuarte:

The King was very pleased with the news and asked Master Elisabad to take down in writing everything the two novice knights had said about Esplandian . . . Thus, as you now hear, did these *Exploits of Esplandian* . . . come to be written . . . by the hand of a man so virtuous that he could not write anything but the truth.   (18.427)

Elisabad's authority as eyewitness is buttressed by the King's authority, but since the King also appeared in the earlier books, his credibility falls under the same suspicion as the feats of Amadis. There is, however, an additional subterfuge involved in this scene. The reader appears to witness the occasion when Elisabad receives a mandate to write the book which he is presently reading; the act of reading thereby becomes analogous to the act of witnessing. The ultimate illusion in the *Esplandian* is that the reader can see with his own eyes that the narrator is an authoritative and reliable eyewitness to the allegedly historical action. The testimonial authenticity of the narrative is established in a scene *within* the narrative itself, so that the distance between narration and action is speciously collapsed into a common dimension in order to achieve an equal credibility for both.

Through such an exercise in reflexivity, Montalvo tries to abdicate responsiblity for his creation altogether and disappear from the text. But his narrative disguise becomes hard to maintain; the pretence of eyewitness narration has serious limitations in a romance characterized by such a proliferation of incident that the prerequisite of ubiquity becomes strained beyond belief. Elisabad is made to trot the globe in order to keep pace with the tireless Esplandian's chivalric adventuring. Since the narrator is just one character among others, he becomes vulnerable to an array of purely practical objections to the feasibility of his movements or to the likelihood of certain occurrences. Once the narrator is required to be at or close to the scene of the action, the act of narration cannot be spontaneously assumed but has to find a rationale in the witnessing. A pragmatic and functional consciousness is thereby engendered in the very heart of the romance, and the confidence of its narrative voice becomes inhibited by the hesitancies and fallibilities of the narrator's fictional persona.

Already in the last book of the *Amadis* one finds an occasional concern with the plausibility of the action. One of the most striking examples occurs in Chapter 113 when Montalvo returns to the hermit Nasciano who had brought up Esplandian. The hermit learns of the rift between Amadis and Lisuarte, and hears that Lisuarte plans to marry Oriana off to another instead of Amadis, a plan which would threaten the irreproachable Esplandian with permanent and canonical bastardy. It is hardly a fate which Montalvo, as a Catholic propagandist, would wish to inflict on his exemplary hero. However, what is interesting about the episode are Montalvo's misgivings about the way he has handled it, and the excuses he uses to meet practical doubts. We are told that the holy man Nasciano had lived in his hermitage in the forest for more than forty years, 'and since it was a very forbidding, remote place, seldom did anyone go there, and so he always maintained supplies sufficient for a long time; and it is not known whether by the grace of God or by means of reports that he was able to hear about the matter' (IV.113.491). Montalvo pre-empts criticism of the sort that would ask how Nasciano could have survived for over forty years without human contact and, if so, how had news of the impending crisis reached him in his hermitage at so opportune a juncture. None of these questions is adequately answered, but it is nevertheless worth noting that they occurred to Montalvo.

Two other examples of such mundane concerns can be found in Chapter 130. In the first place, Amadis and Grasandor leave the Island of the Vermilion Tower 'one Monday morning', and Amadis asks Nalfon, Queen Madasima's majordomo, for a guide to the Rock of the Maiden Enchantress. When Nalfon offers to accompany them himself, Amadis politely declines: 'Amadis thanked him and told him it was not necessary for him to abandon what he had already directed him to do, for he needed only one guide' (IV.130.688). This courteous exchange on the need for a guide seems somewhat banal and otiose, for the hitherto intrepid romance hero has had little need in the past for guides to assist him in his adventures. Once on the Rock, they come to a hermitage and find in it a metal statue wearing a crown and bearing in its arms a large gilded tablet with Greek letters:

Amadis and Grasandor entered the hermitage, sat down to rest on a rock bench that they found in it, and after a bit, got up and went to look at the image, which seemed to them very beautiful. And they gazed at it a long while and saw the letters, which Amadis began to read; for at the time he travelled through Greece he had acquired some knowledge of the Greek alphabet and language, much of which the physician Elisabad had taught him when they were travelling by sea, and he had also taught him the German language and those of other lands, of which he acquired a good knowledge. (IV.130.689-90)

Here we have a wealth of circumstantial explanation. The heroes are understandably tired after climbing up to the hermitage, they take a breather on a convenient bench, admire the statue, and Amadis reads the inscriptions. How can he read Greek? The answer is once again surprisingly plausible: he was taught by Elisabad in order to beguile time during those long sea-journeys he undertook between adventures. In fact, not only did he learn Greek, he also showed a marked flair for German and other languages.

Such passages are few and far between in Book IV of the

Amadis but they are indications of a change of imaginative pitch from the early books. Even though a thoroughgoing preoccupation with verisimilitude is still remote, it is quite definitely in the offing. In the *Exploits of Esplandian* Montalvo's naturalistic scruples assume a more serious form with implications that strike even deeper into the nature of imaginative fiction. In Chapter 3, one reads the following (p. 406):

And because in the present branch of the history concerning this knight there will be many occasions when he will pronounce discourses based on sound Catholic doctrine, some readers might quite rightly say: 'Since he is so young it seems unlikely that he would be capable of dispensing such wisdom, which is more worthy of an old man; nor is it likely that he should deliver it with such modesty, for his youth and extreme valour would incline him to arrogance, yet despite his superb valour, where one might expect him to be cruel, he is in fact merciful.' Indeed such thoughts and misgivings are in some way justified, for it would be reasonable to suppose that these gentle, Catholic sentiments are not the knight's but those of the author, who sought to enhance and embellish the history.

Here Montalvo incorporates a hypothetical objection by a notional reader into his text, thereby revealing the force of his misgivings about his own manipulation of the narrative. For a moment, it would seem, Montalvo contemplates the possibility that his flawless exemplary hero might after all strike the reader as being little more than a fictional robot.

This possibility is soon enough dismissed in the usual manner: Esplandian's wisdom is the fruit of the hermit Nasciano's saintly tutelage, and all men should observe this example and deliver their own sons to the care and instruction of holy men. Although the disclaimer fails resoundingly to answer the question, Montalvo has preferred to paper over the problem with the ever-handy expedient of exemplariness rather than delve into it in any depth.

The problem appears once again in Chapter 16, which is headed as follows: 'In which is explained why the history so often refers to this damsel Carmela.' Carmela was introduced a few chapters earlier as the maidservant of Lisuarte's enemy Queen Arcabona, and she is the daughter of the hermit who is sheltering Esplandian. When she returns to see her father at the hermitage she enters the room where Esplandian is sleeping, hoping to kill him in revenge for his having earlier killed her masters. However, she is captivated by Esplandian's beauty and falls in love with him. Thenceforward she is pledged to a chaste love for the saintly hero, to whom she demonstrates her devotion by running messages and serving generally as a shuttle between the two far-flung poles of the narrative. The fact that King Lisuarte and Esplandian are so distant from each other is, of course, by no means a new feature in romance narrative since romances do not observe unities of time or place. Montalvo's invention of Carmela as a device to cover these distances betrays a naturalistic conception of space within the narrative. The transmission of news is no longer taken for granted, it has to be conveyed by somebody, and the poetic imagination in consequence becomes constrained by the mechanics of distance.

There is, in addition, a difficulty of another order. Carmela's assiduous service as messenger must be explained in some way, she must be given a motive. This motive, predictably, is a selfless Christian love: 'She was ever ready to serve and wait upon him whom she loved more than her own self; she slept in his bed, served him at his table, and never parted from him (16.426). However, as the observation that 'she slept in his bed' shows, this chaste love could easily be misconstrued by the reader, so Carmela's love must be seen to remain pure, especially since her affections for Esplandian might intrude awkwardly in the relationship with Leonorina which will be introduced later in the story. To avoid this difficulty, Montalvo seems to have invented an entirely new episode three chapters later. Here a ship appears and a damsel comes ashore bearing gifts of a set of arms and a horse from Urganda to Esplandian. On the arms there is a device of two crowns, and in Chapter 20 we are told 'the reason why the arms bore a device of two crowns'. Ostensibly it is because in *Amadis* Book III Leonorina gave Amadis the crowns, one for the fairest lady and the other for the fairest damsel. Amadis kept one for Oriana as the fairest lady and placed the second on Leonorina's head. Now Urganda uses the device of the two crowns as a portent of the imminent love between Leonorina and Amadis's son Esplandian. Whatever the intrinsic value of the episode, one of the major reasons for its appearance is that Montalvo wished to lubricate the cumbersome machinery of his narrative by resorting to the supernatural authority of Urganda to solve the purely technical problem of avoiding misunderstandings in Esplandian's relations with Leonorina and Carmela respectively.

As we shall see presently, this is by no means the only occasion where Montalvo invents an entirely new episode or a new device for scarcely any other reason than to get himself out of a technical difficulty. This episode is designed to prevent the development of any unseemly emotional conflicts between Carmela and Leonorina over Esplandian; Carmela in turn owes her existence to the problem of managing the action over long distances; and even the narrator himself, the all-seeing Elisabad, was enlisted to enhance the historicity of the work. In short, Montalvo's response to technical difficulties or aesthetic doubts is to invent a new character or a new episode in the hope of dissimulating the problem. As a result, characters and incidents proliferate seemingly at random because of a growing incapacity on the part of the author to come to grips either with the significance of his work or with the fictional nature of his creative activity. Montalvo, in seeking to establish the value of the work by claiming for it historical validity or religious authority, becomes involved in trying to disguise the fictional nature of his narrative at all costs. These subterfuges, of course, merely compound the problem as the original purpose of freeing the text from its condition of fictionality becomes entangled in an outgrowth of further fictional ramifications.

Towards the middle of the *Esplandian* it becomes evident that Montalvo is tiring of this process. The chapters become shorter, more perfunctory, and less co-ordinated. After Chapter 50 the narrative is atomized into short chapters containing one or two pieces of new information or action, encircled by authorial commentary. Montalvo finally announces to the reader in Chapter 98 that he grew tired of striving 'to revise' such a badly-organized narrative and decided to abandon the task. For the first time Montalvo refers to himself in the first person. While it is true that he still prevaricates about his exact role—whether he is in fact the real author or simply an editor—this direct reference to himself is nevertheless a significant development in the romance. He goes further and begins to narrate aspects of his own alleged experience, reporting that while he was in his chamber he was transported either in a dream or by some other means to a very high rock from where he saw a small boat heading towards him with a maiden on board. The maiden announces that she has been sent to fetch him by her mistress. Montalvo is blindfolded and eventually finds himself inside a beautiful ship. At the far end of a long hall he meets a lady, waited upon by four richly attired damsels, who upbraids him for being 'a simple unlettered man of no learning' and castigates him for attempting to correct a book such as the *Esplandian*. Montalvo accepts that he has indeed erred and invites the appropriate punishment, even suggesting that the book be thrown to the flames. But the lady replies that such an action will not be performed 'for that would be no punishment, but a reason to glory in the elimination of your absurd errors' (98.497). This lady reveals herself to be no less a personage than Urganda the Unknown, and she orders Montalvo to stop writing until he hears from her again. Montalvo then finds himself in that same spot in his room 'where I had earlier dozed off or become unconscious'.

The following Chapter 99 describes how the author received Urganda's orders to proceed with his writing: 'And it so happened that one day when I went hunting, as I usually do, to the Castillejo, a region whose rocky inhospitable terrain makes it an excellent hunting-ground, I caught sight of an owl and although the wind was high I set my falcon on it' (99.497). More details are furnished of Montalvo's personal life in this passage—a place-name, his taste for falconry, the nature of the terrain, even the state of the weather—details which add a qualitatively new dimension to the romance, as if we had discovered a false bottom and were now penetrating through to another level, a different and more realistic world. No sooner are we in this new world of Montalvo's own personal life than he relates how he fell into a deep hole in the ground where he was confronted by a fierce serpent. Shutting his eyes in terror, he opened them again to find that the serpent had vanished and Urganda herself had taken its place.

Here we are back again in the by now all too familiar reality of the Arthurian world. Urganda leads the author through underground passages towards an opening and as he emerges into the light he sees a beautiful fortress. The place is identified as the Firm Island 'by the very same signs that were previously given in this great history' (99.498). Urganda then takes him to a chamber where he finds a group of royal figures sitting motionless on thrones. Montalvo identifies them as the principal characters in his story—Amadis and Oriana, Esplandian and Leonorina, Carmela, Briolanja, and others. Urganda now asks him to pick the most beautiful lady and he rightly points to Briolanja. When asked to choose the most valiant knight Montalvo replies that with the exception of Esplandian, whose efforts were solely directed towards the greater glory of God, such a knight is Florestan, Amadis's younger brother. Urganda is greatly impressed with his perspicacity: 'Although I know from other sources that what you have said is true, it is very gratifying to hear you say it yourself, and judging from what I have known of you in the past I believe that you would not say anything that was not true' (99.500). Since Urganda herself has hitherto acted as intermediary between the temporal and the supernatural worlds in both the *Amadis* and the *Esplandian*, Montalvo offers his reader a warranty of his truthfulness as narrator by showing that his credentials have been validated by no less an authority than the supreme fairy from within his own fiction.

Urganda now explains that these immobile characters are under a spell designed to spare them the crude ignominy of death, just as Morgan La Fay had enchanted King Arthur. When Montalvo asks whether they will return to their former condition she replies: 'My good friend, you must truly believe that if King Arthur returns to rule his kingdom, as I said, these others will also return with him, and if not they shall remain as you now see them until their time comes' (99.500). The non-committal reply is a convenient way of avoiding the issue of what to do with the main characters in the story. The ultimate decision is remitted by Urganda to the higher authority of Morgan La Fay, and a regressive hierarchy of authority is thereby established in the romance reaching far beyond the limited purview of the author himself.

Not surprisingly, critics have discerned some irony in these lines.[42] They display rather too brazen an awareness of the implausibility of these allegedly historical characters. But once again I would argue that there is, strictly speaking, no irony here. Instead of revealing the superior control of the ironist, this episode shows Montalvo in the grip of the contradiction between fantasy and historicity. The reference to Morgan La Fay brings that contradiction to a head, and represents an attempt to put into suspension a problem that Montalvo cannot properly resolve: the necessity of having to end his story with the apotheosis of his faultless hero. If the romance were to end with the hero's death Montalvo would have to devise a conclusion that would in some way bring to significant fruition the otherwise erratic and repetitious crusades of Amadis and Esplandian. Having already, as has been hypothesized,[43] dissolved the tragic ending of an earlier version of *Amadis* for the ideological purpose of exalting the Christian militant Esplandian above his rather too courtly father, Montalvo must have found it beyond his powers to invent a fitting conclusion for no less than two generations of the Amadis clan.

I am therefore inclined to see the famous Chapters 98 and 99 not as evidence of literary maturity, but as a ruse to cover up a failure of imagination.[44] They constitute the end-result of the process I have been describing in both *Amadis* and *Esplandian*. From the very start, Montalvo has been engaged in a laborious attempt to keep up an illusion of historicity in order to mitigate the implausibility of his fiction. But he becomes progressively less confident of his ability to sustain this illusion and so he begins to forestall and anticipate criticism within the romance itself by inventing eyewitness devices that might effect a compromise between the traditional marvels of romance and the demands of verisimilitude. By placing his real self—the historical Garci Rodríguez de Montalvo living in Medina del Campo in the fifteenth century—on the same level as his characters, he stretches the eyewitness device to its furthest limit, where the historically proximate reality of his own life can retroactively extend to and influence the remote unreality of the fictional characters.

These extreme methods of historical authentication are, of course, self-defeating. Montalvo casts himself as an adventitious witness to the reality of Urganda: he meets her maidservant, sails in her ship, visits the Firm Island, and even sees the Arch of Loyal Lovers. In this way the fantasy elements of the earlier books are ostensibly discovered and witnessed by the author. But at the same time the author's own reliability as a witness is eventually attested to by Urganda herself after putting him through the selection test. The first device is contradicted by the second, and one can see why this must be so; although the text purports to be historical, like all Arthurian romance it ultimately seeks its own authority by virtue of its correspondence between the temporal world and the supernatural through the mediation of prophecies, truth-contests, duels, and oracular spokesmen. In this episode, Montalvo resorts, in the first place, to criteria of verisimilitude (ocular testimony of Urganda's existence), but he then follows this up with romance criteria (Urganda's oracular knowledge). Instead of enhancing the historicity of the romance, Montalvo's revelation produces the opposite effect: the author, along with his characters, finds himself in an ontological limbo—neither wholly historical nor wholly fictional. It is no surprise that these two crucial, authenticating chapters should remain shrouded in some nebulous state between dream and delusion. Not only has Montalvo exhausted all his verification techniques, he has also drained the fictive imagination of any possibility of self-justification. The ultimate attempt to abolish fiction is capped by an involuntary recognition of the oneiric flimsiness of the entire romance.

When Montalvo resumes his story he addresses the problem of fiction in a different way. In Chapter 102 Esplandian drives out the Turks from the city of Galatia. This is followed by an 'Exclamation of the Author' where he urges all Christian Kings to fight the Turk, and sets up the Catholic Monarchs of Spain as the supreme example of this ideal. In this instance, the notion of exemplariness becomes a tenuous link between the already threadbare fiction of the heroic Esplandian and the contemporary reality of the Catholic Monarchs. Exemplariness acts as a form of reciprocal justification; it allows the fiction some purchase on the historical world while enshrining the praise of the Catholic Monarchs in the pseudo-glory of Esplandian's exploits.

In a subsequent episode, the relations between history and fiction are settled by a laughably simplistic notion of exemplariness. Chapters 157 to 160 relate the strange episode of the Queen of California who brings her regiments of women and a pack of griffins to assist the Turks in their siege of the Christians in Constantinople.[45] The griffins are quickly dispatched to devour those Christians defending the city from the battlements, but they sadly fail to distinguish between Christian and Turk and fall upon both sides indiscriminately, which turn of events causes great consternation in the heathen ranks. The Californian queen commands the griffins to return to base forthwith by sounding a whistle, and the creatures comply with impressive alacrity.

Such a display of obedience moves Montalvo to utter another 'Exclamation', this time addressed to all Christians. He urges them to forgo their blind, sinful ways and obey their Lord. His pious exhortation is concluded thus: 'And should these holy and most truthful counsels be forgotten, the story of these cruel griffins, which is fictitious and made up, may at least remain in our memories and lead us to consider the case of these creatures who were born in such a wilderness and yet were capable of such obedience' (159.541). Here, then, is a less disingenuous expression of Montalvo's aesthetic opinions: fiction is basically worthless, and only in so far as it may serve to remind readers of their Christian duty does it possess value or truth.

There is, none the less, in Montalvo's statement an implicit admission that fiction may exert more influence than straightforward didacticism. But that curious power is not fully acknowledged, and this omission exacts a price. The risible obedience of the griffins contaminates the author's 'Exclamation' and reduces it to tasteless nonsense. Clearly the gold and silver bands of Christian doctrine can at times become tarnished by the very cheapness and levity of the cork salt-shaker. To point a moral effectively the fiction itself must in some way be made convincing. Montalvo has driven himself through the tortuous narrative paths of his text only to conclude by confronting once again the problem of truth in fiction.

Nevertheless, the *Exploits of Esplandian*, together with Montalvo's revision of the primitive *Amadis*, are of extraordinary interest and importance in any discussion of the development of prose fiction from romance to the novel. For here, at the end of the fifteenth century, we encounter a writer like Montalvo opening out, revising, and writing a sequel to a medieval romance. In doing so he not only introduces many of the aesthetic and ideological preoccupations of his own age into Arthurian romance, but also invents, sometimes with perverse ingenuity, certain narrative subterfuges which express the fundamental Renaissance concern with the conflict between history and fiction.[46] Montalvo borrows devices from historiographical narrative, he increasingly makes use of eyewitness reports, and he even tries to efface his own activity as author in favour of the greater authoritativeness of a character like Elisabad. By using a fictional character as an eyewitness narrator, Montalvo initiates a revolutionary new mode of story-telling whose fuller ironic potentialities were later exploited by Cervantes in Cide Hamete Benengeli.

Even so, in Chapters 98 and 99 of the *Esplandian*, Montalvo contrives to undermine even this device with yet another verification ploy when he ventures to intrude his own historical self into the romance world so as to endorse his authorial probity through Urganda the Unknown. Although the absurdity of these self-referential techniques was to be satirized by Cervantes, the object of such equivocations was a serious one: what Montalvo is striving for, and failing to find with his restless, neurotic inventiveness, is a formula for reconciling creative freedom with some universally acceptable standard of truth like historical veracity or Christian doctrine, a formula that might make good the loss of the authority of the author's imagination.

In this, of course, he is no different from other late medieval or Renaissance authors. But even though he lacked the exuberant genius of Ariosto or the ironic subtlety of Chaucer, Montalvo's adaptation of Arthurian romance was to be of considerable significance for the development of prose fiction. With the help of the printing press, the revised *Amadis* became a best-seller throughout sixteenth-century Europe for its thrilling adventures and love-affairs, the elegance of its style, and for the delightful courtesies it portrayed.[47] So great was its popularity that it achieved the dubious distinction of spawning a whole sub-genre of Arthurian romances in Spain.[48]

The two basic features of this sub-genre are the device of the historian-narrator in the guise of a wise magician,[49] and the absence of an inherent principle of structural necessity, resulting in loose episodic narratives capable of being repeatedly opened out to form extensive cycles of generational sequels. Thus *Esplandian*, which is Book V of the *Amadis*, was succeeded by Book VI on the adventures of Florisando, son of Amadis's brother Florestan; then Books VII and VIII which are about Lisuarte of Greece, son of Esplandian; Book IX about Amadis of Greece, son of Lisuarte of Greece; and so on for another three books, all of which constitute a family monopoly that cannot be challenged even by the rival cycle of Palmerin and his progeny. Other features of the *Amadis–Esplandian* narrative become generic: a rather mechanical conception and handling of the conventions of courtly chivalry; an invariable optimism in the resolution of adventures; the absolute perfection of the hero; a reliance on the sensational escalation of the action as a way of holding the reader's attention; and a recourse to didactic commentaries and authorial asides which produce a dichotomy between pleasure and profit in the narrative. These characteristics of the Spanish romances inevitably attracted criticism from clerics, humanists, and aestheticians.[50] The religious moralists objected to their dangerous indulgence in affairs of the heart and to their obsession with swashbuckling prowess, humanists were offended by their implausibilities, while the aestheticians sought a means of defending the art of poetry from the fantasies and the unruly inventiveness of the romance writers.

CHAPTER THREE

The Break with Romance: Don Quixote's Madness

(i) *Ariosto, Tasso, and the Dilemmas of Renaissance Aesthetics*

For the most important and sustained thinking on the art of narrative in the Renaissance one has to turn to Italy. Here the development of medieval romance had been somewhat different from that in Spain.[1] The main tradition of romance in Italy was concerned with the exploits of Charlemagne and the Peers of France derived from the *Chanson de Roland*. By the fourteenth century this Carolingian matter had acquired many features characteristic of Arthurian romance, principally the code of chivalry, the values of courtly love, and a recourse to magic and enchantments in the recounting of adventures. The Italian romances, however, came to possess a distinctively indigenous style, less idealized than either their French or Spanish counterparts, and incorporating comical episodes which imbued them with a light-hearted ironic tone. This Italian romance tradition—an irreverent hybrid of the Matters of France and Britain—culminated in Ludovico Ariosto's *Orlando Furioso* (1516-32), composed as a continuation of the *Orlando Innamorato* that had been left unfinished by Boiardo in 1494.

Although the *Furioso* is incomparably superior as a work of art to any of the Spanish sixteenth-century prose romances, Ariosto had nevertheless to contend with the aesthetic problems that had taken root in late medieval romance: the profusion of episodes and characters, the pretence of historicity, the role of the marvellous, the relation of pleasure to profit. Ariosto succeeded in creating a coherent structure from the loose, disorganized, and often wearyingly digressive material he inherited from his predecessors by streamlining the technique of *entrelacement* which had remained the standard structural principle of romance since it was adumbrated by Chrétien and developed by the authors of the Prose *Lancelot*. With Ariosto, the rambling structures of the medieval romances are transformed into a firmly marshalled sequence of cantos where the adventures of the various knights are woven harmoniously together without loss of narrative drive. To the conventions of courtly chivalry and the marvels of the Arthurian world, Ariosto brings a sensibility that can still absorb itself in the traditional quandaries of love and honour, celebrating the ideal values of courtly chivalry, while acknowledging all the same the turbulent realities of actual history.

In this regard he was well served by the Italian romance tradition, inasmuch as the sometimes racy, colloquial tone of the oral narrator was capable of striking an ironic compromise between the ideal and the pedestrian.[2] For instance, in the passage that describes the surrender of Angelica's virtue to the Moor Medor, several traditional topics of romance—the tyranny of love, the worthiness of chivalric prowess, the sweet cruelty of the chivalric mistress—are all invoked, only to be deftly skewed towards irony by the puckish tone of the narrator:

If she was not to die of longing she would have to help herself without delay: it was clear to her that there was no time to wait until she was invited to take what she craved. So, snapping the reins of modesty, she spoke out as boldly with her tongue as with her eyes and asked for mercy there and then—which he [Medor], perhaps unknowingly, conceded to her./O Count Orlando! O King of Circassia! Tell me just what good your eminent valour has gained you, what account has been taken of your honour and nobility, what reward your attentions have merited. . ./Angelica let Medor pluck the first rose, hitherto untouched—no one had yet enjoyed the good fortune of setting foot in this garden.   (Canto 19.30-3; p. 220)[3]

Still, even if the narrator's ostensible disapproval of Angelica's ingratitude to Orlando cannot altogether suppress a hint of envy of the infidel Medor's stroke of luck, Ariosto is at other times capable of extolling the virtues of a love that is refined and deepened by the disciplines of Christian chastity. The love scene between Ruggiero and the virginal Bradamant is treated with the kind of awe reserved for the contemplation of an evanescent ideal:

Ruggiero embraced his fair one who blushed redder than a rose; then he culled from her lips the first blooms of their blissful love./A thousand times the two happy lovers renewed their embraces and hugged each other; they were so blissful, their breasts could scarcely contain their joy. . ./Bradamant was ready to concede all the pleasures that an honest virgin may give to a lover in order to keep him from sadness without hurting her own honour.

(Canto 22.32-4; p. 259)

These shifts from the earthly to the sublime require of the artist a high degree of control over his subject-matter. Ariosto himself is a pervasive, dominating presence in the poem, dispelling with his comic irony any illusions that the narrative could possibly be true history. On the contrary, the unfettered creative freedom of the poet sets up an interplay between the world of the characters and the overmastering sway of his own imagination. Ariosto produces abrupt transitions from the reality of the story itself to that of the storyteller entertaining his patron. For example, there is a scene towards the end of Canto 42 where Rinaldo is tempted to put himself through a test that will determine whether he belongs to the Order of Cuckoldry. He is required by the terms of the test to drink wine from a golden chalice: 'Almost persuaded to seek for what perhaps he would rather not have found, Rinaldo reached out, grasped the chalice and made to undergo the test. But then he considered the danger he might be incurring by setting it to his lips. Permit me, however to rest my Lord; then I shall tell you what the paladin replied' (Canto 42.104; p. 509). Such creative whimsy renders the substance of the romance pliable and subjective; whatever truth the narrative might lay claim to must find its ultimate justification in a broad analogy with God's lordship over creation: the poet employs his manifold talents and encyclopaedic knowledge in the fabrication of a rich world of the imagination which he is able to supervise with an authority and confidence comparable to the Almighty's regulation of the universe.[4]

Not long after its appearance, the *Orlando Furioso* gave rise to aesthetic controversies which intensified towards the middle of the century as a result of two factors: the revival of theoretical discussion of literature after the publication in 1548 of Francesco Robortello's commentary on Aristotle's *Poetics*, and the new climate of moral seriousness in art and literature fostered by the Council of Trent. In an age of growing scientific awareness and bitter disputes over the nature of religious truth, the poet's freedom to create fictions becomes hard to distinguish from indulgence in idle fancies. Whereas a medieval writer like Chrétien de Troyes could attribute his literary skills to the grace of God, the increasingly elaborate pretence of later writers that their romances are historically true testifies to the gradual erosion of the belief that the narrative imagination is animated by a transcendent spirit. Renaissance controversies over the marvellous in fiction or over the value of poetic discourse are symptomatic of the more fundamental problem of reconciling the secular artist's powers of invention with classical or religious aspirations to universal truth.

Like the authors of late medieval romance, the classical theorists of the Renaissance were unable to resist the attractions of historical veracity or moral exemplariness as standards of truth for fiction. Although they took Aristotle as their principal authority, much of their thinking, as Bernard Weinberg has shown, was based on distortions or misunder-standings of Aristotle's *Poetics*.[5] One of the most significant distortions concerned the question of mimesis. According to Aristotle, an epic or tragedy was the imitation 'of action and life';[6] Renaissance theorists, however, were inclined to interpret mimesis more narrowly, as the imitation of an action in nature or history. Aristotle's mimesis, a difficult if not enigmatic concept that still allowed for the representation in art of 'actions' that were neither external nor empirically perceptible, crystallized into the Renaissance notion of verisimilitude, which conceived the truth of poetry as conditional upon its approximation to historical reality or empirical plausibility. Such a conception of poetic truth clearly left little place in theory for the ideal or the marvellous.[7] In this respect the doctrine of verisimilitude tended to curtail the freedom of the artistic imagination and detract from its authoritativeness.

Aristotle's ideas of necessity and probability, the twin principles of unity of action, were similarly misunderstood. Given the neo-Aristotelians' diminished confidence in the poetic imagination, Aristotle's unity of action was seen not in terms of an inherent order, or of the intrinsic logic of an aesthetic object, but rather as a vague condition of integrity in which the different parts of a narrative would be related to one another and to the central action on the basis of the unities of time and place, or in a way that was close to neo-Horatian ideas of decorum.[8] These latter largely pertained to the tone and style of the poem, but they were also extended to character and action on the principle of the coherence of natural organisms as opposed to artificial monsters created from disparate parts that did not naturally belong together. Decorum promoted a kind of aesthetic conservatism which required of literary characters that they correspond to fixed types, say fitting things, behave correctly, and generally be consistent with themselves and with their supposed counterparts in nature throughout the duration of the poem.

When it came to a consideration of the ends of poetry, both neo-Aristotelian and Horatian theorists, influenced by Tridentine strictures, place edification above pleasure.[9] The poet must include philosophical reflections, *exempla*, proverbs or sentences in his work so as to enhance its moral utility. Since pleasure was for the most part regarded as a means to moral improvement, the specific aesthetic qualities of the work were assimilated to devices of classical rhetoric whose object was to persuade and instruct an audience.[10]

In all the major areas of theoretical discussion—imitation, unity of action, decorum, and profit—the Renaissance theorists' mistrust of the individual poet's powers of invention corresponds to a phenomenon in Renaissance epic identified by Robert Durling as a loss of confidence in the convention of the inspired narrator.[11] Without a sense of inspiration the poet is a man like any other, unable to find access through his imagination to absolute or universal truth, and therefore bereft of the authority to claim intrinsic validity for his creations. The narrative poet, as a result, loses much of his freedom to follow the inner priorities of his imagination and order the work to suit his own aesthetic intentions.

The dissociation of truth from the imagination engendered a series of dichotomies—verisimilitude – the marvellous, unity – variety, pleasure – profit, poetry – history—whose resolution became a central concern of Renaissance literary theory and practice. Not the least of these dichotomies was the division that separated high art from the popular. In contrast to the comic romances which enjoyed great popularity, there appeared serious epics which aspired to emulate the achievements of Homer and Virgil, such as Trissino's *Italia liberata dai Goti* (1547-8) or Bernardo Tasso's *Amadigi* (1559), this last inspired by *Amadis of Gaul*.[12]

As the major form of lengthy narrative that had survived from the Middle Ages, the romance of chivalry began to attract the attention of theorists who sought to define its generic properties in the light of classical precepts. This gave rise to the famous Renaissance quarrel over Ariosto and Torquato Tasso.[13] In the view of Ariosto's admirers chivalric romance was *sui generis* and could not be criticized from a classical standpoint. Torquato Tasso and his supporters, on the other hand, considered the romances to be modern, degenerate epigones of the ancient epic which needed to be refined in accordance with Aristotelian principles. Tasso's position was, in fact, one of compromise between the strict classicism of poets like Trissino, and the comparative licence of Ariosto. For Tasso noted that, while the *Orlando Furioso* had brilliantly sustained its popularity with the public at large, Trissino's *Italia Liberata*, in spite of its scrupulous observance of classical proprieties, 'was read by few, mentioned by fewer . . . and buried in the libraries of a few scholars'.[14]

In his own epic, the *Gierusalemme Liberata* (1581), and in his theoretical discourses on epic poetry, Tasso relaxed neo-Aristotelian rules so as to accommodate some of the qualities of the *Orlando Furioso* that had captivated the contemporary public.[15] While accepting the neo-Aristotelian notion of verisimilitude as a standard of poetic truth, he recognized the advantages of marvellous episodes, and evolved the concept of a 'legitimate' marvellous based on variety of description, great historical events, Christian miracles, or accounts of exotic lands, in order to acquire for the serious epic the chivalric romance's enviable capacity to produce *admiratio*, those feelings of wonderment aroused by the revelation of unknown or unexpected marvels.[16] Tasso, similarly, insists on unity of action and a sober, heroic style, but these theoretical ideals should be tempered by the inclusion of romantic adventures. The high moral intent of Tridentine literature is also upheld, while acknowledging all the same that the poet must entertain his audience. Torquato Tasso's efforts to combine the precepts of neo-Classical aesthetics with the marvellous delights of romance were directed ultimately towards the same end as Ariosto's comic irony, that is, the achievement of a synthesis in narrative art between heroic and transcendent values on the one hand, and actual experience of ordinary reality on the other. A similar wish to recover the creative freedom of the imagination without thereby sacrificing its authority will characterize Cervantes's own literary endeavours.

The issues that preoccupied poets and literary theorists in Italy became current also in the Iberian Peninsula. Here the Renaissance interest in reviving the ancient epic manifested itself in the composition of serious works on heroic themes of empire, such as Alonso de Ercilla's *La Araucana* (1569-90) and Luís de Camoẽs's *Os Lusíadas* (1572). There was no equivalent to the comic verse epic of Ariosto, even though the *Furioso's* influence on Spanish literature was considerable. It was rather for its heroic and serious elements, its love-poetry and noble sentiments, its lively characterization and dramatic episodes that the poem was admired.[17] Only the prose romance *Tirant lo blanc* (1490) by the Catalan Joanot Martorell displays an ironic tone and comic gusto that foreshadow the *Orlando Furioso*. But *Tirant* turned out to be an isolated phenomenon, its influence curtailed by the success of *Amadis of Gaul* and its myriad successors.

Neo-Aristotelian literary theory filtered gradually into Spain in the second half of the sixteenth century, particularly through the influence of Cesare Scaligero on the poetic commentaries of Fernando de Herrera. It was not until the publication of Alonso López Pinciano's *Philosophia antigua poética* in 1596, only nine years before Part I of *Don Quixote* appeared, that neo-Aristotelian ideas were expounded in a systematic manner in Spanish. Although there is no conclusive evidence to prove that Cervantes derived his familiarity with neo-Aristotelian doctrines directly from El Pinciano, nor, for that matter, from first-hand contact with the Italians during his sojourns in Italy, Cervantes's work, nevertheless, reveals a wide knowledge of Italian literature and literary theory.[18] The *Quixote* contains numerous allusions to *Orlando Furioso*; for instance, the mad knight's imitation on Sierra Morena of Orlando's madness, his mistaking of a barber's basin for Mambrino's helmet, or his ride on Clavileño, a wooden cousin of Ruggiero's hippogryph. Furthermore, the terms in which Cervantes discusses the art of narrative have been shown to be similar to the theories of the Italians, particularly Torquato Tasso's.[19] Not surprisingly, the aesthetic questions at issue in the Ariosto – Tasso quarrel are contained in *Don Quixote*, and are even reflected to this day in critical discussion of Cervantes's novel. For it is natural on the one hand to see in Cervantes's satire of the chivalric romances a desire, like Tasso's, to purge romance of its defects while salvaging its best qualities, and on the other, to associate Cervantes's robustly ironic humour with Ariosto's.

In a widely-influential article, Leo Spitzer cast Cervantes very much in the Olympian mould of an Ariosto: 'High above the world-wide cosmos of his making, in which hundreds of characters, situations, vistas, themes, plots, and subplots are merged, Cervantes's artistic self is enthroned, an all-embracing creative self, a visibly omnipresent artistic Creator who graciously takes the reader into his confidence showing him the work of art in the making, and the laws to which it is necessarily subjected.'[20] Spitzer, however, remains vague about the laws to which the *Quixote* 'necessarily' conforms. These laws have been assumed by other scholars to be the rules of Tasso and the neo-Aristotelians, a view normally substantiated by citing the remarks made by the Canon of Toledo in *Don Quixote* Part I Chapter xlvii, where he criticizes the romances of chivalry for their lack of unity and verisimilitude, their lapses in decorum, and their general disregard of the moral ends of poetry. Nevertheless, like Tasso, the Canon does find something to praise in the romances, namely the freedom they afford a writer to display the full scope of his imagination.

The Canon, what is more, confesses to the priest that he once tried his hand at writing a chivalric romance in which he sought to follow the precepts of the neo-Aristotelians. The project was abandoned, however, when he realized that since the public at large care nothing for the rules of art, his theoretical rectitude would be appreciated by no more than a handful of discerning men (I. xlviii. 427). The Canon's remarks are reminiscent of Tasso's own wry observation on the epic of Trissino that for all its classical propriety it lay gathering dust in the libraries of a few scholars. By making the Canon so dubious of the actual value of rule-based aesthetics, Cervantes is marking his distance from Tasso's attempts to combine Aristotle with Ariosto. For the Canon of Toledo is expressing misgivings not about Trissino's neo-classical epic but about romances written according to the theoretical compromise devised precisely by Tasso himself.

The existence of the *Quixote* is, needless to say, proof enough that Cervantes did not himself share the Canon of Toledo's despair of ever writing literature that would appeal to the general public without losing the esteem of the cultivated minority. Although his narrative fiction shows him, like Ariosto and Tasso, to be in search of a synthesis between transcendent ideals and everyday realities, his approach was that of a working writer rather than a literary theorist. The variety of tone and style, the boldness with which genres are mingled or contraposed in his work suggest an unflagging will to experiment. Indeed, Cervantes's imagination seems to have been a kind of melting-pot in which new literary forms and ideas imported from Italy, like the pastoral novel or the Renaissance *novella*, could exist alongside or even be crossed with narrative styles drawn from popular indigenous sources, such as the literature of roguery running from *La Celestina* to the new picaresque novels. In many respects Cervantes was a hoarder of literary ideas, reluctant ever to discard or disown any of his material even when he was engaged in other modes of writing. For example, in the Dedication of *The Labours of Persiles and Sigismunda* published in 1617, a year after his death, he is still promising his patron the Count of Lemos a sequel to the pastoral novel *La Galatea*, his first lengthy work of fiction published in 1585, even though he had by this time attacked the idea of pastoral as artificial and absurd both in the *Quixote* and in the *Colloquy of the Dogs*.

Cervantes's modes of writing were diverse and concurrent, especially in that intense period of creativity towards the end of his life between the publication of Part I of the *Quixote* in 1605 and his death in 1616. In the course of these eleven years he produced the major part of his work in various genres. There would seem then to be little point in attempting to establish a consistent, chronological order of development in Cervantes's works from the evidence of what he published during that period. Any such pattern would presuppose some ultimate preference for either 'romance' or 'realism', and the signs are that Cervantes felt able to move quite freely from one mode to the other.[21] Just as he could contemplate finishing *La Galatea* after having parodied pastoral elsewhere in his writings, so too could he have been writing the *Persiles*—a Christian romance based on Tasso's aesthetic principles—at the same time that he was composing Part II of *Don Quixote* or some of his *Exemplary Novels*.[22] Cervantes's parody of romance and, as I will argue presently, his conscious attempts to supersede its procedures, would not have precluded his having experimented at broadly the same time with Tasso's advanced ideas on the art of narrative.[23]

Cervantes's search for a synthesis of the transcendent and the natural can be illustrated in his *Exemplary Novels*, where there are two distinct types of story. The more numerous type concerns well-born or aristocratic characters who are involved in an intrigue of love that is articulated, like the stories of the Italian *novellieri*, by means of ingenious plots relying upon coincidences, disguises, sudden reversals, *deus ex machina* devices, and the usual stock-in-trade of the romance author.[24] The other type of story is set in plebeian or low-life milieux. The action is loose and episodic, designed to evoke a particular social ambience and depict characters whose way of life would be exotic or aberrant to the reader, either because they are mad, like the sententious graduate Vidriera who believed he was made of glass, or because they are socially marginal, like the confraternity of boy-thieves in Seville run by the old rogue Monipodio. However, there are two stories, *The Young Gypsy Girl* and *The Illustrious Kitchenmaid*, where Cervantes invents an Italianate love-plot and sets it in a picaresque context, as if to invite quite deliberately an acute conflict between ideal and mundane realities that would call upon his best resources to reconcile. In both these hybrid stories the beautiful young heroine, who would conventionally have belonged in a noble environment, grows up and lives among the common people, either with gypsies or as a serving-girl in a roadside inn. She is eventually courted and won by a lover from a higher social class whereupon it is discovered that she too is well-born and everything ends happily. In both cases, the heroine's beauty and secret aristocratic origins betoken high virtue and ideal qualities in the traditional romance way, but here they survive untainted and inviolate in a promiscuous social nether-world of thieves, tarts, and gypsies.

Much the most intriguing examples of Cervantes's literary grafting of romance and picaresque-style low-life tales are the twinned stories *The Deceitful Marriage* and *The Colloquy of the Dogs*. The former exhibits the well-wrought ingenuities of Cervantes's Italianate manner, while the latter is an unprecedented autobiographical account of a dog's life in contemporary Spain. Formally, the *Colloquy* is a remarkable fusion of picaresque tale (along the lines of *Lazarillo de Tormes* or *Guzmán de Alfarache*), animal fable, and Renaissance philosophical dialogue. The stresses and strains inherent in such an unlikely cross-breeding of high and low are well caught in the personalities of the talking dogs. Berganza is impetuous, voluble, given to gossip and digression when recalling his days of service under different masters. Cipión, on the other hand, is something of an intellectual, and, inevitably, a bit of a prig. He keeps interrupting the other dog, reproving him for straying from the point, interjecting a pompous moral observation here, an aesthetic comment there; in short, he provides a reflective counterpoint to the raw experience of Berganza's adventures.

Unlike the author-dominated plot of *The Deceitful Marriage*, which is full of witty narrative twists and sleights of hand, the dialogue-form of the *Colloquy* allows Cervantes to disappear behind his two canine interlocutors, who are left to muse inconclusively upon the ironies of social life and sundry other topics, chief amongst them being the mystery of their own powers of speech. The connection between the stories is provided by the human protagonist of the *Deceitful Marriage*,

Campuzano, an unreliable soldier just out of hospital where he has been treated for syphilis contracted from the harlot he married. No sooner does he finish telling his friend Peralta the story of his marriage than he announces that he once overheard two dogs conversing one night while he was lying awake in his hospital bed. He gives Peralta the text of the *Colloquy* which he swears is a faithful transcript of what passed between the dogs.

The indecorous linking of two such disparate stories seems calculated to stir up all the fundamental dilemmas of neo-Classical aesthetics. Where the *Deceitful Marriage* is verisimilar, the *Colloquy* is outrageously implausible; where its action is unified, the *Colloquy*'s is varied and open-ended. Conversely, if the *Colloquy* strives after edification, the *Marriage* is entirely ruled by pleasure; and while the dogs yearn for some transcendent authority, their enigmatic existence must be taken on trust from a decidedly shady character like Campuzano.[25] Indeed, by pulling the two stories together around a pox-ridden swindler, Cervantes creates a startling figure of the debauched and rather uninspiring condition of the narrative imagination. Unlike other *Exemplary Novels*, there is in the twinning of the *Marriage* and the *Colloquy* no sign at all of synthesis. Instead there are complex, unresolved tensions cultivated knowingly by Cervantes as though in despair of ever regaining the authoritativeness of his predecessors.

From this perspective, the *Quixote* will be seen to occupy a unique place in the melting-pot of Cervantes's imagination. For here alone does he renounce altogether the Renaissance quest for a synthesis of the ideal and the real, and creates instead a sharp, comical antithesis between them. Such a break with romance cannot be accounted for solely by the fact that the *Quixote* is a parody. Both the *Orlando Furioso* and *Tirant lo blanc* also contain parodic elements. The critical difference lies in the nature of Cervantes's parody. For all their misgivings about the idealized world of chivalry, Ariosto and Martorell are ultimately trapped by genre: the conventions of romance determine the structure of their narratives and shape the experience of their characters. In the *Quixote*, however, the entire world of chivalric romance exists nowhere other than inside the mad hero's head. All the absurdities for which the romances of chivalry had been taken to task by neo-Aristotelian theorists and Counter-Reformation moralists now become quite simply the stuff of lunacy. Aesthetic quarrels and moral disputes are thus superseded at a stroke by the fortuitous birth of a comic idea whose elaboration will lead Cervantes out of the dichotomies and deadlocks of Renaissance aesthetics. Literary theory is not, however, abandoned, it acts as a constant frame of reference. The 1605 Prologue, in fact, evinces a high degree of theoretical self-consciousness as well as Cervantes's pride in the innovatory character of his comic narrative.

(ii) *The 1605 Prologue*

Nowhere better than in the Prologue to Part I of *Don Quixote* can one analyse Cervantes's own attitude to his work. Addressed to the unoccupied reader, it immediately broaches the problem of evaluating the fruits of his 'sterile and ill-cultivated' wit. What else could it produce but some impoverished, capricious invention? Cervantes affects to recognize his incapacity to judge its true worth since a loving father is often blind to the faults of his son. Such a self-deprecating attitude should, of course, put the alert reader on his guard. It is the classic stance of the Socratic ironist, cunningly abasing himself the better to lull the presumptuous into a self-betraying complacency.[26] One can sense an ironic trap being set in the depths of a long, winding sentence, shaded by an array of nuances:

> But I who appear to be the father am in fact the stepfather of Don Quixote, and I will therefore not swim with the tide of custom nor implore you, almost with tears in my eyes, like others do, dearest reader, to forgive or overlook whatever faults you might find in this my child, for you are neither a relative nor a friend of his, and you have a soul in your body and a free will as good as the next man's, and what is more you are in your own house, of which you are master as the king is master of his taxes, and you are aware of the popular saying that 'under my cloak I will kill the king'.[27]

Cervantes's liberal invitation to the reader to judge the work as he pleases swells rhetorically in tones of unctuous good will, reaching a climax in the image of the self-sufficient reader, king-like in his authority to judge and dispose. But there would seem to be a sting in the tail of such generosity: the apparently all-knowing reader must also surely be acquainted with the common saying that 'under my cloak I will kill the king'.[28] The 'king' here refers to the reader who has just been invited by Cervantes to view himself as the sovereign judge of the text. This old proverb, which evokes the cloak-and-dagger stealth of a regicide, following anti-climactically as it does after the highest pitch of a crescendo of flattering encouragement, represents a declaration of ironic intent by Cervantes: whatever regal authority the reader might arrogate to himself when evaluating the novel should be tempered by a degree of circumspection lest there be surprises in store which might upset overconfident judgements.[29] The entreaties and special pleading to the reader by other authors, especially those of Spanish romances, are replaced here by an attitude which is dialectical, implying a relationship between author and reader which is fraught with ironic possibilities.

As a foretaste of things to come in the main narrative, Cervantes proceeds to engage his reader in some devious ironic banter. He protests that he had originally intended to present the novel without the conventional introductory paraphernalia of prologues, sonnets, epigrams, and encomia such as grace other books. He graphically describes how he had been seeking to compose a suitable prologue for his novel without making much headway until a friend came into the room and asked what was troubling him. In Cervantes's explanation of his difficulties we again experience the evasive obliquity of his irony.

He starts by playing down his talents once more, professing to be abashed by what the public might say if they found such a paltry work presented to them bereft of the customary trappings such as marginal commentaries or maxims from philosophers like Aristotle and Plato, chosen to assure the reader of the author's learning and authority. But in the sentences that follow one detects a degree of ironic criticism of such practices. Under the guise of admiring other authors' readiness to quote Sacred Scripture in their fictions, Cervantes points out the inaptness of such citations, as when, for example, an ecstatic lover is depicted by the author only to be followed immediately by 'a little Christian homily'. Here one finds Cervantes covertly attacking the sort of indecorous juxtaposition of profane fantasy and sanctimonious didacticism which we have previously encountered in Montalvo's *Esplandián*. The irony is aimed at what we have called the didactic alibi of the romance author, who uses didacticism as a pretext for fantasy or, worse still, for a form of salaciousness. Cervantes professes to be inhibited by the fact that he is unable to provide these spurious marks of respectability: 'For I find myself incapable of supplying them because of my inadequacy and scanty learning, and because I am too spiritless and lazy by nature to go about looking for authors to say for me what I can say myself without them' (p. 27). The passage ends with another unexpected ironic sting. His self-deprecation is suddenly converted into a sharp dismissal of the whole panoply of authoritative props; he can very well say what he has to say without corroboration from anybody.

Nevertheless, Cervantes is still pretending to baulk at the reader's expectation of authoritativeness. The friend slaps his forehead in amused exasperation and chides Cervantes for his obtuseness: how could a witty, intelligent, and talented man like him be stumped by such a trivial obstacle? The reader's desire for signs of authority can be satisfied by inventing whatever sonnets, epigrams, and encomia he likes and appending some grand-sounding name to them. As for citations from the Bible or from authors of Antiquity, all he need do is quote anything which comes to mind or which can be conveniently dug up and that will be that. When the friend gives various examples of commonplace classical and biblical maxims, the Prologue turns into a malicious parody of the citation of authorities. A venerable and ancient literary tradition is overturned and mocked, demonstrating just how shallow and deceitful such impressive paraphernalia can be in the hands of dishonest writers.

Cervantes's introduction of an imaginary friend into his Prologue is a device that permits him to dramatize the state of affairs between a contemporary author and his public. He and his friend act out two contrasting authorial attitudes towards a notional reader. For himself he reserves the role of a writer reluctant to practise the chicanery of his fellows but who is none the less anxious that a reader might despise him for his conspicuous lack of authority. Cervantes clearly relishes this image of himself as a timid, painfully honest writer, neurotically inhibited from publishing the fruits of his imagination for fear of being rejected on the whim of a despotic reader. By way of contrast we have the cavalier cynicism of the friend who urges Cervantes to pay lip-service to tradition and yet remain true, if he must, to his sincere wish to present his story as fiction, 'naked and unadorned'. The friend is thus made responsible for whatever opprobrium might attach to the real Cervantes's underhand approach to his reader. He blithely suggests that Cervantes append to his text a transparently irrelevant list of authorities going from A to Z, a ploy that is recommended because its ironical duplicity will not fool the intelligent reader, since the deception is so obvious, but might take in simpletons or pedants (p. 29). The friend agrees with Cervantes that since his novel is merely an invective against the romances of chivalry it has no need of any authorities to buttress it, nor of support from Aristotle, St. Basil, or Cicero, nor should its 'fabulous nonsense' ('fabulosos disparates') be confused with 'the niceties of truth', with 'astrological observations', 'geometrical measurements', 'rhetorical argument', or even preaching, which would only lead to 'mingling the human with the divine' (p. 30).

Now such an appraisal of the province of fiction is radically distinct from that of the writers of Arthurian romance and of the neo-Aristotelians. Not only does it situate fiction squarely in the realm of the human imagination without mention of divine inspiration, it clearly extricates it from other branches of knowledge and other departments of truth, especially the truths of religion. Cervantes will be left free to operate in a self-sufficient aesthetic context, absolved from the need to defer to or seek justification from other quarters. Clearly the friend can proclaim this marvellous creative freedom for Cervantes because *Don Quixote* has no higher aim than to discredit the absurd romances: 'Keep your aim steadily fixed on overthrowing the ill-based fabric of these books of chivalry, abhorred by so many yet praised by so many more; for if you achieve that, you will have achieved no small thing' (p. 30). The friend does not refer to a mere parody of the books of chivalry but to the overthrow of the entire machinery of chivalric romance which is alleged to be unsound.

Cervantes's friend, in fact, offers positive advice on how to set about this task. From his comments one can extrapolate elements of an aesthetic attitude which would have informed Cervantes in the composition of the *Quixote*. In the first place there is a reference to 'imitation': 'In what you are writing you have only to make use of imitation, and the more perfect the imitation the better your writing will be' (p. 30). Now the word imitation here is vague but it has an unmistakable Aristotelian ring to it. Nevertheless, Cervantes would seem to be talking about imitation in a way which differs from that of the neo-Aristotelians, as something that is not exactly identical with the reader's sense of verisimilitude. Good writing born of imitation, it implies, derives from the author's own intimate engagement with his subject-matter. Significantly, Cervantes chooses the progressive subjunctive to describe the author's activity: 'en lo que fuere escribiendo', suggesting thereby that mimesis is the striving after a truth perceived primarily by the author in the process of creation.

This notion of imitation is elaborated a few lines later when the friend again tells Cervantes that he has no need to go begging maxims from philosophers or seek the counsels of Sacred Scripture, but should see that he uses plain, well-turned sentences that will 'depict your intention as far as possible and to the best of your ability' ('pintando en todo lo que alcanzárades y fuere posible, vuestra intención'). The curious phrase Cervantes uses—'to depict' or, more literally, 'to paint' one's intentions—provides an apt image of a creative writer who is not directly concerned with reflecting an historical action or an everyday experience, but is engaged rather in a form of imaginative self-realization, where success is in any case uncertain, as is indicated by the recourse once again to the subjunctive ('lo que alcanzárades y fuere posible'). We have here the ideas of imitation ('pintando') and purpose ('vuestra intención') closely bound up together in a transitive relationship between an author's artistic skill and his creative will.[30] Thus in Cervantes's account of mimesis the object of imitation has as much to do with the artist's own purposes as with the reader's sense of verisimilitude. By implicitly distinguishing between an aesthetic object and a natural object Cervantes avoids the neo-Aristotelian bias towards referentiality which made the validity of literary discourse conditional upon its appearing to denote things in the external world.[31]

There can be found in the friend's statement of the purpose of the *Quixote* a similar emphasis on specific aesthetic values rather than on historical verisimilitude. Cervantes's objective, he declares, should be twofold—to give harmless pleasure to the public, and to win praise for the author's artistic skills, even from the most disobliging reader: 'Be careful too that the reading of your story makes the melancholy laugh and the merry laugh louder; that the simpleton is not confused; that the intelligent admire your invention, the serious do not despise it, nor the prudent withhold their praise'[32]. A distinction is made here once more between simple and intelligent readers.[33] The first kind read the story or history (for there exists this ambiguity in the Spanish *historia*) purely for amusement, content merely to react to the various comic incidents without bothering to consider its artistic merits; for these readers the question of whether the narrative is fictional or historical does not arise.

Intelligent readers, however, should be encouraged to see beyond the *historia* to the *invención*, and they will then, it is hoped, respond with admiration, respect, and praise. Cervantes, therefore, conceives of the *Quixote* as operating on two levels: the *historia*, which would correspond to the fraudulent referentiality of narrative fiction, its imitation of history, and the *invención*, where the author has 'depicted his intentions' and where aesthetic value consequently resides.[34] The difficulty for the narrative artist lies in making artistic invention compatible with pseudo-denotation, in effecting, that is, a convincing transition from ostensibly historical reference to distinctive aesthetic form.

This passage from the pseudo-historical to the aesthetic is less problematical in symbolic or allegorical modes of narrative. Chrétien de Troyes could circumvent the problem of identifying his romances with history not just because he and his audience might genuinely have believed that the romances referred to real events but chiefly because the standard of truth was in any case not held to be that of verisimilitude. With Chrétien the aesthetic is coterminous with the spiritual: the truth of the romances inheres in the essential beauty of the structure (the *bele conjointure*) that Chrétien's skill has fashioned from inherited legendary material; this ability to find a beautiful structure is due to the grace of God. For Cervantes, however, such an explanation of the aesthetic had become unavailable; the literary imagination could no longer claim to have been inspirited to creation by a transcendent power. Instead, author and reader of fiction were in thrall to historical verisimilitude as the only credible alternative to outright fantasy.

It is in this context that one can best appreciate the historic significance of Cervantes's creative stance in the *Quixote* as expressed in the regicidal proverb: 'under my cloak I will kill the king'. For although he exempts his reader 'from every respect and obligation', and grants him the freedom to 'say anything you think fit about this story, without fear of being abused for a bad opinion, or rewarded for a good one', his threat to kill the king suggests once more that the narrative works on two levels: a surface level at which the reader is free to judge as he pleases, but also at a further level that is 'under the cloak'; it is here that the despotic, king-like reader whom Cervantes affects to be in awe of when he asks his friend for advice with his Prologue, may, as it were, be 'killed'. The old Jewish proverb to all intents and purposes sets forth a formula for narrative irony that envisages the superficial sense of the *historia* being reversed or contradicted by the thrust of the *invención*: Don Quixote's career may seem to be little more than a 'history' of a madman's laughable clashes with reality, but Cervantes's inventiveness will transform these adventures into a pattern of aesthetic experience capable of eliciting from the know-all reader responses whose value cannot be determined by considerations of historical plausibility. Cervantes's ironic formula thus provides a solution to the fundamental Renaissance dilemma of reconciling the individual writer's powers of invention with his need to acknowledge empirical reality.[35] At a superficial level verisimilitude is observed, and yet, by articulating the narrative on the basis of ironic surprises, Cervantes will divert the reader's attention from the story's denotative accuracy to an appreciation of the imaginative order it embodies.

The 1605 Prologue amounts to a defence of the imagination, a vindication of the writer's creative freedom from the dead hand of verisimilitude, historicity, or didacticism. Blowing away all the nervous dissimulation of fictionality, Cervantes embraces the pleasures of invention, exposing the didactic alibi of late medieval romance and abolishing the contradiction between historicity and imagination which had got the Spanish romance writers into such knots of self-justification.[36] Now all that tangled flotsam from the wreckage of Arthurian romance is used to trick out and festoon the narrative personae Cervantes adopts in the *Quixote*. The crabbed, disingenuous subterfuges of such as Montalvo are inspired with an ironical breeziness: Cervantes masquerades as the editor of an obscure and unreliable historical text; at one point the narrative is broken off abruptly in the middle of a fight between Don Quixote and a Basque while the editor explains 'that the author of this history left the battle in suspense at this critical point, with the excuse that he could find no more records of Don Quixote's exploits than those related here' (I.viii.74); Cervantes now intrudes details of his own experience, as Montalvo had done in Chapters 98 and 99 of the *Esplandian*, to describe how he happened upon an Arabic version of the missing history among some parchments and old papers being sold off by a young lad in the Alcaná of Toledo, a street of Jewish merchants; having bought up the parchments for only half a *real* when he was, in fact, quite prepared to offer six, Cervantes had them translated back into Spanish from the Arabic by a *morisco* who 'promised to translate them well, faithfully and very quickly' for fifty pounds of raisins and three bushels of wheat; after the history is resumed we find ourselves in the hands, not of Montalvo's infallible historian Elisabad, but of a degenerate avatar, Cide Hamete Benengeli, a shifty Moor with pretensions to historical truth that will rise at times to a breathtaking degree of testimonial scruple without yet managing to win the reader's trust quite. The history of the idealistic knight thus comes down to us after having transmigrated through a variety of languages and textual variants, and changed hands several times over in the market-place of a bustling town.

It would be a simple reader indeed who could be taken in by the *Quixote*'s 'illusion of historicity'. But while gesturing at the wholly fictitious character of his story, and renouncing any *a priori* claim to special truthfulness or authoritativeness, Cervantes sets out to win respect for his imagination even from the most 'prudent' and 'serious' readers with his ironic formula of 'killing the king'. For as we shall presently see, over the specious verisimilitude of the *historia* is thrown the cloak of Don Quixote's madness behind which Cervantes's wit will be ever ready to defeat the expectations of his readers. The knight's madness acts therefore as a mantle of comedy that allows the author a creative space beyond verisimilitude in which to assert the freedom of his imagination against the sovereignty of the reader's judgement.

(iii)   *The Nature of Don Quixote's Madness*

When he made his hero mad, Cervantes broke decisively with romance: the Platonist world of Arthurian chivalry was converted into a fantasy and set against a reality defined by common sense and ordinary experience. In *Don Quixote* empirical truth is the scourge of fantasy; the mad knight is mocked and ridiculed for ignoring it with astonishing cruelty at times. But if Cervantes, unlike Ariosto or Tasso, does not attempt to reconcile verisimilitude with the marvels of romance, creating instead a sharp antithesis between them, how did he salvage the possibility of producing *admiratio*, that species of pleasure considered by theorists and writers of the period to be indispensable to narrative art?

Admiratio, in epic and romance, was thought to consist in the element of surprise and wonderment caused by the telling of such exotic, supernatural or magical events as would transport the reader's imagination into the realms of the unknown. The systematic ridiculing of romance marvels in the *Quixote* might, therefore, suggest that Cervantes renounced *admiratio* as part of his literary purpose. Nevertheless, Cervantes himself points out that laughter should not be the sole response to the knight's lunacies, 'for Don Quixote's adventures must be honoured either with wonder [*admiración* in the Spanish] or with laughter' (II.xliv.748). *Admiratio*, just as much as mirth, forms part of his intention in the *Quixote*; but if as a desired effect it is entirely traditional, the means of achieving it is novel.

Where his predecessors sought to retain *admiratio* by effecting some sort of compromise between the marvellous and verisimilitude, Cervantes effectively re-defines the nature of the marvellous by seeking it, not in the supernatural, but in the madness of his protagonist: although the madness is consistently mocked, it is used all the same to turn the tables on the reader, whose common sense is never actually confounded but neither is it ever decisively triumphant over the knight's inspired lunacy. Don Quixote's enormously resourceful wit, alluded to in the *ingenioso hidalgo* of the original title, thus produces *admiratio*—the surprises, reversals, and unsuspected discoveries that were formerly sought in the magical and the supernatural. The ultimate source of wonder in the *Quixote*, after all, is the fact that the hero's madness should endure for so long and through so much adversity. By all normal reckoning, the knight's chivalric nonsense should have collapsed well before his second sally, and yet, without once offending the reader's alerted sense of verisimilitude, Cervantes prolongs the madness in repeated defiance of common-sense expectations. It is a *tour de force* of narrative wit, a triumphant vindication of the author's creative freedom from the restrictions of verisimilitude.

Nevertheless, Don Quixote can be used so effectively to outwit common sense because his madness is not arbitrary; there is a method in it which regulates his behaviour and structures his arguments, rescuing him from the status of a mere puppet in a knockabout farce, and endowing his chivalric mission with a peculiar cogency. This method is derived from the concepts and conventions of Arthurian romance. Set in the context of chivalric ideology, Don Quixote appears no less mad, but his wildest adventures and craziest pronouncements will not then seem entirely pointless. Much modern interpretation of the *Quixote* is based on the supposition that the knight's madness is totally irrational and whimsical. Romantic and Perspectivist critics believe, with varying degrees of intensity, that this is a good thing, and so tend to convert the madness into a metaphor of some kind of faith.[37] Other critics, disapproving of the knight's alleged irrationality, see his madness as a manifestation of pride or ambition, which, as a result of being chastized by Cervantes's comedy, gradually abates; the knight's recovery of reason is held to mark his achievement of wisdom and virtue.[38] 'Soft' and 'hard' critics, and most of the others in between, tend to agree on two fundamental points.[39] First, they dilute Don Quixote's madness by turning it into a metaphor of sorts; the knight cannot just be downright mad, he must also be an actor, or a myth-maker, a visionary tormented by doubt, or even a Christian saint.[40] Second, now that most critics have abandoned the extreme Romantic view epitomized by Unamuno's glorying in the knight's refusal to face facts, it is widely accepted that the movement of the novel is best described as the madman's progressive return to his senses.[41] One view follows from the other: if the madness is taken to be a metaphor of faith or sin, then it is tempting to interpret the novel either as a process of loss or a path of perfection.

Don Quixote's madness, however, is not a metaphor of anything in particular, it is completely *sui generis*, inexplicable, and absurd. What is more, it can be shown that it does not decline during the course of the novel, for what gives the comedy its edge is the relentless earnestness with which the lunatic pursues his mission despite mounting evidence of its futility. Were the madness to abate, the reader's common sense would meet with no resistance, and the novel's capacity to cause *admiratio* would correspondingly diminish. Yet if the madness symbolizes nothing and does not progressively decrease, can one describe the development of the narrative other than as an endlessly repeated series of collisions between illusion and reality? I believe that by analysing the rationale of Don Quixote's madness, seeing its basis in a kind of romance logic, it is possible to produce a reading of the *Quixote* which does no violence to the text while allowing it still a definite movement and shape.

All we are told about Don Quixote's madness is that it was induced by excessive reading of romances of chivalry, which led him to believe that everything written in them was literally true. Cervantes fastens on this simple cause and provides no further explanation. Medical or psychological theories of insanity—whether modern or contemporary—would offer very little that could be relevant to an understanding of the nature of the *hidalgo's* madness.[42] On the other hand, the fact that he is mad pre-empts any kind of moral judgement on his behaviour, for a madman is absolved of responsibility for his actions and cannot therefore commit sin. Don Quixote's madness is no more than an artistic *donnée* which allows Cervantes the freedom to mock the absurdities of Spanish romances of chivalry.

The immediate objects of Cervantes's literary satire become clear in the opening pages of the novel. He is attacking the bombastic prose-style of romance writers such as Feliciano de Silva, the implausibilities of romance typified by the exaggerated number of wounds received by Sir Belianis of Greece, and the rambling narrative structures that seem positively to invite sequels and continuations. But, above all, the knight's madness makes a mockery of the hoary subterfuges employed by writers to justify their unwieldy fictions, namely the illusion of historicity and moral exemplariness. For Don Quixote's madness, as Cervantes presents it, is based on two distinct errors: first, a passive belief in the absolute historical truth of the romances, and following this primary fit of insanity, there appears a militant desire to imitate their heroes' example in the actual world:

> In fact, now that he had utterly wrecked his reason he fell into the strangest fancy that ever a madman had in the whole world. He thought it fit and proper, both in order to increase his renown and to serve the state, to turn knight errant and travel through the world with horse and armour in search of adventures, following in every way the practice of the knights errant he had read of. (I.i.33)

Although the madness has its origins in a literary joke, the way in which Cervantes has made passive belief and militant action interdependent allows for the possibility of extending the satire to the ideals and values enshrined in the romances as well as their purely literary shortcomings.

In the knight's speech on the Golden Age (I.xi.85-7), where he evokes a period in which the highest spiritual and moral ideals actually obtained in the world, there is little evidence of direct authorial mockery. Don Quixote spells out the benefits of that happy condition which he now plans to restore: everything was held in common, there was no labour, no strife, women's freedom of choice in love was entirely respected, there was 'no fraud, deceit, or malice mingled with truth and sincerity', perfect justice reigned, and legal interpretation was unnecessary 'for there were none to judge or be judged'. The state of affairs celebrated here corresponds exactly with the ideals towards which chivalric romance tends: a timeless condition of harmonious integrity in which everything is of a reassuring transparency, since whatever is internal, hidden, or unseen can find uncomplicated expression, there being no self-interest, no lies, no sophistication, and presumably no irony.

However, the tone and style of Don Quixote's Golden Age speech, and the fact that it is addressed to goatherds, reveals Cervantes's attitude to the utopian ideology implicit in chivalric romance: it is indistinguishable from that of pastoral romance, which in the *Colloquy of the Dogs* is quite openly mocked as an absurd literary illusion. What Cervantes is attacking in both pastoral and chivalric romance is not so much the desirability of these ideals in themselves as the means by which romance represents their fulfilment. In so far as they seem to provide ready-made codes of conduct that will guarantee success, the romances foster a moral automatism which compromises the credibility of the lofty ideals they propound. Don Quixote's resolve to 'follow in every way the practice of the knights errant he had read of' leads, in fact, to a crass devaluation of human experience: the hackneyed plots of the Spanish books of chivalry are taken to represent the ideal pattern of life.

Don Quixote's description of a knight errant's career for the enlightenment of Sancho Panza sounds uncannily like a plot-summary of the *Amadis*: the knight errant should prove himself by seeking adventures until he is so well known by his deeds that the king of some country will recognize him from the moment he sees him, a princess will fall in love with him, and he will successfully complete an adventure against all the other knights at court which will show him to be the best knight in the world; then he goes to war against the king's enemies, defeats them, marries the princess when it is revealed that he is in fact the son of a king himself, and eventually succeeds to the throne, bestowing high rewards on his trusty squire (I.xxi.165-8). So strongly is Don Quixote convinced of the truth of this train of events, that he presents it to Sancho as a certain vision of their future, as though his believing in it were sufficient guarantee of its successful outcome.

The description begins in the Spanish text with the use of the subjunctive mood, alternating with verbs in the future tense.

But Don Quixote gets so carried away by the prospect he is describing that the speculative use of subjunctive and future is intermittently replaced by a present tense which soon takes over entirely. As he actualizes this archetypal pattern of romance fiction through his subtle changes of tense, he endows it with the necessary force of a law of nature. Thus a knight errant's destiny becomes a foregone conclusion that can even be referred to in the perfect tense, as when he later rebukes Sancho for suggesting that he should marry the princess Micomicona instead of Dulcinea: 'Who do you think has conquered this kingdom and cut this giant's head off, and made you a marquis—for I take all this as an accomplished fact—if it is not the might of Dulcinea, employing my arm as the instrument of her exploits?' (I.xxx.264). Don Quixote's belief in the inevitable success of chivalric action is absolute, and his attachment to the forms and methods of romance will remain unbreakable throughout the novel.

What does change is the confidence he displays in the *immediacy* of his success, given the increasing interference of wicked enchanters in his life. Even though he is eventually obliged to renounce his activism, we shall see that he refuses adamantly to give up his belief in the validity of romance; at this substantive level he remains hopelessly mad to the last. This, of course, does not mean that Don Quixote fails to evolve as a character; he does indeed, but not as a result of a piecemeal recovery of his senses after a process of self-doubt. Rather he develops only within the stubbornly unaltered bounds of his obsession with romance: he does no more than concede that he may perhaps not have been called to fulfil his destiny as a knight errant as early as he had imagined. In other words, Don Quixote is forced to *postpone* the secondary, active level of madness, but the primary, passive level remains wholly undiminished in the strength of its original conviction.

The entire novel, then, is elaborated from the disjunction that exists between Don Quixote's unwavering belief in the truth of the romances and his capacity to put this belief into practice. There would, in this regard, have been little scope for narrative development were Don Quixote's madness to have involved nothing more subtle than hallucination. But we have seen that Cervantes refers to the knight's ingenuity, and Don

Quixote's ability to reason his way out of the tightest spot suggests that he has been endowed with a conceptual framework which is flexible enough to appreciate other points of view, cope with criticism, and generally adapt itself to unforeseen circumstances.

The basis of the madman's thinking is best illustrated from his explanation of Dulcinea's identity (I.xxv.208-11). He begins by admitting to his squire that the lady Dulcinea can neither read nor write and has never received a letter from him (p. 208):

For our love has always been platonic, and never gone farther than a modest glance. And even that so occasionally that I can truly swear that in all the twelve years I have loved her more than the light of these eyes which the earth will one day devour, I have not seen her four times. And perhaps on those four occasions she did not even once notice that I was looking at her; such is the reserve and reclusion in which her father, Lorenzo Corchuelo, and her mother, Aldonza Nogales, have brought her up.

It seems clear from this that Don Quixote's madness does not involve a crude distortion of visual perception, it amounts rather to a kind of perverse misreading of everyday situations caused by a desire to make them fit his chivalric obsession: the peasant girl Aldonza's 'reserve' is not due to chastity or shyness, more likely it reflects her utter indifference to an old *hidalgo* giving her the eye. Thus, although Don Quixote fully realizes that Aldonza is the daughter of a peasant, he deduces—quite wrongly, as it happens—from his observations of her behaviour that she possesses hidden qualities which transcend her actual circumstances and suggest that she is really a chivalric princess. In basing his arguments on a careful distinction between his lady's actual, empirical condition as Aldonza Lorenzo, the daughter of a peasant family, and her ideal self, the princess Dulcinea del Toboso, Don Quixote is clearly drawing upon the medieval Platonism inherent in Arthurian romance with its distinction between appearances and essences, the formal and the real, the actual and the potential.[43]

There is, of course, a vital difference between Don Quixote and his chivalric predecessors. Earlier knights like Yvain, Cligés, or Amadis were 'upholding' or 'maintaining' the order of chivalry, they were adopting a defensive posture against evil and the corruptions of time. Don Quixote, on the other hand, finds himself in the position of having to *restore* the order of chivalry in a world where the ravages of time and evil are so far advanced that actual appearances have become grossly unfaithful to their real character. The mad knight sees reality much as other people do, but he believes things to be potentially superior to their actual appearances: his task, as in the case of Aldonza Lorenzo, is to identify the romance potential concealed within the humdrum reality he is condemned to live in so as to draw it out for others to see.

In this awesome endeavour he can rely only upon his knowledge of the books of chivalry, for his senses are treacherous, they perceive nothing but the decadent forms of an Age of Iron where the whole phenomenal texture of reality itself has degenerated.[44] For example, when he comes across a village barber wearing a brass basin on his head to shield himself from the rain, Don Quixote declares the basin to be the enchanted helmet of the Moorish King Mambrino captured by Rinaldo in *Orlando Furioso*. Once he has this glorious prize in his possession the knight is disconcerted by Sancho's persistence in calling it a barber's basin:

Do you know what I think, Sancho? This famous piece, this enchanted helmet, must have fallen by some strange accident into the hands of someone who did not esteem it in all its true value. So, not knowing what he was doing, and seeing that it was pure gold, he must have melted down the other half for the sake of the metal, and made from this half what looks like a barber's basin, as you say. But, however that may be, its metamorphosis is of no consequence to me, who knows what it really is. (I.xxi.163)

It is as though the world had been metamorphosed into a banal travesty of itself: the golden helmet of Mambrino appearing to be a barber's basin, the peasant girl Aldonza masking the lady Dulcinea, and he, Don Quixote, having spent a good fifty years of his life in the unprepossessing figure of Alonso Quijano.

And yet, as the Mambrino's helmet episode illustrates, the entire enterprise of changing phenomena back to their traditional romance features hangs on the judgement of Don Quixote, who alone can perceive the true nature of things. Surprisingly enough, the madman is aware that his judgements might appear arbitrary and subjective to other people. In the passage referred to above, where he reveals to Sancho the identity of Dulcinea, the sceptical squire expresses amazement at his master's choice of a lowly village girl as a mistress. The knight counters this with the story of a rich widow who fell in love with a strapping young friar. When asked by the superior why she had chosen such a coarse, ignorant fellow, there being so many learned men in the house, she replied that her choice was not at all bad, 'seeing that for all I want of him he knows as much philosophy as Aristotle, and more' (p. 210). The moral drawn by the high-minded knight, immune as ever to carnal innuendo, is that: 'for what I want of Dulcinea del Toboso, she is as good as the greatest princess in the land'. That is to say, like a lover who is sometimes alone in appreciating the hidden virtues of his beloved, he believes Aldonza has the qualities required to make a proper chivalric mistress, for she has the power to inspire him to reveal his own potential as a knight errant, much as love-poets invent ladies 'so that [they] might be taken for lovers, or men capable of being so'. What Don Quixote, in short, wants of Dulcinea is that she should bring out the best in him and thereby act as the supreme conductor of romance realities, converting what is as yet mere potentiality— unseen, unknown, but none the less true—into something palpable and convincing to other people. Unlike the love-poets, Don Quixote is not inventing an imaginary mistress, he is addressing the real woman, Aldonza Lorenzo, who he is confident will soon appear in her ideal aspect.

The knight realizes, however, that to ignoramuses like Sancho, Dulcinea appears to be a figment of his imagination; he therefore roundly proclaims the chivalric truth in the tones of one who wishes to defy, even though he cannot quell, the doubts of a contemptible audience: 'I imagine all I say to be true neither more nor less, and in my imagination I draw her as I would have her be both as to her beauty and her rank. . . . Let anyone say what he likes, for though the ignorant may reproach me for it, men of judgement will not condemn me' (pp. 210-11).[45] Sensitive to the incredulity of others, Don Quixote will be perennially at pains to prove that his chivalric insights have objective validity; he is aware that without concrete chivalric successes he will be unable to demonstrate that the world of romance exists anywhere other than in his own imagination. Don Quixote's enterprise can be interpreted, then, as a kind of mad epistemological argument over the true nature of reality, an argument conducted in the knowledge that other people will not be easily persuaded to a romance view of the world and will inevitably assume that he is seeing things.[46]

The lunatic's fundamental problem is not one of hallucination, it is one of recognition: perceiving reality as others do, he still has to distinguish between phenomena that are meaningless in terms of romance, and those that are susceptible of chivalric interpretation. In the rather dicey task of identifying covert romance features, he adopts the venerable medieval criterion of resemblance or analogy: whatever reminds him of the books of chivalry is seized on as a providential sign of romance identity and proclaimed as such in the teeth of any empirical evidence to the contrary. After all, Don Quixote's assertions about the nature of reality cannot be validated by empirical methods, since that would involve self-contradiction; they can only be tested coherently by his engaging allegedly romance phenomena in an appropriate chivalric manner; if the response obtained complies with romance tradition then the truth of the assertion will have been objectively demonstrated. When in doubt Don Quixote goes by the books of chivalry; the whole of his epistemology is founded on the authority of literary reminiscence.

(iv) *Don Quixote's Career in Part I: A Qualified Success*

In his first sally Don Quixote is fortunate to meet with favourable circumstances. His arrival at the inn coincides with the blowing of a pighorn which exactly matches his expectations and confirms his prior assumption that the inn is a castle. The good-humoured innkeeper and the two whores comply with his eccentric wishes and cushion him in his affirmations. Again, his success at dispersing the muleteers and other interferers during his vigil (I.iii.44), and his rescue of the unfortunate boy Andrew (I.iv.47-9), further reinforce his confidence that he is able to recognize and interpret signs of romance phenomena. In the Andrew adventure he adjudges the nature of the sounds he hears: 'These cries come no doubt from some man or woman in distress, and in need of my protection and assistance' (p. 47). He challenges Andrew's tormentor to pick up his lance and mount his horse for he will then demonstrate the cowardliness of his actions: ' . . . and I will teach you that you are acting like a coward' (p. 47). Don Quixote threatens combat so as to make evident to the tormentor the moral nature of his actions on the assumption that, once having appreciated this, he will desist. For the mad knight, evil is a form of aberration or ignorance; it is sufficient to reveal the truth for everything to fall into its proper place.

Immediately after this victory, the knight finds another opportunity to imitate the romances of chivalry. When he encounters the merchants of Toledo, he blithely chooses to accost them in a traditional chivalric manner by proclaiming Dulcinea to be the most beautiful woman in the world and challenging anyone to contradict his assertion. When one of the merchants asks him to show them the lady, Don Quixote indignantly replies: 'If I were to show her to you what merit would there be in confessing so obvious a truth? The essence of the matter is that you must believe, confess, affirm, swear and maintain it without seeing her' (I.iv.51). This reply, of course, appears absurd both to the merchants and to the reader, but it makes sense within a chivalric scheme of things. The merchant is asking for direct ocular proof, an empirical proof based on the nature of surface appearances, whereas Don Quixote, as a knight errant, knows that appearances in this Iron Age are especially misleading. He possesses a much more reliable principle of verification in armed combat. Combat, as we have seen in Arthurian romances, is a means of revealing truth in an otherwise confusing situation. The victor of the fight will have won because his particular assertion was the true one; with this form of proof, why rely on the precarious evidence of the senses?

In the adventure of the windmills (I.viii.68), Don Quixote's self-confidence makes him even more reckless. When he proclaims the windmills to be giants, he deliberately ignores Sancho's warnings that he is mistaken. Here, and in the adventure of the flocks of sheep (I.xviii.134), there is some phenomenological basis for Don Quixote's assertion. Windmills, from a distance, could be said to have the shape or silhouette of an oversized man waving his arms about, and in the case of the sheep, the dust-clouds and the sound of hooves could conceivably bring to mind, at least momentarily, a vision of two rival armies. With Don Quixote, however, such flimsy sensory evidence is seized on and asserted as the truth. Anybody could at first believe that windmills from a distance looked like giants, or flocks of sheep like charging armies, but one would normally look for further sensory evidence to check and substantiate that initial impression. Don Quixote, nevertheless, is content to go on initial impressions, provided they seem to conform with chivalric precedents. If things appear to be giants or armies, if certain phenomena remind him of the world of chivalry, then that is taken as a sign that they possess an underlying romance character, and he will respond to them in a chivalric manner. To seek further sensory evidence would be self-contradictory, for once having taken the decision to believe the romances of chivalry, Don Quixote is committing himself to rely on their authority rather than on his sense-perceptions. There is, therefore, little need to sift true from false perceptions; all phenomena are potential signs of spiritual realities, and it is incumbent upon him to discriminate between meaningful signs and non-meaningful ones; the distinction is not between fact and fantasy but between intelligibility and non-intelligibility. This may explain why he acts on his intuition that the windmills are in reality giants; the very fact that he can recognize a certain phenomenon in this fallen world as having a meaning within the romance scheme of things is a sign of the existence of the old order beneath the confused surface of the Iron Age.

Thus on many occasions he moves from vague recognition to public declaration and to undoubting action. When he happens upon the strange procession led by two Benedictine monks wearing riding-masks and carrying sun-shades, he says to Sancho: 'Either I am much mistaken, or this will prove the most famous adventure ever seen. For those dark shapes looming over there must, beyond all doubt, be enchanters bearing off in that coach some princess they have stolen; and it is my duty to redress this wrong with all my might' (I.viii.71). Cervantes presents the movement of Don Quixote's thought very accurately: the initial speculation of 'must be' ('deben de ser'), quick excited progression to 'beyond all doubt' ('y son, sin duda'), followed by the urgent necessity for action. He goes from recognition to proclamation to deep conviction (his reply to the protestations of the monks is: 'No fair speeches for me, for I know you, perfidious scoundrels'). Sancho, of course, appeals to his master to look again, to see for himself, but Don Quixote brushes him aside as a man ignorant in matters of chivalry. Indeed, he reacts to Sancho's warning as to a challenge to prove the superiority of the chivalric system of cognition over that of the senses: 'What I say is true, and now you will see it.' The madman goes into battle to maintain his chivalric assertions against Sancho's perceptions.

In this particular case Don Quixote wins a victory which vindicates his version of reality. Sancho has to agree, and he rushes forward to strip the unhorsed monk of his habit as legitimate spoil of battle. The mad knight then proceeds to implement the chivalric system by asking the liberated 'damsel' to report this deed to his lady Dulcinea at El Toboso. So far as Don Quixote is concerned his proclamatory method seems well proven, he has objectively established his assertions about the romance nature of reality over those born of Sancho's empiricism.

But in spite of his initial exuberance, Don Quixote is capable of admitting the possibility of error in identifying the signs of romance. Such an occasion arises in the adventure with the corpse, when he comes across a torchlit procession of sinister figures dressed in white surplices (I.xix.143). Cervantes actually comments that it was an adventure 'that did not require any contrivance actually to look like one' (p. 142). Both Sancho and Don Quixote are terrified, but it immediately occurred to Don Quixote, says the narrator, that this was a chivalric adventure. He rides up and challenges the people to declare their identity and their business, 'either to punish you for the wrong you have done, or to avenge the outrage done upon you' (p. 144). A fight ensues and Don Quixote routs the unarmed men in white. Sancho is forced to admire his master: 'There's no doubt that my master is as valiant and mighty as he says' (p. 145). For Sancho, once again, Don Quixote's actions are proof of the truth of his declarations about the nature of reality.

However, when Don Quixote is informed of his error he apologizes, saying that the white figures should not have appeared as they did, 'for you truly looked like some evil things from the other world. I could not therefore refrain from fulfilling my duty by attacking you' (p. 146). The knight admits he was mistaken only because their appearance was confusing since it coincided with chivalric signs. And yet, one of the most curious aspects of this adventure is that Don Quixote feels he was obliged to intervene. He apologizes to his victims for the injury 'which he had been unable to avoid doing them' (p. 146), but he excludes the possibility that he may have had no business interfering at all, as is illustrated by his false antithesis: 'either to punish you . . . or to avenge you'. Once initial impressions remind him of a romance situation, they seem to trigger off an automatic reaction, leaving little room for doubt; all that has to be settled is what sort of action is required, mistaken impressions or erroneous identifications can be rectified after the event.

The most extreme example of the superiority of chivalric ideas over sense-impressions is found in the episode of the Moorish enchanter (I.xvii.125-7). Don Quixote and Sancho are recovering in the dark of the dormitory at the inn from the drubbing they have received at the hands of a muleteer after the misadventure with the kitchenmaid Maritornes. The knight explains to Sancho that the treasure of Maritornes' beauty must have been reserved for another knight and guarded by some Moorish enchanter. At this point an officer of the Inquisition enters the dormitory and lights a lamp. Sancho asks his master if that could be the Moorish enchanter but is told that it cannot because enchanters are invisible. The officer asks Don Quixote how he is feeling, but addresses him patronizingly as 'my man', to which the knight replies with an outraged insult. The officer of the Inquisition hits him over the head with his oil-lamp and leaves under cover of darkness. Sancho observes ruefully that without a doubt that must have been the Moorish enchanter, and Don Quixote has to agree: 'You are right . . . but there's no point in taking any notice of matters of enchantment, nor in getting angry and enraged about them. For, as these magicians are invisible and supernatural, we shall find no one to take vengeance on, however hard we try.' He then tells Sancho to ask the 'governor of the fortress' for ingredients to make the balsam of Fierabrás: 'Indeed, I think I

am in much need of it, for I am losing a great deal of blood from
the wound that apparition gave me.' Not even the impact of
pain and blood is sufficient to jolt Don Quixote out of his
obsession with romance. To the reader the explanation of this
blow from an oil-lamp as being the work of 'an apparition'
appears to be an extreme rationalization, to say the least, of a
straightforward situation, but for Don Quixote the chivalric
explanations are immediately more persuasive. If there is a
contradiction between chivalric ideas and sense-perceptions it
is the senses that must be mistaken, and if these contradictions
should persist, a good romance reason for them must be found;
hence the existence of enchanters.

So, in Don Quixote's view, the appearances of the world,
fallen as it is, are being made even more treacherous by the
presence of enchanters who are expressly confusing the
chivalric signs in order to make his enterprise of restoration
doubly difficult. As he says to Sancho, who complains that the
helmet of Mambrino is really a barber's basin:

> Is it possible that all this while you have been with me you have not
> discovered that everything to do with knights errant appears to be
> chimaera, folly and nonsense, and to go all contrariwise? This is not
> really the case, but there is a crew of enchanters always amongst us
> who change and alter all our deeds, and transform them according to
> their pleasure and their desire either to favour us or injure us. So what
> seems to you to be a barber's basin appears to me to be Mambrino's
> helmet, and to another as something else.   (I.xxv.204)[47]

Don Quixote is not saying that one man's view is as good as
another's. The effect of the work of the enchanters is to make
everything topsy-turvy, thereby producing an *apparent*
relativism and perspectivism in the world of phenomena, but
Don Quixote is quick to point out that it does not follow from
this that there is not a single unified reality behind it all: the
enchanters' intention is 'to make what is really and truly
Mambrino's helmet seem to everyone a basin' (p. 204).

Here, once again, the mad knight has been forced by
circumstances back onto his basic chivalric premises, which
he can only reiterate baldly without any objective proof that the
basin really is, despite appearances, the helmet of Mambrino.
He is, therefore, in the very difficult position of claiming to be
the sole perceiver of truth. Clearly, for the age of chivalry to be

restored, the whole chivalric system must be seen by others to work *independently* of his actions and claims. To this end, Don Quixote attempts in the Sierra Morena to set the chivalric system in motion by imitating the penitential 'madness' of Amadis or Orlando.

The concept of imitation in this case takes on a particular meaning, it is a form of spiritual exercise. Don Quixote imitates Amadis in the hope that by *acting* like him he will eventually come to *be* like him: 'The knight errant who best copies him will attain most nearly to the perfection of chivalry' (p. 202). Since outward action in the chivalric world betokens inner spiritual qualities, successful imitation amounts to a kind of proof of inner worth, and so, in the Sierra Morena, Don Quixote seems to be attempting to reproduce effectively, in the present Iron Age, a traditional sequence of chivalric events which we have previously encountered in *Yvain* and the *Amadis*.

In both these romances the hero is cut off from the love of his lady; Yvain because he broke his promise to Laudine, Amadis because of a misunderstanding with Oriana. In each case the knight retires to a wilderness, mourns his loss, and then eventually wins back the lady's love by acquiring glory under a surrogate identity—Yvain's 'The Knight with the Lion' or Amadis's 'Beltenebros'. The sequence can be broken down into the following essential components: (A) mutual love between knight and lady; (B) rejection of knight by lady, with resultant loss of knight's chivalric identity; (C) period of grief or madness; (D) assumption of surrogate identity and regaining of glory; (E) lady appreciates the significance of knight's feats of arms and duly responds; (A^1) mutual love restored. The sequence presupposes the existence of love between knight and lady, a form of circuit of spiritual life which is interrupted at point (B), but which is eventually reconnected when the lady, whose good will is indispensable to the knight, recognizes the true worth of the hero and responds to his love again.

Don Quixote, however, can only intervene at point (C) by declaring that he loves Dulcinea and imitating the exemplary penitential madness; then he could at best move to point (D) by assuming a surrogate identity and embarking on adventures. But the crucial step is that between (D) and (E): Don Quixote may acquire as much glory as he can, but this must be recognized by Dulcinea and she must return his love. The purpose of Don Quixote's penance, then, is to invite this kind of response from Dulcinea in an effort, not, of course, to restore the circuit, but merely to put one into operation. He therefore appeals to Sancho to watch his actions closely: 'Impress on your memory what you will see me do here, so that you may tell and recite it to the sole cause of it all' (I.xxv.205). Here Don Quixote unwittingly exposes the flaw in his endeavour: Dulcinea is not the real cause of the proposed sequence of events, she has merely been declared to be such by him.

Having already spotted the mistake, Sancho points out that the other knights at least had a reason for their suffering but what cause has he to go mad? Don Quixote replies that whether there is a real cause or no is immaterial for his purposes, 'the thing is to do it without cause; and then my lady can guess what I would do in the wet if I do all this in the dry' (p. 203). For Don Quixote the actual cause is not as important as getting through to Dulcinea, making her recognize him, thereby eliciting some response from her. He is aware that (A) and (B) are absent from his proposed circuit, for he has arbitrarily declared that he is in love, but if he could get a favourable reply from Dulcinea it would, in effect, provide him with an independent token that his proclaimed love-service is indeed grounded in objective truth. Hence his anxiety to get Sancho to visit Dulcinea and report his actions.

The irony is that, so far as Don Quixote is concerned, the circuit *does* come into operation. The first sign of this is the fact that Dorothea, in her disguise as the princess Micomicona, claims to have come from afar to seek out Don Quixote de la Mancha whose fame is trumpeted abroad (p. 253). The knight is at last seeing independent, unsolicited evidence of his reputation spreading far afield. For the first time another character has, without prompting, recognized him for what he has declared himself to be. But the really critical evidence that his restoration of romance is properly under way comes when he questions Sancho about the meeting with Dulcinea. Sancho says it went well and reports that Dulcinea wishes to see Don Quixote, and that the defeated Basque did in fact visit her, although the liberated galley-slaves had not yet done so (I.xxxi.270). Don Quixote is immensely pleased: 'So far so good.' His satisfaction is, in fact, so great that he disregards or rationalizes away the degrading details Sancho intersperses in his reports about Dulcinea's rustic ways. These can be dismissed as the ignorant squire's mistakes, which count for very little against the most welcome news that not only has Sancho seen Aldonza in her ideal form as the lady Dulcinea, but that the peasant girl has actually responded to his overtures in the manner of a chivalric princess: her ideal potential is emerging in actuality, the process of restoration of romance is well in train.

Now, like Yvain or Amadis before him, Don Quixote finds himself deliciously torn, as all true knights should be, between his public duty and his private obligations: 'On the one hand I am perplexed and harassed by the desire to see my lady, on the other incited and summoned by my pledged faith and the glory I shall gain in this enterprise' (i.e. the killing of the giant who has usurped Princess Micomicona's rightful place). Sancho, who is lying, tries nervously to persuade him that he should first perform the latter feat, to which Don Quixote agrees because that would only increase his renown even further before actually meeting his lady.

After this episode Don Quixote is enthusiastic and very much more confident. It now seems to matter less to him that appearances are being mischievously turned upside down by enchanters because at last there are others who, it appears, share his chivalric vision and interests. When Sancho tries to tell him after the battle of the wineskins that Princess Micomicona is really Dorothea, Don Quixote is puzzled until Dorothea declares that 'I am the same today as I was yesterday' (p. 335). This assurance satisfies Don Quixote who blames Sancho for talking 'nonsense that put me into the greatest perplexity I have ever known'. Then, after finishing a meal in the company of Dorothea, Don Ferdinand, and all the other guests gathered in the inn, Quixote is moved to remark in wonderment:

Most truly, gentlemen, if the matter be deeply considered, great and most extraordinary are the experiences of those who profess the order of knight errantry. For who is there of all men living upon earth who would judge us and know us for what we really are, if he were to come in now through the gate of this castle and see us as we appear at present? Who would be able to guess that this lady at my side is the great queen we all know her to be, and that I am that Knight of the Sad Countenance, so trumpeted by the mouth of Fame? Now there is no doubt that this art and exercise is greater than any discovered by man, and must be more highly valued the more perils it is subject to.

(I.xxxvii.340)

Comforted by the presence of people knowledgeable in matters of chivalry, Don Quixote marvels at the ironies generated by his campaign to restore romance; for they can be savoured only by the select few who are capable of perceiving the glories of ideal truth camouflaged by such humdrum appearances. Don Quixote's capacity to appreciate the positive irony typical of romance—where things turn out to be far better than anticipated—is an index of his satisfaction with the progress of his enterprise:[48] Aldonza has been transformed into Dulcinea, she has sent him her blessing through his squire, a princess in distress has spontaneously sought his services, and here he is dining in a castle with persons of rank.

But if at this juncture Don Quixote is confident that some others can also see through the inaccurate appearances of the Iron Age, and through the added confusion wrought by enchanters, he is soon enough reminded that not everybody enjoys this privileged insight. The barber, from whom he had previously won the helmet of Mambrino, and from whom he had allowed Sancho to take the harness of his horse as booty, turns up at the inn to reclaim his basin and ass's pack-saddle (I.xliv.402). Don Quixote, naturally, is annoyed by the irate barber's frontal assault on his chivalric account of reality; but, secure in the knowledge that Dorothea, Don Ferdinand, and the others can appreciate the truths of chivalry and will therefore perceive romance reality correctly, he declares that he will not argue over the question of the pack-saddle, which has doubtless been transformed from a horse's harness by an evil enchanter, he will simply ask Sancho to fetch the helmet of Mambrino in order to prove conclusively that the barber is lying.

The empirical Sancho is alive to the hazards of Don Quixote's approach;[49] merely to proclaim the nature of reality will not suffice: 'Good Lord, sir, if we've no better proof of our case than what your worship's saying, Malino's [sic] helmet is as much a basin as this good fellow's harness is a pack-saddle' (p. 403). In the event, Don Quixote's friends back him up on the question of the helmet but defer to him on the question of the pack-saddle. Don Quixote now declares that he does indeed see it as a pack-saddle, but this might be due once again to the tricks of wicked enchanters, especially in this castle where he has already suffered various enchantments. He therefore leaves the final judgement to his companions, for the following reason: 'Perhaps, since none of you are knights, as I am, the spells in this place will have no effect on you, your understanding will be free, and you will be able to judge of the affairs of this castle as they really and truly are, and not as they appear to me' (p. 405). Now this statement is not a 'perspectivist' admission by Don Quixote that perceptions of reality are relative, nor does it amount to a confession that his own perceptions might be erroneous, it simply shows Don Quixote attempting to be scrupulously, patronizingly, fair to the barber. He concedes that the enchanters may have been up to their tricks and leaves it to the other chivalric *cognoscenti*, who are quite possibly immune to the spells of the castle, to scotch the importunate claims of the wretched barber. When Dorothea and the others declare his version to be the correct one, Don Quixote is triumphantly confirmed in his beliefs, and so he remains hermetically sealed within the circularity of his chivalric vision while the empirical truth of the situation is recalled for the reader when the priest secretly pays the wronged barber for the loss of his property (p. 411). Both versions of reality remain tangential to and unaffected by each other.

For the rest of Part I Don Quixote remains fairly pleased with the way things are turning out, for he has seen objective evidence that romance is being restored. Further mischief from enchanters does not worry him unduly. When he is carried back home in a cage he finds himself happily arguing with Sancho that he is truly enchanted. His arguments are clever, and not without consistency; they can be reduced to the shape of a simple deduction: he is a knight errant, he knows he cannot move, therefore, because he has never read that knights can be immobilized other than by enchantment, he must be enchanted (I.xlviii-ix.430-4). This reasoning is not defective in itself so long as one is agreed on the premiss that Don Quixote is a true knight errant and therefore subject to the conditions of knight errantry such as they are portrayed in the romances. If this is accepted, his arguments become valid. However, since Sancho does not seem to accept it, or at least is sceptical of that premiss, Don Quixote is again forced back into assertive bluster: 'I most certainly know that I am enchanted, and that is sufficient to ease my conscience' (p. 434).

As a result of his enchantment, he is condemned to reiterate his belief in his own intrinsic worth and in the books of chivalry to the sceptical Canon of Toledo: 'I can say of myself that since I became a knight errant I have been valiant, courteous, liberal, well-bred, generous, polite, bold, gentle and patient' (I.l.442). This is all very well, but he should be able to demonstrate such virtues and not merely affirm them. Don Quixote is very much aware of the need to make these inner qualities shine forth through heroic action, and he adds: 'I expect by the valour of my arm, if Heaven favours me and fate is not against me, to find myself *in a few days* king of some kingdom, in which I can display the gratitude and liberality enclosed in this bosom of mine' (p. 442; my emphasis). Even though he is for the present rendered impotent by a spell, the mad knight is in good spirits, for he is still confident that the day is not far off when he will realize his chivalric destiny.

(v) *Don Quixote's Career in Part II: The Absence of Providence*

As far as Don Quixote is concerned, the difference between Parts I and II is that he will now be less confident of the *immediacy* of the restoration of romance. Indeed, at a certain point, his morale will sink low enough to make him doubt that his chivalric destiny will be fulfilled at all. In Part II, therefore, the mad knight is more circumspect about chivalric proclamations because he is highly sensitive to the dangers of enchantment; he will concentrate instead on seeking supernatural endorsements of his romance aspirations.[50] Rocinante's neighing, which Don Quixote takes to be an omen of good fortune (II.iv.494), indicates the direction Cervantes's parody will take. The appearance in this second Part of omens, dreams, apparitions, oracles, prophecies, and other manifestations of the supernatural shows Cervantes striking deeper into the heart of romance. His parody is aimed increasingly at two of its most basic premisses: that there is direct intercourse between the material and the spiritual worlds, and that the destiny of the hero is guided by Providence. Without these assumptions, as we have seen in previous chapters, romance will founder in a chaos of destructive irony, duplicity, and indeterminacy of meaning.

Don Quixote's decision to embark on his third sally by first visiting Dulcinea in El Toboso conforms to this new trend in the novel. It is no arbitrary indulgence, rather it makes good chivalric sense, after the bewildering effects of his enchantment in a cage and the no less debilitating experience of the enforced comforts of home life, for the knight errant to nourish his spirits by seeking the blessing of his lady: 'For so long as I see her it is all the same to me whether it is over walls or through windows, or chinks or garden grilles. For any ray reaching my eyes from the sun of her beauty will illuminate my understanding and fortify my heart, so that I shall be unique and peerless in wisdom and valour' (II.viii.515). In addition to being sound in terms of romance logic, the knight's decision is also psychologically right, since it is understandable that he should want to capitalize on what he assumes to be his one enduring success of Part I: the peasant Aldonza's idealization into the regal lady Dulcinea del Toboso.

When master and servant enter the village of El Toboso, Don Quixote is eager to find where Dulcinea lives, but in the dark they fail to come across anything that looks like a palace. Sancho grows nervous lest his lie is discovered, and asks to be allowed to look for the palace on his own because, having only seen the place once before, he cannot quite remember where it is. After all, he says, Don Quixote himself cannot find it even though he must have been there thousands of times. This taunt exasperates the knight: 'You will drive me to despair, Sancho. . . . Look, you heretic, have I not told you a thousand times that I have never seen the peerless Dulcinea in all the days of my life, nor ever crossed the threshold of her palace, and that I am only enamoured of her by hearsay, and because of the great reputation she bears for beauty and wisdom' (II.ix.522).

Why does Don Quixote lose patience with Sancho here? Surely because the ignorant squire has still not grasped the basic point of the whole enterprise: Don Quixote had set out to transform Aldonza Lorenzo into her ideal self, the peerless Dulcinea. Sancho has previously claimed to have had an audience with Dulcinea, whereas he, Don Quixote, having seen the peasant girl Aldonza barely four times, has never actually set eyes on her *transfigured into the lady Dulcinea*. This is precisely what he has come to witness in El Toboso, and his use of the word 'palace' clearly indicates that he is referring to the regal Dulcinea as opposed to the rustic Aldonza. It follows that his love for Dulcinea cannot be based on ocular evidence but rather on something that approximates to hearsay or renown since it relies as always on a form of inspired chivalric intuition that beneath her humble appearance, Aldonza, like, say, the poor maiden Enide in Chrétien's romance, possesses the qualities of a princess.

Though it may strike us as comically absurd, Don Quixote's claim to be in love 'by hearsay' is based on the traditional chivalric notion of *amor de lonh* or love from afar which John Stevens has shown to be intimately associated with the nature of the romance heroine, who is presented as 'distant, mysterious, desirable, inaccessible and beautiful'.[51] Far from indulging in sophistry, let alone lying, Don Quixote is here scrupulously spelling out the truth of the matter to the obtuse Sancho, whose crude intelligence fails to appreciate these conceptual niceties of courtly chivalry, except to seize on the idea of 'hearsay' as a way of letting the truth about his alleged visit to Dulcinea leak out in terms his master might just find amenable to chivalric interpretation: 'I would have you know that my seeing her and the reply I brought back were by hearsay too; for I no more know who the lady Dulcinea is than I can punch the sky' (p. 522). As usual, from Don Quixote's point of view, Sancho begins to take serious questions rather too flippantly and so loses sight of basic truths. To make matters worse, an omen cuts short these arguments; a voice singing a heroic ballad is suddenly heard and the knight takes it to be an adverse chivalric augury. But the peasant who was singing the ballad is a stranger to the town and is unable to tell them the whereabouts of Dulcinea's palace. Don Quixote is naturally disappointed and Sancho, sensing danger, tries a second time to get his master out of the village so that in pretending to carry out the search on his own he can gain time to think of something to cover up his deception.

Luis Rosales has interpreted the whole scene as indicating that the mad knight is deliberately seeking to be deceived by Sancho so as not to have to face up to the implications of the non-existence of Dulcinea.[52] I would agree that here Cervantes has mischievously given us just a hint that Don Quixote might be protecting himself from disappointment, especially when he waits for nightfall before entering the village. But in the context of the knight's initial eagerness to find the palace, his apprehensive sensitivity to the significance of the ballad, his understandable irritation and frustration over Sancho's defective recollection of the place, it is psychologically plausible that he should now prefer to give in to Sancho's repeated request that the search be left to him. Sancho, what is more, cunningly hits on the perfect chivalric reason for getting his master to retire: 'Is it to our wenches' house we're going, like their keepers, who come and call and enter at all hours of the day and night?' (p. 521). The squire, therefore, volunteers to seek an audience with Dulcinea and receive her instructions on 'how you may see her without damage to her honour and reputation' (p. 523). For Quixote to present himself unannounced before Dulcinea, without first doing her the courtesy of sending his squire to ask permission for an audience, would be unchivalrous in the extreme. Rosales greatly overstates the extent of Don Quixote's collusion with Sancho in order to hang upon this exaggeration the view that in Part II the knight is wilfully credulous and deliberately predisposing himself to being deceived by others. The next chapter of the novel demonstrates that Don Quixote is not fooling himself over the problem of Dulcinea.

When Sancho returns from the village and says that he has seen the lady (p. 527), the madman is overjoyed. But the alleged princess turns out to be a peasant girl on an ass; and Don Quixote, broken-hearted, realizes that even the earlier transformation of Aldonza into Dulcinea has now been undone by the evil enchanters who have been so cruel as to change her back, not to the handsome peasant girl Aldonza, but to a rebarbative travesty of her former self: 'Do you see now what a spite the enchanters have against me, Sancho? See to what extremes the malice and hatred they bear me extend, for they have sought to deprive me of the happiness I should have enjoyed in seeing my mistress in her true person' (p. 531). However, the interesting point is that Don Quixote sees the repellent girl as she is; he does not create a consoling myth by agreeing with Sancho that she looks like a princess. Nor is Don Quixote, as Mark Van Doren believes, play-acting here; his attempts at being a knight errant must clearly be genuine, not hopeful self-deception or make-believe. He accepts the empirical reality, even though it is so wounding, because, unlike the windmills or flocks of sheep, he has not *himself* recognized and proclaimed the romance character of the peasant girl.

This episode constitutes the ultimate proof of Don Quixote's absolute honesty. He is deceiving no one and falsifying nothing. It also confirms the epistemological authority of literary reminiscence for Don Quixote: in a situation where phenomena do not remind him of romance, he does not attempt to transform empirical reality. Because the coarse peasant girl, unlike the lovely Aldonza Lorenzo, is so far removed from the world of romance, she fails to stir the knight's imagination. But since Sancho claims to see this ugly girl on an ass as Dulcinea in full apotheosis, Don Quixote must try to reconcile the absolute nullity of his own perceptions with the gratifying evidence that romance realities retain some objective validity beyond his own subjective declarations. He therefore assumes, quite logically, that he has been singled out and deliberately victimized: Dulcinea must have been enchanted in such a way that only he sees her as a repulsive peasant whereas others see her as he knows her to be—a princess.

Don Quixote, nevertheless, is in the horrifying position of depending *faute de mieux* upon Sancho to tell him about the real Dulcinea in circumstances where he himself has been prevented from seeing 'my mistress in her true person'. Whereas he could once confidently instruct Sancho on matters of chivalry he has now to rely on his squire's evidence for the most vital aspect of his mission. Naturally enough Sancho begins to get it wrong. As in the earlier Sierra Morena episode, Don Quixote quizzes him on what Dulcinea looks like, and he begins to give provocatively inappropriate answers, partly through malice and partly through incompetence. The knight, for example, objects to Sancho's comparison of Dulcinea's eyes to pearls, saying that her eyes must have appeared more like emeralds, with two rainbows for eyebrows; the pearls should more properly be transferred to her teeth because Sancho must surely have got her eyes mixed up with her teeth. To which Sancho archly replies: 'Anything's possible . . . for her beauty confused me, as her ugliness did your worship' (II.xi.533).

Finding himself in the unfortunate and dangerous position of having to rely upon Sancho's word as the only support for his assertions about Dulcinea, Don Quixote immediately directs his efforts to finding more reputable evidence. He suggests they try an experiment ('una experiencia') to discover if the knights and giants he defeats can see Dulcinea in her true form (p. 534). After his victory over the Knight of the Mirrors (II.xiv.559), he imposes the traditional chivalric terms that he go to El Toboso and put himself at the disposal of Dulcinea. This time, however, Don Quixote adds that the Knight of the Mirrors should *return* from El Toboso and seek him out by following the trail of his feats to report what passed between Dulcinea and him. This stipulation amounts to a chivalric, non-empirical experiment designed to elicit an independent response from his lady and so extricate his knowledge of Dulcinea's existence from its unsatisfactory dependence on Sancho's eyewitness testimony.

The inability to see Aldonza in her true state as Dulcinea was in effect a blow to the heart for Don Quixote, it saps his energy and makes him despondent. For example, when Don Diego de Miranda's son, Don Lorenzo, casts doubt on whether there are or have ever been knights errant in the world, Don Quixote wearily replies that this is a mistaken belief but he knows from experience that it is impossible to prove this fact to sceptics: 'Unless Heaven miraculously convinces them to the contrary, any labour undertaken for that purpose must be in vain, as experience has many times shown me' (II.xviii.583). Don Quixote's weariness is of course a far cry from his tireless enthusiasm during most of Part I, but there are no traces of actual doubt in him. He still considers Don Lorenzo's attitude to be an error and remains confident that his chivalric mission is correct. However, by this stage, he seems to be chary of argument or verbal persuasion; he must rely on more substantial verifications that will conform with chivalric tradition.

A suitable opportunity arises a few chapters later when he decides to explore the Cave of Montesinos (II.xxii). The whole episode is shrouded in mystery if not actual mystification on the part of both the narrator and Don Quixote. The knight's account of what he saw inside the cave possesses all the characteristics of an hallucination or a dream: a jumble of strange associations which combine ill-assorted elements of romance with instances of crude realism, evincing both delusions of heroic grandeur and pathetic fears of inadequacy.[53] Don Quixote describes how he fell into a deep sleep while sitting on a ledge inside the cave and then awoke to find himself in a pleasant meadow in front of a castle where he is recognized and welcomed by Montesinos himself who shows him the enchanted figures of Durandarte and Belerma, characters from Spanish pseudo-Carolingian romance.[54] But most important of all, Don Quixote claims to have seen Dulcinea, albeit travestied still as an ugly peasant. Montesinos tells him that in due course he will find a way of disenchanting all the people who inhabit that nether-world (p. 622).

When Sancho hears his master claiming to have seen the enchanted Dulcinea, he is convinced that he is totally mad, since it was he who had invented the whole story simply to get out of a tight corner. He now appeals to Don Quixote to renounce these vacuous fantasies, but the knight replies in the usual way: 'As you are not experienced in the affairs of this world, anything that has any difficulty about it seems to you impossible'; and he insists that the truth of what he saw 'admits of no reply or controversy' (pp.623-4). Don Quixote is now asserting, against Sancho, Sancho's own earlier assertion about the enchantment of Dulcinea. The problem, as ever, is how to get beyond rival assertions onto a more objective footing. Don Quixote can, nevertheless, draw a good deal of comfort from the experience in Montesinos' Cave. He now knows of Dulcinea's enchantment from Montesinos himself, a more reputable romance authority than Sancho, and furthermore, he has been given the welcome responsibility of disenchanting not only Dulcinea but all the other romance characters that reside in the cave.

Subsequently, the knight will attempt to verify the Montesinos' Cave experience at any suitable opportunity. When he comes across the prophesying ape he consents to Sancho's suggestion that he ask it about the Montesinos episode, 'though I have certain scruples about it' (II.xxv. 637). This incident is significant because the ape is a kind of oracular source of truth and, as such, corresponds functionally to the sign-machines and prophetic devices of the romances through which the supernatural could communicate with the temporal world. But even on this occasion Don Quixote receives unsatisfactory, equivocal replies. The ape, according to its owner Master Peter, says that 'part of what your worship saw or experienced in the said cave is false and part true, and that's all he knows about this question'. Sancho declares that the ape has vindicated his contention, but Don Quixote merely replies that time will tell who is right.

Sancho's persistent scepticism about the Montesinos vision, together with the ape's equivocations, underline even more sharply the difference between Don Quixote's life and that of former knights errant. In the romances, the hand of Providence showed itself at strategic points in the hero's career, either to reveal the significance of an adventure through some intermediary like the hermits in the Prose *Lancelot* or Urganda in the *Amadis*, or to rescue the knight when he had reached the limits of his human powers, as in the case of Yvain's faithful lion. But where his predecessors were freely offered these revelations, Don Quixote, in spite of strenuous efforts, can find no sure signs of favour. As a result, he comes close at this juncture to losing confidence altogether in his destiny as a knight errant.

The significance of the Enchanted Boat adventure on the River Ebro (II.xxix) can be seen in the context of Don Quixote's waning self-assurance. This episode may appear to be unique in Part II because it alone recalls the adventures of Part I when the knight exuberantly transformed everyday situations into romance fantasies.[55] Although exceptional in this sense, the adventure is still consistent with the new direction of the knight's madness in Part II, where he is seeking providential signs that the maleficent hold of the enchanters will be broken. The pleasant shores of the Ebro inspire in the knight 'a thousand amorous thoughts'—of Dulcinea, no doubt. These, in turn, remind him of his vision in the Cave of Montesinos, 'for although Master Peter's ape had told him that part of it was true and part false, he leaned rather to its being true than false: the very opposite view to Sancho's, who considered it all one great lie' (p. 656). Brooding thus on the uncertainties and controversies that plague him, it is no wonder that when he espies an empty boat tethered to a tree he should seize that as an opportunity of adventure offered by Providence as a sign that his luck has changed. So heartened is he by this augury of good fortune that he plunges into the sort of reckless chivalric action that characterized his behaviour in the early days of Part I, in the declared belief that the boat has been put there by a benevolent enchanter so that he may succour someone in distress.

When the adventure turns out badly, Don Quixote is fairly bewildered but he does not discard the notion that the adventure had been spontaneously offered by an enchanter. He now thinks that it has either been reserved for another knight or a second, malevolent enchanter is frustrating the good intentions of the former: 'God help us, but this whole world is tricks and devices, one against the other. I can do no more' (II.xxix.661). More than ever, he feels the need of direct assistance such as knights errant could depend on in times of crisis. However, his 'I can do no more' ('Yo no puedo más') is not quite a cry of existential despair or of moral capitulation,[56] it is rather Don Quixote's understandable protest that without providential aid he can do but his level best; in such adverse conditions, little more could be expected of him.

Still, in this phase of the novel, Don Quixote is at a very low ebb indeed. There are, as Madariaga has observed, signs of a progressive weariness of spirit, of confusion, even of doubt. But despondency does not puncture his romance illusions; Don Quixote explains the nature of his plight and expresses misgivings about his destiny in terms that are entirely defined by the system of romance. Even at the outset of his career he was able to conceive of failure; knights of old, he had pointed out to Vivaldo in Part I, won glory largely through their own efforts but 'if those who did rise so high had had no enchanters or sages to help them, they would have been defrauded of their desires and cheated of their hopes' (I.xii.98). Fear of this peculiarly chivalric desolation, rather than scepticism about the truth of the romances, is what haunts the mad knight in Part II.[57]

It is a measure of Cervantes's skill in modulating the ups and downs of Don Quixote's morale that after having let the knight down so badly he should next reward him with the best piece of evidence so far in Part II that his chivalric identity is attaining to objective status. When he happens across the Duke and Duchess, he is taken to their castle and given an astonishing reception as 'the flower and cream of knights errant'—the traditional formula of praise accorded to heroes in the romances. It is no wonder that 'this was the first time that he was positively certain of being a true and no imaginary knight errant, since he found himself treated just as he had read these knights were treated in past ages' (II.xxxi.667). His claims to being a knight errant, which have hitherto aroused such controversy and drawn repeated charges of subjectivism, are confirmed here in a totally unequivocal manner: his potential chivalric identity has become a palpable actuality.

Don Quixote's renewed confidence is put to the test once more when the Duchess raises the delicate issue of Dulcinea's existence. She accepts the mad knight's assurances that he did not simply invent Dulcinea, but confesses to entertaining one scruple that calls in question the greatness of her lineage; to wit, Sancho's claim to have seen the princess Dulcinea winnowing a sack of corn while he delivered the letter from his master. Don Quixote launches into a lengthy rebuttal of Sancho's allegation, arguing that when his squire first visited Dulcinea she must also have been transformed by enchanters into a peasant girl. He cites as evidence of this kind of metamorphosis the fact that on his own recent visit to El Toboso he saw her as a peasant himself whereas Sancho was rewarded with the sight of her 'in her proper shape' (p. 682). The whole argument is fundamentally absurd, of course, because Don Quixote has never once set eyes on Dulcinea in her true form yet he uses Sancho's *second* alleged vision of Dulcinea as proof that his first was defective, even though the second vision clearly depends on Sancho's having already had an audience with Dulcinea.

But the argument, it must be said, is not altogether without a semblance of coherence; Don Quixote accepts Sancho's word that an interview with Dulcinea did take place, although he now casts some doubt on the accuracy of his squire's visual perception of the lady in order to reject the humiliating suggestion that she could stoop to winnowing corn. The knight goes so far as to concede that Dulcinea may have been winnowing—a kind of pastoral activity after all—though he declares that it was not a sack of corn but 'grains of oriental pearl'. The inspired lunacy of such a qualification has a crazy beauty about it which is quintessentially quixotic, for it captures in a single image both the knight's poignant devotion to an ideal of aristocratic excellence, and the hair-splitting futility of the arguments that sustain it. The impression of casuistry is part of Cervantes's comic purpose here, amusing as it is to have the knight find complicated reasons for not seeing what is blindingly obvious to everyone, but there is no sophistry strictly speaking since there is little cause to impute bad faith to the knight. On the contrary, Don Quixote cuts a sad figure, given the mad earnestness with which he clings to any shred of 'objective' evidence that Aldonza has already been idealized into Dulcinea.

The debate with the Duke and Duchess about the status of Dulcinea is yet another failed attempt by Don Quixote to establish his romance point of view through argument. But the lunatic himself, as we know, is aware by this stage that romance truth cannot be demonstrated through argument alone, it must be accompanied by practical proof in the form of a successful adventure or a supernatural sign. In the short term his fears are allayed by the elaborate chivalresque pageant mounted by the Duke to delude him. A cortège appears bearing some famous wizards of romance—Lirgandeo, Alquife, Arcalaus, and Merlin (II.xxxiv.698-701). This last addresses Don Quixote directly and prophesies that Dulcinea will be disenchanted when Sancho inflicts 3,300 lashes on his buttocks (II.xxxv.701). Sancho is exhorted to accomplish the task by 'Dulcinea' herself who appears next to Merlin in the carriage. The mad knight is all too easily taken in by this unexpected appearance of such a gathering of romance authorities, and it gives him confidence henceforward in his long-running argument with Sancho over the Montesinos vision.

The dispute is by and large settled in the Clavileño episode, where master and servant are blindfolded and mounted on a wooden horse said to be capable of flying. When they descend from Clavileño, Sancho's extravagant account of their flight meets with general scepticism, not least from Don Quixote who haughtily assures the audience that they could not have flown as high as Sancho claims because they would have had to traverse the region of fire: 'So, seeing that we are not burnt, either Sancho is lying or Sancho is dreaming' (p. 734). The knight is delighted to find that Sancho is in a position identical to his own after he emerged from the Cave of Montesinos. With a kind of vindictive pleasure he is able to whisper in his squire's ear: 'Sancho, if you want me to believe what you saw in the sky, I wish you to accept my account of what I saw in the Cave of Montesinos. I say no more' (p. 735). As the terse exultancy of the last phrase indicates, Don Quixote believes he has finally demonstrated to his squire the ineffectiveness of verbal persuasion or even empirical assurances if one's audience is not predisposed to believe.

From this point until his final defeat, the madman's faith in the ultimate disenchantment of Dulcinea remains inviolate, but the vicissitudes of life on the road, and the absence of sure signs of a decisive upturn in his fortunes, begin to take their toll. On a number of occasions, for instance when his squire is awarded an island by the Duke (II.xlii), or when he comes across the statues of four warrior-saints (II.lviii), he is struck by the ironic discrepancy between his own hapless career and the traditional experience of a knight errant.

And yet this discrepancy does not make him any saner, nor does it encourage him to abandon his inveterate habit of seeing everything in terms of chivalry. Even his defeat at the hands of the Knight of the White Moon fails to shock him out of the world of romance; if anything it confirms that its influence is undiminished, for Sampson Carrasco must bend to its laws in order to get the madman to go back home. As Don Quixote returns to his village after having promised to give up arms for a year, he may be depressed by the defeat—he is no longer the invincible hero of his earlier vision—but he has a perfectly good chivalric explanation for it all: Dulcinea's enchantment has sapped the spirit needed to foil the enchanters' conspiracy of envy against him. He is, nevertheless, confident that once Dulcinea is disenchanted the restoration of romance can be resumed.

There are only two instances in the text where Don Quixote may appear to be less mad than before. Both involve his not mistaking roadside inns for castles in the way he used to do in Part I. The first instance occurs the day after he is painfully trampled by a herd of bulls, and it may be read as a sign that this terrible humiliation has taken the wind out of his sails for a while (II.lix.848). On the second occasion, the narrator explains that 'since his defeat he spoke on all subjects with a sounder judgement, as will now be shown' (II.lxxi.924). This is the only time Cervantes appears to state unequivocally that Don Quixote's madness is abating, and it appears to provide textual evidence for the progressive sanity of Don Quixote in Part II. But the subordinate clause 'as will now be shown' could only refer to the ensuing scene where Don Quixote and Sancho see two very badly executed paintings, one of the abduction of Helen by Paris, the other of Dido and Aeneas. As evidence of the knight's soundness of judgement, we have the historical reflection prompted by the subject-matter of the pictures: 'These two ladies were most unfortunate not to have been born in the present age, and I even more unfortunate not to have been born in theirs. Had I encountered those gentlemen, Troy would not have been burnt nor Carthage destroyed; for all those calamities would have been avoided simply by my killing Paris' (II.lxxi.924). With this statement Don Quixote reaffirms his madness in all its primitive vigour, for in the first chapter of the novel it is reported that his response to the epic of Roland was that 'he would have given his housekeeper and his niece into the bargain, to deal the traitor Galalon [sic] a good kicking' (I.i.33). Since the knight's madness is characterized by a literal belief in epics and romances, coupled with a desire to plunge into similar heroic action, these beliefs and aspirations are as undiminished in their potency at the end of the novel as they were at the beginning. The author's comment on Don Quixote's soundness of mind turns out to be another ironic feint, a mild joke at the expense of the reader.

Since Don Quixote is still as mad as ever when he arrives home, there is no moral to be drawn from the history of his adventures. As if to pre-empt any kind of moralizing, Sancho performs a little parody of the theme of the prodigal's return when they arrive within sight of their village. He falls to his knees and intones a mock-heroic address to their 'beloved country', urging it to open its eyes to see 'your son Sancho Panza returning—if not rich yet well beaten', and to open its arms to receive 'your son Don Quixote too, who, though conquered by another, has conquered himself—which, as I have heard him say, is the very best kind of victory' (II.lxxii.930). But the temptation to elevate the mad escapades of an old *hidalgo* into some form of spiritual mastery of self is disallowed by Don Quixote's ill-tempered reply to Sancho's raillery; 'Stop these fooleries . . . and let us enter our village right foot foremost. Once there, we will give play to our imaginations and devise the scheme of the pastoral life we mean to follow'.[58] Impervious to the lessons of experience, his words merely breathe new life into the old obsession with romance literature, transmuted now into pastoral form. Not until his final illness does Don Quixote step outside the bounds of romance; his pastoral project is but a temporary diversion, referred to by the author as a 'fresh craze' (p. 932), before reverting to the real business of knight errantry after a year.

Don Quixote comes to his senses for a brief interval before his death, and this only after an obscure illness which strikes 'when he least expected it' and whose cause is unknown even to the narrator: 'Whether that event was brought on by melancholy occasioned by the contemplation of his defeat or whether it was divine ordination, a fever seized him and kept him to his bed for six days' (p. 934). Don Quixote's release from the grip of madness is as sudden and unaccountable as its onset. Just as it is impossible fully to explain the reasons why Alonso Quijano succumbed to the delusion that he was a knight errant, so too are the reasons for his emergence from it inexplicable. Till the very end, however, he remained convinced that the restoration of the world of chivalry was possible, never once did he admit otherwise, nor did he seek to compromise his adherence to the chivalric code by resorting to empirical methods of verification.

The novel does not describe a progressive movement from madness to sanity. Don Quixote always sees empirical phenomena as they appear unless they remind him of chivalric reality. He is aware that appearances are deceptive in a fallen world, so he wants to go beyond appearances to the essence of things. But more and more he is obliged either by circumstances or by deception to fall back on subjective assertions. In Part II especially, he is forced to return to first principles and to argue, reason, and expostulate in order to overcome his inability to act successfully.

The remarkable thing is that Don Quixote should persist through so much adversity in rigidly maintaining the validity of his chivalric enterprise, brooking no counter-argument and tirelessly searching for a break-through. One can only marvel at his inability to see the obvious, and here one arrives precisely at the source of his fascination as a character. It would have been much easier for Cervantes to have made Don Quixote gradually see sense, but the real challenge to Cervantes's powers of invention was to make Don Quixote *not* see, to prolong his madness as far as possible without allowing it to pall on the reader. If Cervantes had been interested in correlating mental and moral health so as to draw his hero back towards sanity, the episode where Don Quixote goes to visit the non-existent Dulcinea in El Toboso would have provided an excellent moral climax to the novel by confronting him with the emptiness of his illusions. Instead, Cervantes places this episode at the very beginning of Part II and makes Don Quixote pursue the most difficult course open to him: that of believing what Sancho says about the gross peasant girl, and spending the rest of the novel trying to unravel the problem on his own romance terms.

The comic energy of the *Quixote* is largely drawn from the way in which Cervantes keeps putting the madman in situations where it seems impossible that he should not realize his folly; and yet, time and again, he is allowed to wriggle out of his corner and indulge his remarkable gifts of rhetoric and dialectic to salvage his chivalric mission.[59] The basic device used to seal Quixote off from reality is that of enchantment, and it is in the handling of this device that one can best appreciate

Cervantes's narrative mastery, for enchantment could easily have degenerated into an all-purpose excuse used to disguise difficulties and evade problems. Cervantes, however, orchestrates it so subtly that he is able to wring fresh delights from it. What, in fact, prevents the theme of enchantment from becoming unconvincing is that it appears to form part of a logic derived from the theory and practice of chivalric romance, for Don Quixote's whole approach to the world is dictated by the insidious power of fiction, a power that is so pernicious precisely because the madman does not recognize its existence.

CHAPTER FOUR

Irony and the Relics of Romance

(i) *Don Quixote's Ideal Language*

Having discussed the various ways in which Don Quixote attempts to implement his belief in the truth of the romances, I propose to look more closely at the implications of this fundamental delusion. In holding fictional discourse to be literally true, Don Quixote evinces a strong inclination to assume that words must always refer to real things. The most extensive illustration of the knight's inability to comprehend the non-denotative nature of fictional discourse is found in his reply to the Canon of Toledo's contention that the people and events described in the romances are wholly imaginary (I.1).

Don Quixote maintains that the detailed account of the heroes' lives and actions given in the romances is sufficient to recommend their historical truthfulness. But, more interestingly, he claims that the very vividness of the narrative, its ability to make the reader almost see in his mind's eye the characters and situations depicted, is conclusive proof of its authenticity as history. Don Quixote adduces as evidence the pleasure got from reading; by implication, the greater the pleasure derived the more certain one can be of the denotative truth of the language. He does not restrict himself to abstract argument but illustrates his point by recounting a brief tale of a knight errant who jumps into a boiling lake when invited by a mysterious voice to discover the marvels submerged under its surface. Although at the beginning of his story Don Quixote recognizes the fictional status of his tale (viz. his qualifying 'as we might say'; p. 440), he emphasizes the vivid actuality of this imaginary world by insisting on the verb 'to see': 'What finer sight, then, than after all that to see them take him to another room where the tables are laid so magnificently that he is speechless with amazement? And to watch him sprinkle on his hands water all distilled of ambergris and sweet-smelling flowers? And to see him seated on an ivory chair? And to see all the maidens serve him, still preserving their miraculous silence' (p. 441). Moreover, his mode of narration accentuates the minutiae of time and space; it is interspersed with 'here' and 'there', and characterized by such a frequent recurrence of the phrase 'and then' that the action seems to take on a momentum of its own and sweep irresistibly towards its climax.

The euphoria generated by the narration of the story causes Don Quixote to lose sight of the reason for telling it in the first place. He assumes his argument is proven: 'I will enlarge on this no further, for you can gather from what I have said that any passage from any story of knight errantry is bound to delight and amaze a reader' (p. 442). Literary pleasure is itself taken to be a sufficient index of veracity. The mad knight obviously begs the question by telling this tale as proof of the truthfulness of the romances, but Cervantes has given us a marvellous demonstration of the process by which romance addles the brains of the unfortunate *hidalgo*: the vivacity of the literary representation leads to a belief in the real existence of the thing represented, causing him to blur the fundamental distincton between fictional language and language that refers to the real world.

Don Quixote's reluctance to admit the concept of fiction is all of a piece with the sentiments he expresses in his speech on the Golden Age: 'In those days the soul's amorous fancies were clothed simply and plainly, exactly as they were conceived, without any search for artificial elaborations to enhance them. Nor had fraud, deceit or malice mingled with truth and sincerity' (I.xi. 86). Plain speaking is related to truth, whereas artificiality is suspiciously akin to falsehood; even the 'fancies' of a lover must refer accurately to his true sentiments. In such an account of language and communication, the 'lie' or artifice of fiction must appear to be an aberration, if not an outright evil.

The madman is nevertheless prepared to concede that the language of poets in the present Age of Iron is non-denotative and artificial because it describes a kind of beauty that exceeds the bounds of common experience. The poet employs illusory words because he wishes to display the quality of his moral nature and sensibility. Don Quixote asks Sancho rhetorically whether he believes that all those Amaryllises, Phyllises, Sylvias, Dianas, Galateas, and Phyllidas were actually ladies of flesh and blood: 'Not a bit of it. Most of them were invented to serve as subjects for verses, and so that the poets might be taken for lovers, or men capable of being so' (I.xxv.210). Writing poetry is a means by which a man can give public testimony to the inner worth of his soul. In this regard the poet is no different from a knight errant like himself: 'I am quite satisfied, therefore, to imagine and believe that the good Aldonza Lorenzo is lovely and virtuous; her family does not matter a bit ... for my part, I think of her as the greatest princess in the world.'

But if the poet merely invents his lady as a fictional peg to hang words which mirror his own spiritual complexion, Don Quixote, as we have seen, refuses to accept that Dulcinea is a figment of his imagination; she is a genuine, living creature for whom he is prepared to do and die, as he demonstrates consistently throughout the book to the bitter end. This attitude qualitatively distinguishes Don Quixote's words from the poets'; the latter use language as an outward sign of their own subjective condition whereas he *acts* upon his words, thereby committing himself to the objective validity of their referents. Love-poetry may be an arbitrary spiritual exercise, and poetic language correspondingly void of true referential meaning, but in attempting to revive the world of romance Don Quixote hopes to recover for the language of the romances and, by extension, the language of poetry, its capacity to denote real people and real things without inviting disbelief or contempt. In the course of his discussion with Vivaldo about the truth of the books of chivalry, Don Quixote evokes the beauty of Dulcinea, which is declared to be 'superhuman':

... for in her are realized all the impossible and chimerical attributes of beauty which poets give to their ladies; that her hair is gold; her forehead the Elysian fields; her eyebrows rainbows; her eyes suns; her cheeks roses; her lips coral; her teeth pearls; her neck alabaster; her breast marble; her hands ivory; she is white as snow; and those parts which modesty has veiled from human sight are such, I think and believe, that discreet reflection can extol them, but make no comparison. (I.xiii.100)

Dulcinea is the referent to which the seemingly hollow language of poetry points, and which it is his duty to render manifest in the world once again. Don Quixote is, therefore, inclined to deny that Dulcinea is simply a metaphor or symbol, her name does not simply possess figurative meaning, it actually denotes an existing, tangible reality.

The question of Dulcinea's status—upon which hangs Don Quixote's conception of language—is brought to a head when the Duke and Duchess subject the knight to the most searching interrogation in the entire novel. The problem of Dulcinea is introduced by the Duchess who declares that 'this same lady does not exist on earth, but is a fantastic mistress, whom your worship engendered and bore in your mind, and painted with every grace and perfection you desired' (II.xxxii.680). Don Quixote's response to this familiar charge is meticulously honest. He admits his difficulties with a kind of resignation: 'There is much to say on that score . . . God knows whether Dulcinea exists on earth or no, or whether she is fantastic or not fantastic. These are not matters whose verification can be carried out to the full' (p. 680). His reply echoes the one he gave to Don Diego de Miranda's sceptical son on the question of whether knights errant had ever existed. There Don Quixote had pointed out that no matter how much trouble one takes to persuade sceptics it will be in vain 'unless Heaven miraculously convinces them' (II.xviii.583). As far as Dulcinea is concerned, only God really knows whether she objectively exists, and it is not the sort of knowledge one can arrive at through importunate empirical investigation of what are, in any case, for Don Quixote, the misleading appearances of a degenerate world. In the last resort, chivalric knowledge is a form of grace, a gift of God. It does not follow that he has simply invented Dulcinea: 'I neither engendered nor bore my lady, though I contemplate her in her ideal form, as a lady with all the qualities needed to win her fame in all quarters of the world' (p. 680).

By resorting to the notion of contemplation the knight endows his love with a kind of mystical character: Dulcinea is an object to which he can direct his aspirations, just as in a different though kindred context a mystic might contemplate the Godhead without incurring the charge of solipsism or self-delusion. On an earlier occasion Sancho had noticed the parallel between Don Quixote's love and religious or mystical devotion: 'That's the kind of love . . . I've heard them preach about. They say we ought to love our Lord for Himself alone, without being moved to it by hope of glory or fear of punishment' (I.xxxi.273). Don Quixote's courtly love-service possesses a similar disinterestedness because it appears to have no visible, material object. The trouble is, of course, that he is not satisfied with granting Dulcinea a purely abstract, spiritual status, she must have a material existence too. After ascribing to her a series of superlative moral qualities which merit this dedicated, selfless service, he concludes his paean by affirming her high lineage, 'for with good blood beauty shines and glows with a degree of perfection impossible in a humbly born beauty' (p. 681). Now this assertion is, of course, problematical, and it elicits from the Duke the expected objection that even though one may concede that Dulcinea exists and is beautiful, she surely cannot be better born than classic romance princesses like Oriana, Alastrajea, or Madasima.

In reply to this Don Quixote at first appears to retreat and fall back upon the argument that even though Dulcinea may be humbly born her beauty and virtue make her the equal of any lady: 'As to that I may say . . . that Dulcinea is the daughter of her works, that virtues improve blood, and that the virtuous and humble are to be more highly regarded and prized than the wicked and exalted.' But this turns out to be a case of *reculer pour mieux sauter*, for the knight then claims that not only does Dulcinea's beauty make her anybody's equal, there are very real possibilities of her becoming a queen: 'Dulcinea has a vein in her which may raise her to be a queen with a crown and sceptre, for the merit of one lovely and virtuous woman is sufficient to perform even greater miracles; and if not formally, at least virtually, she has greater fortune stored within her.' The knight's distinction between the formal and virtual qualities of Dulcinea lays bare the Platonist basis of his thinking. But this is Platonism with a very special, mad twist to it, for it envisages the 'miraculous' materialization of what is virtual: the regal vein stored within Dulcinea has the capacity to transform itself into a palpable reality, making the peasant girl a queen 'with a crown and sceptre'. It is a hope which constitutes the very nub of Don Quixote's madness inasmuch as it reveals the tenacity with which he clings to the notion that truth depends ultimately on the possibility of attaching demonstrable referents to words. Although he is prepared to admit the concept of potentiality as regards Dulcinea's present status, he immediately links it with the idea of actualization by a miracle, as if potential unrealized would before long become indistinguishable from the empty promise of metaphor.

Don Quixote's approach to language has a precedent and a model of sorts in the tradition of biblical exegesis we had occasion to mention in the first chapter.[1] In the notion of the *figura* history was converted into a form of allegory where events both prefigured later events and also referred to the invisible transactions of the spiritual life. The language of Scripture consequently enjoyed a unique privilege: its sacred symbolism was not devoid of reference since it denoted things which were, if anything, more real and important than the historical events themselves. In this regard, biblical language was the very opposite of fictional discourse, for in so far as its tropes and symbols were securely grounded in denotation, it could be neither fantastical, nor empty, nor gratuitous.

An analogy may be drawn between biblical language and the status accorded by Don Quixote to the language of the romances. The madman's literal belief in the books of chivalry radically denies their fictional character and endows them with a plenitude of reference akin to that of Holy Writ. But if the romances depict true historical reality, it is clear even to the madman himself that this reality is incongruent with the one he inhabits. The actual world Don Quixote lives in is but a confused copy of the real world, and the knight's professed task involves its restoration to pristine clarity. And so, as Don Quixote's replies to the Duke and Duchess make plain, he considers Dulcinea to be not a symbol of some abstract ideal, but a concrete, historical fact. The obvious contradiction between the peasant Aldonza and the regal Dulcinea—both of whom are alleged to be materially real—must logically arise from a conflict between two versions of historical existence, one of which is corrupt and the other true. The corrupt version is that recorded by sense-perception, and it is to this version that Aldonza Lorenzo belongs; on the other hand the correct version is the one given in the romances of chivalry, and it is here that Dulcinea comes into her own. Owing to neglect of chivalry, the true version of historical reality has suffered the ravages of time and evil, and appearances, as a result, belie their true character. By reviving the practice of chivalry Don Quixote will refurbish the phenomenal surface of reality so that it may again be read symbolically as a sort of *figura* where the direct 'literal' level of experience would point to its spiritual meaning; for instance, Aldonza's physical beauty would then be accepted, without trying quibbles and disputes, as signifying her peerless virtue and nobility.

However, Don Quixote's anxiety to see words securely tied to the things they denote makes him behave very much as if the coining of a new word were capable of calling into existence a new object of reference. When he seeks a new name for himself, his horse, and his lady, he takes a good deal of care and effort to choose words that are sonorous and meaningful (for his horse he finds a name that is 'alto, sonoro, y *significativo*', and for his lady one that is 'músico y peregrino y *significativo*'). Such fastidious concern for meaningfulness is, nevertheless, central to the restoration of romance because the new name should make manifest an essence which appearances had hitherto concealed and had caused to be called by a false or unworthy name.[2] Language becomes for Don Quixote an important medium for the reformation of the Age of Iron. Just as he hopes to reveal through adventure the true essences of misleading phenomena, so must he organize the loose language of everyday life into its essential meanings. Hence his abhorrence of the linguistic howlers perpetrated by Sancho; to abuse the lexicon is to debauch meaning itself and introduce confusion into the true order of things.

Don Quixote, by contrast, likes to make words and concepts as precise and clear-cut as possible. Like a scholastic thinker he loves to draw distinctions.[3] He embarks on fairly lengthy disquisitions on the differences between the career of Arms and that of Letters (I.xxxviii), or between worldly Herostratian fame and chivalric renown (II.viii), liberty and confinement (II.lviii), or between the several forms of knighthood (II.xvii), or the two types of beauty (II.lviii). Each activity, condition, state, or concept belongs to a unique and distinctive category.

Needless to say, the knight carries his fondness for definition to absurd lengths. After he is beaten up by the Yanguesans (I.xv), he rationalizes his humiliation by distinguishing between an 'affront' and a 'disgrace'. His misfortune is not a 'disgrace' because 'wounds dealt with instruments which are accidentally in the hand do not disgrace a man; that is expressly laid down in the law of the duel. So if a shoemaker strikes a man with the last he is holding, even though it is of wood, it shall not therefore be said that the man whom he struck was cudgelled' (I.xv.116). For Don Quixote wounds can be distinguished generically according to their different essences; they have, it could be said, a distinguishing mark which identifies them. What matters ultimately is not the wound itself but the category to which it belongs; the wounds they received at the hands of the Yanguesans do not constitute a disgrace. For Sancho, however, a thrashing is a thrashing, and there is no going beyond that to enquire into the different categories of a good beating. In Part II Chapter xxxii, Don Quixote makes a similar distinction between an 'offence' and an 'affront' after the churchman has insulted him at the Duke's table: 'For between an offence and an affront there is this difference. . . . An affront comes from one who is capable of giving it, gives it, and maintains it, but an offence can come from anyone without carrying an affront with it' (p. 676). He then illustrates this distinction with various examples and concludes that he need not resent what the churchman said to him.

Don Quixote is in fact employing a mode of reasoning that has a long medieval pedigree: that of scholastic realism, which Cervantes here reduces to absurdity.[4] For an extreme medieval realist these terminological distinctions would not be hair-splitting; they would reflect the realm of essences. Sancho, however, effectively denies this invisible reality for the actuality of existence. In Sancho's eyes, there is no difference between an affront, an offence, or a disgrace; they are all quite sufficient synonyms for the single experience of pain, but his master sorts his painful experiences into neat categories, each possessed of its own special character.

Don Quixote's committed literalism, what we might call his verbal essentialism, becomes the target of much of Cervantes's irony. The knight tries to exclude figures and metaphors from language, or to attach rigid, preconceived definitions to ambiguous situations in his efforts to reduce perplexing appearances to prescribed meanings. The episode of the galley slaves (I.xxii) aptly reveals Don Quixote chivvying tropes into plain statement with the help of his sword. On coming across the chain-gang and learning from Sancho that they are 'men forced by the King', the knight is horrified: 'What! Men forced? . . . Is it possible that the King uses force on anyone?' Sancho tries to explain, but Don Quixote is struck by the fact that these men 'go by force, and not out of their own free will'. He immediately fixes on the one word 'force' (*fuerza*), whose true meaning he seeks in the chivalric code which enjoins the knight to 'overcome force' (*desfacer fuerzas*), instead of investigating the meaning of 'force' in the actual context of the galley-slaves.

Even when Don Quixote asks the prisoners the reason for their punishment they reply in euphemistic slang which the knight cannot understand. One says that he has been punished for 'being in love', the other 'for being a canary'. Of course, Don Quixote has to seek clarification; he cannot understand the meaning of the words because 'love' and 'canary' are quite clearly being used as whimsical metaphors which even the uninitiated would recognize if not perhaps fully understand.[5] Don Quixote, who is keen to see an orderliness in language, is at a loss to transform the whole thing into intelligible chivalric terms. However, even though he manifestly cannot appreciate the moral complexities of each individual case (and his failure to recognize the ironical metaphors illustrates this), he copes with perplexity in the usual way, by resorting to chivalric action and pronouncing these criminals to be needy, oppressed persons whom it is his duty to succour. The niceties of the King's temporal justice are disregarded in order to establish the higher claims of 'natural' or chivalric justice, and so, after releasing the galley-slaves from their royal shackles, he presses them into chivalric service by extracting from them a promise to report to Dulcinea.

This adventure illustrates just how the rigidity of Don Quixote's concentration on the literal meaning of words leads him so disastrously to misinterpret situations and miss the very object he is aiming at. He blindly follows the books of chivalry when faced by complicated issues; any term or phrase which he fancies has a chivalric ring will evoke a prescribed response, much as alleged traces of romance reality are transmuted into full-scale adventures in his mind. As a result of this rigidity Don Quixote cannot avoid projecting his preconceptions on to the everyday world.

An example of this response is his attempt to help the shepherdess Marcela (I.xiv. 110), after she has delivered an eloquent and spirited defence of her rejection of Grisóstomo's importunate complaints against her, and has withdrawn into the woods. Some of the shepherds make as if to follow her whereupon Don Quixote reaches for his sword and warns them against doing so. His rather superfluous action is motivated by the feeling that 'this was an occasion to exercise his chivalry by the succouring of a maiden in distress'. Now Marcela, who has so splendidly taken care of herself by rejecting unwanted lovers, can only be described as a 'maiden in distress' in a limited sense, as a single woman whose honour may be in need of the kind of chivalric protection against attack referred to by Don Quixote in his Golden Age speech. In wishing to attach Marcela to that chivalric formula of 'maiden in distress', Don Quixote excludes all the other facets of the girl—her real intentions, her independent will—which make her much more complex than a story-book damsel. What is more, this elimination of significant nuances in favour of a single, inflexible meaning prevents him from grasping the central truth of the situation: that Marcela is the victor and Grisóstomo the victim in the particular situation. The usual chivalric pattern where the woman was virtually always the passive object of men's actions is actually reversed here, but Don Quixote seems unaware of the possibility that an accumulation of contextual nuances can sometimes be great enough to outweigh and radically alter, if not actually contradict, a literal or formulaic meaning.

Far from clarifying reality, such a fixation on the literal encloses Don Quixote in a vulnerable subjectivism which blinds him to the most damaging attacks on his dignity and ideals. Even when his cherished lady Dulcinea is being savagely burlesqued by one of the Duke's servants, he is taken in because of his unwillingness or inability to register the ironies of tone and style which undermine the literal sense of the speech. The counterfeit Dulcinea implores Sancho to whip himself so as to break the spell she is under: 'Lash, lash that thick hide of yours, you great untamed beast; raise up from sloth that spirit which inclines you to eating and more eating, and set at liberty the smoothness of my skin, the meekness of my temper and the beauty of my countenance' (II.xxxv.702). She then pleads with Sancho to do it at least for the sake of his poor master 'whose soul I can now see stuck in his throat, not ten inches from his lips'. On hearing this, Don Quixote feels his throat and remarks to the Duke: 'By God, sir, Dulcinea has spoken the truth for here is my soul sticking in my throat like the nut of a crossbow.'

The knight's tendency to seek a denotative sense to language makes it particularly difficult for him to adjust to the metaphorical nature of art as it manifests itself in everyday life. When Don Quixote comes across the actors on the waggon of the *Parliament of Death*, he at first thinks he has found a new adventure (II.xi.534). He halts them in traditional chivalric fashion in order to root out their true identities: 'Carter, coachman, devil, or whatever you may be, tell me instantly who you are, where you are going, and who are the people you are driving in your coach.' Like a good knight errant he wants to get at the substance of this phenomenon and resolve the troublesome accidental ambiguities of its appearance. The driver obliges him by painstakingly spelling out his business and identifying the real people behind the actors' costumes. Don Quixote listens to this exposition of each actor's metaphorical *alter ego*—one of whom says he represents the Devil—and then expresses amazement at such a wilful perversion of appearances. But just when he seems to have grasped the nature of the theatrical metaphor, he unexpectedly runs into trouble with one of the clowns, who causes him to be thrown off Rocinante. The metaphor now slips back into a literal meaning as the capital letter of allegory is particularized into lower case in the following exchange initiated by Sancho: 'Sir, the Devil's carried Dapple off'; to which the knight replies 'What devil?'; and when he is told by Sancho, he says: 'Then I shall get him back . . . even if he were to lock him up in the deepest and darkest dungeons of Hell' (p. 536). The knight immediately reacts as if it were a real devil, whom he is prepared to chase into Hell itself if necessary. However, he is so bemused by what is happening that he finally urges Sancho to turn away: 'Let us leave these phantoms and return to our quest for better and more substantial adventures' (p. 538). He finds it hard to accept these actors merely as actors: either their allegorical costumes must denote true identities, or else they must be phantoms, yet another trick of the enchanters.

On a similar but more famous occasion, when Don Quixote settles down to watch Master Peter's puppet show, he appears at first to recognize the difference between the literal and the metaphorical (II.xxvi). In fact, so carried away does he become by the dramatic action that he leaps to the rescue of the persecuted puppets and, having smashed the Moorish army single-handed, loudly extols the virtues of knight errantry. When apprised of his error, he apologizes and blames it as usual on the enchanters, who change and controvert appearances: 'I assure you gentlemen that all that has passed here seemed to me a real occurrence. Melisendra was Melisendra; Sir Gaiferos, Sir Gaiferos; Marsilio, Marsilio; and Charlemagne, Charlemagne' (p. 643). He seems at this point to have admitted his mistake in taking the puppet show literally and agrees to compensate Master Peter for the damage. As the puppet-master reckons the cost and asks two *reales* and twelve *maravedís* for the broken-nosed and one-eyed Melisendra, Don Quixote observes with wry satisfaction: 'Well, the devil is in it . . . if Melisendra and her husband are not over the French border, at least, by now. For the horse they were on seemed to me to fly rather than gallop' (p. 644). It turns out that Don Quixote is even now incapable of fully appreciating the scenes as metaphorical. He is loath to concede that the puppet-play did not refer to any event in the real world, and clings instead to his conviction that Melisendra and Gaiferos did, after all, escape to France. Master Peter, seeing that Don Quixote 'was rambling back to his old theme', rapidly changes his tune and declares that if the puppet is not Melisendra, it must be one of the damsels who served her, and correspondingly, he reduces his claim to sixty *maravedís* (p. 645).

In all the examples discussed above Don Quixote becomes a

victim of irony because he takes words at their face value, as if they were always tied to their ostensible referents regardless of the utterer's intentions. In his anxiety to get things straight he actually diminishes the range of meanings language can generate through indirection and suggestion. Metaphor, hyperbole, irony, burlesque, parody, all the artifice of discourse, the restless, posturing masquerade of language is reduced by the mad knight to a ritual celebration of certainty. Don Quixote seeks to restore to language a virtue which it appeared to enjoy in romance, and which the chivalric code—with its truth-seeking duels, its system of pledges and inescapable obligations—was meant to preserve against time or evil, namely, its capacity to serve as an unequivocal medium of communication which even in its figurative usages, in symbolic or allegorical discourse, could still be relied upon to denote some knowable if transcendent reality. In making Don Quixote the proponent of this utopian linguistic stability Cervantes demonstrates all the more effectively the opposite, the true, condition of language: its disconcerting emptiness, and the resultant possibility of using it to conceal intentions and mislead.

(ii) *Sancho's Sense of Irony*

Because a good part of Don Quixote's enterprise involves defining concepts, fixing words to their literal meanings, respecting distinctions, and upholding stringent standards of decorum, his relations with the peasant Sancho are of particular importance in this regard. From the beginning of their long relationship Cervantes establishes the fundamental difference between them. After Don Quixote is hurt in the adventure of the windmills he tells Sancho that if he does not complain of the pain it is because knights errant are not supposed to do so (I.viii.69-70). Sancho for his part assures Don Quixote that he would complain of the slightest pain. That night Sancho sleeps while Don Quixote meditates on Dulcinea; at the break of day Sancho eats, whereas Don Quixote 'determined to subsist on savoury memories' (pp. 70-1); the knight regulates his behaviour by the laws of chivalry as he remembers them from the books, but Sancho cannot even read or write; Don Quixote is an educated *hidalgo* interested in ideas and moral precepts, whereas Sancho is an ignorant peasant who wholeheartedly follows his natural inclinations.

This difference is, of course, one that Don Quixote recognizes as natural since it confirms the traditional distinction between knights errant and the rabble. But the madman does not wish to leave things as they are, he has determined to make his companion act in the manner of a squire. Although unfit to be a knight errant, Sancho cannot be allowed to remain in his benighted condition as a gross peasant, he must be educated so that he may take his rightful place in the reconstituted world of romance. The *hidalgo* therefore instructs his servant not to intervene on his behalf against other knights because a squire must only defend himself against the low-born. Sancho replies that he will obey, 'but as to defending myself, sir, I shan't take much notice of those rules because divine law and human law allow everyone to defend himself against anyone who tries to harm him' (p. 71). Don Quixote agrees but insists that 'in the matter of aiding me against knights, you must restrain your natural impulses'.

From time to time, however, Don Quixote has to resort to force in order to subject Sancho's natural impulses to chivalric laws. For example, when the knight invites Sancho to celebrate the victory over the Basque by granting him the privilege of sitting and eating with his master, Sancho declines the honour because he is too hungry to bother with polite manners. Don Quixote insists and pulls Sancho down beside him, making the reluctant squire co-operate willy-nilly in the practice of chivalry (I.xi.85). By and large Sancho is disposed to co-operate with Don Quixote only out of self-interest. After the victory over the Basque, Sancho asks his master for the promised island but Don Quixote urges him to be patient, for adventures 'of this kind are not adventures of isles but of cross-roads, from which nothing is to be gained but a broken head and the loss of an ear' (I.x.80).

Not too long after this, the fickleness of Sancho's greed and the vicissitudes of circumstance will begin to make him feel rather sceptical about his master's chivalric pretensions. The first occasion arises when both knight and squire are lying on the ground after having been beaten up by the Yanguesans. Sancho notices the woeful discrepancies between their painful experience of chivalric adventure and Don Quixote's accounts of their lofty precedents. Thus when his battered master declares that he would not feel disgraced to ride on Sancho's ass to some castle where his wounds might be cured, citing the illustrious precedent of Silenus who once stooped to riding on an ass, Sancho observes that 'there's a great deal of difference between riding astride and being laid across like a sack of dung' (I.xv.117).

Sancho's capacity to see through the proprieties of chivalric decorum grows when he is subjected to his traumatic blanket-tossing. After this experience he wants to return home but Don Quixote's reaction, typically, is to chide him both for his faint-heartedness and his ignorance of chivalric lore, declaring that there is no greater pleasure in the world than 'winning a battle and triumphing over an enemy' (I.xviii.133). But Sancho, not surprisingly, does have doubts about this, although his reply this time is less forthright: 'That may well be ... for all I know. But I do know that since we have been knights errant—or your worship has, for I cannot count myself of that honourable number—we have never won a battle except that one over the Basque.' Here he feigns agreement with his master's sentiments but conveys his feelings obliquely by appearing to acknowledge the virtues of chivalry yet pointing to their failure. Sancho's emerging sense of scepticism about Don Quixote's enterprise and, more especially, his ironic expression of this, evolve paradoxically from this distance Don Quixote imposes between them; the servant's inability to have it out man-to-man with his crackpot master obliges him to look to more circuitous methods of communication when the need arises or a crisis is imminent.

Sancho's relations with the knight change decisively and irreversibly in the adventure of the fulling-mills (I.xx). He is terrified when he hears the thunderous noises in the night, but Don Quixote rejects his frightened appeals to desist from investigating their source and abandon the place. Sancho tries all manner of pleading and concludes by adopting chivalresque language: 'In God's name, sir, do me not this wrong' (p. 151; 'Por un solo Dios, señor mío, que non se me faga tal desaguisado'). He urges Don Quixote to postpone the adventure until the morning, which according to the 'science' he learned as a shepherd cannot be more than three hours away. When Don Quixote asks how he can know this if there are no stars visible, Sancho replies that fear has many eyes but that, in any case, through proper reasoning ('por buen discurso') it is possible to tell that it will not be long till dawn. Not only does fear prompt Sancho to use chivalresque language, it makes him appeal in desperation to the laws of a 'science' that appears to proceed, if necessary, through reasoning alone without reference to sense-experience, much as Don Quixote's chivalric 'science' is elaborated deductively according to its own abstract laws of reasoning.

When this ploy fails, and Don Quixote still persists in his wish to find the cause of the noise, Sancho is forced into the unprecedented act of lying to his master. He ties Rocinante's legs and then addresses the mad knight in a style which aspires to an unaccustomed dignity and cultivation: 'See, sir, the Heavens are moved by my tears and prayers. They have ordained that Rocinante shall be unable to stir. If you persist in urging, spurring, and striking him it will be provoking Fortune and, as the saying goes, kicking against the pricks' (p. 151). Here Sancho manages an erudite reference to Fortune and an allusion to Scripture, and Don Quixote, amazingly, responds to this line of approach, agreeing to await the dawn. The knight relents because he is predisposed to believe the type of argument about divine intervention which his squire puts forward. For Sancho it is a special triumph: he has learned to beat Don Quixote at his own game and to advance his interests at the same time.

What starts out merely as a need to communicate develops fortuitously, through a mixture of incompetence and wilfulness, into parody. As the night wears on Sancho needs to relieve himself, and even though he tries to conceal this from Don Quixote, he cannot contain himself. Hearing Sancho, the knight enquires about the new sounds that have now been added to the original ones, and the squire archly replies: 'I don't know, sir. . . . It must be something fresh, for these adventures or misadventures never begin for nothing' (p. 155). The sounds he perpetrates are thus converted into a source of mystery, precisely like those other sounds Don Quixote is waiting to investigate. With new-found artfulness Sancho mockingly converts his digestive travails both verbally and acoustically into a brief ironic travesty of his master's adventure-seeking.

When Don Quixote realizes what has happened he becomes irritated and again imposes a proper distance between himself and Sancho, attributing the latter's lack of respect to an excess of familiarity. But after the noises in the night are discovered to have been caused by a fulling-mill, Don Quixote, although dismayed at first, notices Sancho trying to hold back his amusement and breaks into laughter himself. The sight of his master laughing unleashes uncontrollable convulsions of mirth from Sancho, who quickly indulges in a gleeful parody of the knight's bravado upon first hearing the noise: ' "You must know, friend Sancho, that I was born by the will of Heaven in this our iron age to revive the age of gold, or the golden age. It is for me that are reserved perils, great exploits, and valorous deeds" ' (p. 158). Don Quixote reacts to this brazen mockery with great fury, and hits Sancho with his lance, but a while later he admits the funny side of the matter. Even so, he defends his outburst of censorious anger at Sancho's disrespect by making it clear that one should interpret situations circumspectly, with an eye to how they may be maliciously distorted by others: 'I do not deny . . . that what happened to us is a thing worth laughing at. But it is not worth telling, for not everyone is sufficiently intelligent to be able to see things from the right point of view ('poner en su punto las cosas')' (p. 159).

Here Don Quixote argues that one is not entitled to put just any construction on experience, a moral effort must be made to perceive its proper significance. Such is the implication of the Spanish phrase he uses: 'poner en su punto las cosas', which can also be rendered as 'assigning things to their proper place', or 'giving things their due weight'. Moreover, since not everybody can be entrusted with this task, a special authority is reserved for the discerning minority able to exercise this moral discrimination. Sancho apologizes and vows not to make light of chivalric matters again, swearing to honour Don Quixote 'as my master and natural lord'. The mad knight is well pleased with these sentiments and endorses them with some grandiloquence: 'In that case . . . your days will be long on the face of the earth, for next to our parents we are bound to honour

our masters as we would our fathers' (p. 160). The momentary
anarchy of the fulling-mills episode is overcome, and the
paternalistic distance between master and servant restored.
Hierarchical order, of a sort, reigns once again.

Sancho's promise to honour his master as his 'natural lord' is
rather short-lived. When he returns from his visit to El Toboso,
he is forced to lie about his meeting with Dulcinea, which, of
course, never took place at all (I.xxx-xxxi). In his enthusiasm,
Don Quixote supplies Sancho with details of what ought to
have occurred according to the customs of chivalry. Sancho
responds by consciously degrading his noble version with
cruelly realistic details, playing on the literal meaning of the
word 'high' and on the quality of Dulcinea's personal odours
(p. 269), but pointedly refraining from altogether destroying
the chivalric image of Dulcinea; he refers to her as 'the lady
Dulcinea' and reports that she wishes to see Don Quixote, that
the Basque had been to pay homage to her, though not as yet
the galley-slaves (p.270). Sancho is clearly deriving malicious
enjoyment from tantalizing Don Quixote; he does not present
the knight with an entirely desired picture nor with a totally
degraded one either, rather he teases his master by combining
elements of the two, thereby savouring a form of covert power,
an underhand control of the other's responses.

For the first time, Don Quixote comes up not against reality
(e.g. windmills), nor against other people's version of reality
(e.g. the barber's basin), but against a deliberate travesty of
reality designed both to satisfy and annoy him. Don Quixote is
not, as with Dorothea-Micomicona, so much the victim of a
well-intentioned lie as the dupe of Sancho's ironic intentions.
Sancho's words are more than lies, they are meant as secret
amusement and mockery of his master, they are a covert
expression of a power which is based upon the knowledge of
Don Quixote's fundamental weakness: Dulcinea does not exist,
and Sancho knows this because his complete fabrication is
believed by the madman. Had he merely been interested in
defensive lying, Sancho could have played along fully with Don
Quixote's desires and presented him with an acceptable picture
of the non-existent princess. But as it is, Sancho offers him some
titbits and wantonly withdraws others, rendering his master,
on this occasion at least, into a creature of his will.

Sancho's deception inaugurates a new phase in the narrative where there is a conscious split between a character's real intentions and the surface meaning of his words and actions. His ironic play with the existence of Dulcinea contaminates the very core of Don Quixote's chivalric world. From then on the knight has to contend with a romance dimension to experience which appears to accord with his expectations (albeit with some disturbing inconsistencies) but which in fact has been contrived by Sancho and, increasingly, by other characters. This factitious romance overlay increases in structural importance and ironic sophistication as the novel progresses; in Part II it becomes an indispensable narrative feature with the so-called enchantment of Dulcinea and its far-reaching consequences in and beyond the Duke's castle.

When Don Quixote attempts to restore the age of chivalry he is seeking to re-open access to that transcendent reality which in Chrétien's romances corresponds to the *sen* or the spiritual sense of experience, that is to say, the symbolic level of the narrative which unifies and gives meaning to the disparate adventures.[6] In other words, Don Quixote attempts to find a similar unity in his words and actions by relating them to a spiritual reality beyond the material surface of the world. However, given his inability to establish this spiritual reality independently of his assertions, his persistent efforts at transcendence simply collapse back into the empirical.

On the other hand, when Sancho fashions his lie about Dulcinea from the material Don Quixote provides, he encourages the construction of a rather rickety superstructure of romance reality beyond immediate experience. Sancho achieves this through irony, by imposing a duality in his own language between surface and real meaning. His irony therefore introduces a new level of reference in the narrative; but this is a travesty of romance symbolism since it does not, of course, genuinely correspond to the spiritual order of things Don Quixote aspires to reach through his chivalric practice. The knight's stubborn search for a higher romance reality has only succeeded in forcing Sancho to resort to irony, thereby giving rise to the wholly different problem of hidden intentions.

In direct contrast to Don Quixote's concern for denotative truth and moral responsibility in all forms of discourse, Sancho uses language as the ductile medium of his desires and fears. He becomes in consequence a potentially anarchic element in his master's scheme of things by unsettling words in their stable relation to meaning; his ironical activity inevitably undermines Don Quixote's wish to preserve a sharply outlined profile for words and concepts, an immovable, substantive structure of truth and value in the shifting world of human experience.

Cervantes, therefore, alludes in the Quixote – Sancho relationship to some conflicts of very general and serious import; conflicts between literal and metaphorical levels of discourse, between symbolism and irony, or between authority and individual interest. Indeed Don Quixote's search for unity and coherence is not altogether absurd; there are parallels between the mad knight and the author of fiction which did not escape Cervantes's notice.

The introduction of irony into a narrative is potentially anarchic. Unless they are subsumed in a framework of symbolism or allegory, as in Chrétien's romances, ironic meanings are liable to proliferate and produce a sense of complete relativism. The author's own judgements and values will then appear unstable to the reader, and the fictional world can lose its substance and slip into farce. Even if he lacks the authority, in Don Quixote's phrase, 'to assign things to their proper place' ('poner en su punto las cosas'), the writer of fiction has still to set some objective limits to his ironic freedom in order to distinguish his invention from the sheer arbitrariness of fantasy. Having explicitly rejected any claim to special authority, Cervantes, as we shall see, was none the less very much alive to the dangers inherent in irony and farce.

(iii) *The Ironic Author*

I have so far confined myself to Sancho's ironic opposition to Don Quixote. Nevertheless, Sancho's attitude is shared by many other characters, principally, in Part I, by Dorothea, the priest and barber, and later by Sampson Carrasco, the Duke and Duchess, and Altisidora in Part II. But the main accomplice in Sancho's duplicity and ironic undermining is unquestionably Cervantes himself, the ironic author.[7] The most significant ironic adversities Don Quixote encounters, so to speak, come in the form of the tricks the invisible author plays on him. Cervantes employs a great many ironic devices of varying magnitude and subtlety. Because of the manifold and elusive nature of irony itself, it becomes impossible to catalogue minutely each instance in the narrative. I therefore propose to discuss some major devices, especially those which have a fundamental, structural bearing on the novel.

The most obvious technique is, of course, that of flat contradiction. When Don Quixote (or for that matter some other character) says or does something, the narrator will contradict him by producing a contrary situation or statement. This, of course, is fairly close to the common definition of irony as the saying of one thing and meaning another. Cervantes sharply upsets the expectations of Don Quixote in most of the straightforward adventures into which the mad knight launches himself. The device is not much different from that employed in Greek drama, where the hero is blind to certain events produced by an adverse Fate which will eventually frustrate his human striving and destroy him.

A variant of this basic ironic pattern is to have the clash occur, as in the fulling-mills episode, between two characters, resulting in a misunderstanding where one is deliberately concealing some information from the other so as to exercise power or control over him. The ironic relations are far more unstable than in the formula for tragic irony where the victim has no chance against forces beyond his human ken or control. Here the victim may be momentarily taken in, but since the ironist is also human, he is equally vulnerable to the subsequent manœuvres of his victim. Roles can be reversed, and so the ironic confrontation has the makings of a power struggle with the possibility of reciprocity, interaction, and shifting relations.

Cervantes introduces further ironic variations into his narrative by combining the two devices in different ways. For instance, he takes up a particular character's words and incorporates them into his own narrative description, thereby producing a discrepancy between the character's subjectivity and the narrative's objectivity. The following is a brief example: 'Don Quixote went out of the *inn* to be sentinel of the *castle*, as he had promised' (I.xlii.386; my emphases). This device is frequently used and it is relatively straightforward, but it leads to a variant which is extremely fruitful for ironic play. Cervantes sometimes appropriates the discourses of two characters and plays them off within his own narrative discourse, not only preserving the original clash between the characters' motives, views, and value-judgements, but introducing a further clash with the objectivity of the actual narration. When the priest, the barber, and Dorothea ask after Don Quixote on Sancho's return from seeing his master in Sierra Morena (I.xxix.250), Cervantes indirectly narrates Sancho's report on his visit. Not only is the reader informed of the actual conditions of Don Quixote's penance but also, through Sancho's comically inept reproduction of Don Quixote's archaic chivalresque language ('estaba determinado de no parecer ante su fermosura fasta que hobiese fecho fazañas que le ficiesen digno de su gracia'), he is able to appreciate the lunatic stubbornness of the knight. In addition to this, the reader can gauge something of Sancho's own interest in the matter. His anxiety that Don Quixote might not become an emperor or an archbishop is conveyed by the syntactical construction of the last two sentences of the reported account ('Y que si aquello pasaba adelante, corría peligro de no venir a ser emperador, como estaba obligado, ni aun arzobispo, que era lo menos que podía ser. Por eso, que mirasen lo que se había de hacer para sacarle de allí'). The arrangement of the various subordinate clauses imbues the narrative discourse with a petulant tone which reflects Sancho's urgent desire to extract his master from the Sierra Morena so that he might all the quicker marry a king's daughter and give him an island to govern.

By setting off Don Quixote's reported speech against Sancho's within the mainstream of his narrative, Cervantes is able to ironize both characters at once for different reasons. The narrative is not merely descriptive, nor does it merely report what the characters have said, it goes beyond reportage to adopt their verbal style and assimilate this to the description. It is a technique which foreshadows the *style indirect libre* in its flexibility and subtlety. It enjoys the best of two worlds since it retains the descriptive impartiality of the narrative while incorporating the subjective values of the characters. It is as if the narrator had stepped off his historian's pedestal of scrupulous detachment and descended into the embroiled world he describes as a protean presence who assumes and discards the rhythms and tonalities of his characters' actual speech.

By appropriating his characters' discourses, Cervantes increases the possibilities of manipulating them. Taking up a particular tone or rhythm and placing it in a broader context, the narrator can throw into relief certain hidden qualities or at least condition ironically the significance of the original. An excellent example of this occurs in the first chapter of the novel where Cervantes reports Don Quixote's views on the romances. It is best to give the original Spanish:

Decía él que el Cid Ruy Díaz había sido muy buen caballero pero que no tenía que ver con el Caballero de la Ardiente Espada que de sólo un revés había partido por medio dos fieros y descomunales gigantes. Mejor estaba con Bernardo del Carpio, porque en Roncesvalles había muerto a Roldán el encantado, valiéndose de la industria de Hércules, cuando ahogó a Anteo, el hijo de la Tierra, entre los brazos. Decía mucho bien del gigante Morgante, porque, con ser de aquella generación gigantea, que todos son soberbios y descomedidos, él solo era afable y bien criado. Pero, sobre todos estaba bien con Reinaldos de Montalbán, y más cuando le veía salir de su castillo y robar cuantos topaba, y cuando en allende robó aquel ídolo de Mahoma que era todo de oro, según dice su historia. Diera él por dar una mano de coces al traidor de Galalón, al ama que tenía y aun a su sobrina de añadidura.[8]

The interest of this passage lies not so much in what it seems to be doing—i.e. reporting on what Don Quixote used to say about the world of the romances—but rather in its actual syntactical organization. The report's narrative equanimity is ruffled by the inflections of a more colloquial tone which suggests the cavilling, disputatious quality of Don Quixote's own speech, and thus catches the form of his feelings about the romances as well as their actual content. Because it is a report and not a literal transcript, a certain amount of apparently legitimate compression occurs; the second and third sentences convey a rather breathless compilation of heroic feats which manages to put across the opposite of what it intends: rather than inspiring admiration for these heroes, as the *hidalgo* would presumably have expected, it invites ridicule.

The mechanisms of irony are well stowed beneath the

surface, awaiting the reader's perception of the minimal discrepancies that exist between the reported words and their narrative setting. Once the ironic signals have been recognized, the narrative yields up messages which differ substantially from the overt statements. Don Quixote's enthusiasm now appears as an absurd obsession; his richly detailed arguments, his taste for erudite references and measured comparisons, are squeezed in the narrative into a manic pseudo-logical zeal; his lofty sense of history is transformed by the use of a temporal adverb ('cuando'), a change of tense (from 'veía' to 'robó'), and the seemingly innocuous insertion of a demonstrative adjective ('aquel ídolo'), into a strange chimera existing only within his own fractured mind. In the last sentence the underswell of Don Quixote's emotions rises uncontrollably to the surface; with the phrase 'y aun a su sobrina de añadidura', we capture the immense frustration of the home-bound *hidalgo*, who would give anything to rid himself of the nagging of housekeeper and niece, and leap bodily into the life of the romances.

Cervantes's insidious narrative technique enables him to steal behind the character's own consciousness and so reveal secret pockets of motivation of which even Don Quixote himself seems unaware. However, the intensification of this technique of assimilating various styles and voices to the main narrative is potentially anarchic. By unsettling conventional styles or mingling levels of diction, Cervantes is able to construct entire scenes whose comic energy is drawn from just such an indecorous miscegenation of words, concepts, and values. As we shall see from the extended example below, Cervantes's comic exhilaration is nevertheless punctuated by glances at the underlying issues of poetic truth and authorial responsibility for the selection and ordering of material. And yet, even these references to serious issues are conditioned by the all-absorbing irreverence of the ironic narrative.

In Part I Chapter xvi, the kitchen-maid Maritornes has given her word to one of the guests, a muleteer, that she will visit him that night: 'And it is told to the credit of this good girl that she never made such promises without fulfilling them, even if she made them far away in the mountains and without any witness at all. For she prided herself on being a maiden of breeding, and did not feel degraded by serving in an inn' (p.

121). Here is Cervantes beginning to equivocate on the subject of keeping one's promises—a virtue which is not only the hallmark of good breeding but also, with combat, one of the cornerstones of the system of courtly chivalry. On this occasion the virtue of fidelity is displayed in a very dubious context indeed. The scene switches to the guests' dormitory where Don Quixote, Sancho, and the muleteer have settled down for the night. Suddenly, Cervantes's scruples as editor of the 'history' obtrude in the narrative. The reason for the muleteer's current prominence in the history, he says, may well be explained by the fact that he was known by and is even said to have been a kinsman of Cide Hamete's: 'But, however that may be, Cide Hamete Benengeli was a very exact historian and very precise [*puntual*] in all his details, as can be seen by his not passing over these various points, trivial and petty though they may be' (p. 121). Benengeli's devotion to historical truth is such that he cannot but include in his chronicle trivial incidents like the muleteer's assignation with Maritornes, in contrast to other 'grave historians' who are so selective in their narratives that they leave in their ink-horns 'the most substantial part of their work'. Cervantes goes on to praise the author of the romance of *Tablante de Ricamonte* and the writer of the chronicle of the exploits of Count Tomillas 'for the exhaustiveness [*puntualidad*] with which they describe everything'. Now Cervantes has shifted the equivocal virtue of fidelity from Maritornes to the story-teller or historian. Does *puntualidad* mean that he should emulate Benengeli and chronicle every sordid detail in the interests of fidelity to the truth, even if this gives rise to prurience, or should he attempt to follow the practice of 'grave historians' who exercise the selective discrimination recommended by Don Quixote when he tells Sancho after the episode with the fulling-mills that one should seek 'to see things from the right point of view' ('poner en su *punto* las cosas')? Must the historian pass over in silence things that actually happened because they fail to live up to his moral standards, or should he include everything?

The transference of the notion of *puntualidad* from the unseemly ethos of Maritornes and her muleteer to that of Cide Hamete's allegedly historical narrative poses the fundamental problem of moral authority in imaginative fiction. Cervantes seems to be saying, at least in this passage, that just as we all know what lies behind Maritornes's 'punctuality', we know too what motivates people to write or read about love-affairs, stories about kitchen-maids and lustful muleteers. Despite all the roundabout efforts by chivalric authors at moral rationalization, it is by and large sheer salaciousness which they offer their readers in the guise of historical comprehensiveness.

On the face of it, Cervantes is only making fun of romance story-tellers who clothe their meretricious intentions in high-minded rhetoric, but he has nevertheless touched upon a serious problem for any narrative writer: the difference between poetic and historical truth. If the writer is concerned with historical truth alone he may well invoke this principle in order to include all manner of scurrilous material under the pretence of documentary thoroughness or truthfulness to life. However, and this is the sly point Cervantes is really making, even if a writer claims to be guided by impeccable moral principles, by a high sense of poetic truth, he could still indulge in titillation so long as he dressed his subject-matter in an acceptable moralistic package. Beyond theories of poetic or historical truth, Cervantes would seem to be implying, there lies the fundamental problem of the author's genuine moral disposition. Questions of poetic truth will remain insoluble unless imaginative literature is illuminated by some transcendent power or inner moral conscience. Without a sense of inspiration—a belief in creative writing as an essentially spiritual activity liable to manifold distortions in the absence of divine guidance—there can be no effective means of ensuring moral probity in fiction.

Having raised these weighty issues, Cervantes leaves them in suspension as the narrative presses on: 'But to return to the story. After the carrier had visited his mules and given them their second feed, he stretched himself on his packsaddles and awaited his most punctual [*puntualísima*] Maritornes' (p. 121). Here at least is one quality the good kitchen-maid shares with her tirelessly inquisitive historian. The notion of *puntualidad*, transferred back to its former context, undergoes a further ironic twist, for the superlative that now admiringly enhances Maritornes's exemplary reliability in these matters also captures, in the circumstances, the lecherous self-congratulation of the waiting muleteer. But not only does it lay bare the *état d'âme* of the muleteer, the well-placed superlative alludes to, and so short-circuits, the potentially endless debate about moral responsibility in literature, drawing the entire question into the gathering swirl of comedy.

The comic narrative now begins to spiral through successive twists of irony (pp. 121–4). While Don Quixote lies awake in his bed he persuades himself that Maritornes is the chatelain's daughter, who has pledged herself to come secretly to his chamber that night and lie with him. This sets him worrying about how he will resist her advances. Maritornes does indeed enter stealthily at this point to 'keep faith' with the muleteer, but when Don Quixote hears her he grabs her arm and forces her down on to his bed, whereupon he begins to protest his unyielding devotion to the peerless Dulcinea. In the gloom of the dormitory the muleteer begins to suspect his *puntualísima* Maritornes of having wantonly defected to Don Quixote's bed. He creeps up to investigate, fearing 'that the Asturian maid had broken her promise to him in favour of another' ('le hubiese *faltado la palabra* por otro'). Noticing her struggle to free herself from Don Quixote's clutches, he raises his arm and deals the knight a terrible blow ('*enarboló* el brazo en alto y *descargó* tan terrible puñada sobre las estrechas quijadas del enamorado caballero'). Later, when he sees that his 'lady' is locked in combat with Sancho, the muleteer goes to 'succour' her ('viendo . . . cual andaba su *dama*, dejando a don Quijote, acudió a dalle *el socorro* necesario'). I have emphasized those words and phrases which transform the muleteer, in a further fantastical twist to the earlier equivocations on the notion of *puntualidad*, into a grotesquely punctilious knight errant rescuing his damsel from dishonour. Cervantes crosses the two styles as he describes the misunderstanding: the stately precepts of the chivalric honour-code find an occasional echo in the behaviour of the lustful mule-driver, whereas the love-lorn knight is in turn rather painfully caught up in the sordid affair of Maritornes and her fancy-man.

These are not the only ironic fluctuations in the scene. When Maritornes is liberated by her champion, she hears the innkeeper approach to investigate the rumpus and flees in terror to Sancho's bed where she 'huddles up in a ball' ('todo medrosica y alborotada se acogió a la cama de Sancho Panza, que aún dormía, y allí se acurrucó y se hizo un ovillo'). This picture of coy vulnerability is soon shattered by the landlord's arrival: 'Where are you, you whore? This is all your doing; I'm sure of it' (p. 123). In the narrative discourse the simple kitchenmaid becomes verbally diffracted into several incompatible guises by the diverse treatment she receives from Don Quixote, the muleteer, the innkeeper, Sancho, and the narrator. She is a 'beautiful lady' ('fermosa doncella') and a 'goddess of beauty' ('diosa de la hermosura') for Don Quixote, but only a 'wench' ('coima') for the muleteer, although his subsequent zeal in rescuing her seems to transform her into an ironic 'lady' ('dama'); in her own estimation she is an honourable lady ('muy hidalga'), and then she appears retiring and vulnerable ('medrosica', 'alborotada', 'se acurrucó y se hizo un ovillo'), yet a moment later she is for the innkeeper no more than a hardboiled 'whore' ('puta'); finally, for Sancho, whose sleep she interrupts, she is a 'nightmare' ('pesadilla') which he tries to fight off. Depending on the designs they have on her, or on the way she affects them, each character has a different name for or conception of Maritornes. Cervantes contrives a farcical situation where the conflicting intentions of the characters distort Maritornes into something other than her essential self.

Language in this turbulent, ironic episode becomes flexible and even flirtatious in its changeability, it appears to have lost its respect for the anchored meanings and fixed references of Don Quixote's ideal romance discourse. Through a series of coincidences, overlapping actions, and violent cross-purposes, the situation becomes progressively more confusing and more unreal until the whole scene degenerates into a chaos of flying fists and blows: 'And then, as the saying goes, the cat chased the rat, the rat chased the rope, the rope chased the stick. The carrier beat Sancho, Sancho beat the maid, the maid beat him, the innkeeper beat the maid, and they all laid it on so fast that they never took a moment's rest. While, to improve the joke, the innkeeper's lamp went out and left them all in a heap in the dark, lamming out unmercifully and dealing great execution wherever they hit' (p. 124). Such a thorough breakdown of order and sense is, of course, the result of the narrator's crazy piling-up of ironies, one leading to another at such a speed that the whole thing becomes a whirligig of non-sense, a semantic nightmare for the likes of Don Quixote.

What has occurred in this episode is that Cervantes has used irony so intensively that he has produced a farce. The characters give the impression of having been arbitrarily manœuvred and therefore manipulated by an excessively despotic author. But the author's power here does not make for order, it is not so much evidence of authority as of a licence to unsettle the coherence of his characters' world. The resultant discord is far worse even than the disharmony which Cervantes, using the Canon of Toledo as a mouthpiece, criticizes in the Spanish romances of chivalry: 'For the delight that the mind conceives must arise from the beauty and harmony it sees, or contemplates, in things presented to it by the eyes or the imagination; and nothing ugly or ill proportioned can cause us any pleasure' (I.xlvii.424). In the fracas at the inn there is little to delight the mind; the hurly-burly of farce will produce laughter rather than *admiratio*, or more likely that 'monkey-grin' which Cervantes refers to as an alternative to either laughter or wonderment (II.xliv.748).

The ironic author appears to relish the absence of any effective authority that could, in the words of Don Quixote, 'assign things to their proper place'. The innkeeper's attempt to impose order by punishing Maritornes, 'under the impression that she was the sole cause of all that harmony' (p. 124), fails because he too gets swept up in the discord. So does the officer of 'the Ancient and Holy Brotherhood of Toledo', who, 'seizing his wand of office and the tin box with his warrants in it', rushes into the room crying halt in the name of justice and the Holy Brotherhood, only to collide in the dark with the recumbent body of the senseless knight.

Temporal authority is impotent to restore order and justice to the fictional world because 'the cause of all that harmony' is not the wretched Maritornes but the author himself whose power transcends the compass of his creatures' designs. We have in the convulsive energy of the ironic author an inverted image of the transcendent power of the author of romance, who intervened providentially in his fictional world to direct it towards benign ends. Such ironies as the romance author indulged in were positive because they bettered the expectations of his characters, but Cervantes's fast-paced ironies in this episode are calculated systematically to disappoint. A romance author like Chrétien de Troyes could attribute to the grace of God his ability to find a beautiful order (*bele conjointure*) in his subject-matter. Cervantes, for his part, is no less able to name the source of ironies that can make his fictional world collapse like a house of cards.

The identification is made in a more extended outbreak of farce later in Part I. It occurs, significantly, at the height of a mounting succession of interpolated stories and adventures which accumulate appearances of new characters, mad outbursts by Don Quixote, amazing discoveries of identity, and a series of spectacular coincidences; in short, farce breaks out at the climax of a narrative crescendo, after the author has been steadily winding up the action to a pitch where the narrative is threatened with the loss of coherence and plausibility. At that point the romantic love-story of Don Louis and Doña Clara (the last of the interpolated episodes) is about to be resolved, but the narrator remarks that 'the Devil, who never sleeps, ordained the sudden arrival at the inn of that barber from whom Don Quixote had taken Mambrino's helmet' (I.xliv.402). Where the omnipotence of the romance author is God-like in its providence, the negative ironies of farce have the whiff of Satan about them. And so, Don Quixote's dispute with the barber over the helmet leads to a general affray that recalls the earlier fracas: 'Don Quixote drew his sword and fell upon the troopers. . . . The priest was shouting; the landlady screaming; her daughter wailing; Maritornes weeping; Dorothea was distracted; Lucinda in a flurry; and Doña Clara in a faint. The barber was mauling Sancho; Sancho pounding the barber . . . ' (I.xlv.407).

The chaos at the inn reminds Don Quixote of the discord in the camp of King Agramante in the *Orlando Furioso*, and he calls on the judge and the priest to settle the issue, invoking the authority of romance and even of God Himself to inspire them: 'Come, then, Sir Judge, and you, Sir Priest; let one of you stand for King Agramante, the other for King Sobrino, and make peace amongst us. For, by God Almighty, it is a great villainy that people of such quality as we are here should slay one another for such trivial causes' (p. 407). The mad knight's attempt to rid his world of the dangerous trivialities of farce appears to succeed for a while, although the foundations of the peace are absurdly unstable, as the narrator insinuates: 'Thus this tangle of quarrels was resolved by the authority of Agramante and the wisdom of King Sobrino' (p. 408).

The spirits of these two worthies of romance are obviously no match for the ever-active fount and origin of all the forces of irony: 'However the enemy of concord and adversary of peace, finding himself slighted and mocked, and seeing how little fruit he had reaped from plunging them all into this labyrinth of confusion, decided to try his hand again and bring some new quarrels and disturbances to life' (p. 408). When this next outbreak of discord is finally settled, it is not the work of Providence but a whim of Fortune: 'And as by now good luck had begun to shift obstacles and smooth difficulties in favour of the lovers and the brave folk in the inn, so Fortune was pleased to complete the task and bring everything to a happy ending' (I.xlvi.411).

In the absence of divine inspiration the ironic author becomes the agent of Chance, when he is not actually the accomplice of the Devil himself; the uneasy freedom afforded him by irony is incapable of producing the kind of harmony and concord that would move his reader to feel wonderment at the inherent order of the universe. Instead, when the hollowness of fantasy threatens to engulf the creatures of his imagination, the ironic author can disarm his reader's incredulity by provoking the raucous mindlessness of farce.

The narrator's equivocations on the *puntualidad* of the historian and the *puntualísma* Maritornes point ahead to the episode of the fulling-mills four chapters later where Don Quixote cuts short Sancho's mockery with the assertion of his right to 'poner en su *punto* las cosas'. Even though Cervantes, as ironic author, is apt to join Sancho in mocking Don Quixote, his occasional glances at the issue of poetic truth betray a regret for a fixed point upon which to construct a stable narrative order. For the sort of moral authority that Don Quixote craves would be required ideally by the writer of prose fiction if he is to escape the charge of fantasizing and so resolve fully the question of poetic truth. In the figure of Don Quixote Cervantes could be said to have embodied the author's nostalgia for the authority of divine inspiration, but in the ironic Sancho, and in the two farcical episodes at the inn, he explores the slippery perils of writing in a wholly profane context, where language is the all too malleable medium of suspect motives.

(iv) *The Mad/Sane Paradox*

The relationship between Don Quixote and Sancho Panza possesses the virtue of attracting to itself and polarizing universally significant themes, a virtue which doubtless has its source in the nature of Don Quixote's madness. The paradoxes of language and art created by the madman's literal belief in fiction seem capable of ramifying into questions about the nature of reality, or the illusions and contradictions of human consciousness. There is, in consequence, a tendency for modern readers of the *Quixote* to conceive the Quixote–Panza relationship in symbolic terms which reproduce general conflicts between, say, faith and scepticism, idealism and empiricism, spirit and matter, art and life. The merit of this kind of symbolic dualism is that it provides a structural framework based on the interaction of knight and squire which acts as a fixed point of reference around which the manifold whims of the ironic author can be organized into some sort of intelligible order.

The tendency towards symbolic interpretation is further stimulated and reinforced by the intervals of lucidity which illumine the words of the madman in the course of the narrative. It appears that Cervantes is interested in eliciting from his reader a degree of intellectual and moral identification with Don Quixote. There are occasions when the contemporary reader at least would have found himself in complete agreement with the ideas of the demented knight. After Don Quixote's Discourse on Arms and Letters (I.xxxvii-xxxviii), for example, 'his hearers were moved once more to pity at seeing a man, apparently of such sound intelligence and with such understanding of everything he spoke of, lose it entirely on the subject of his foul and accursed chivalry' (p. 345). Again, in Part II, Don Diego de Miranda is amazed by the knight, 'for Don Quixote's words were consistent, elegant and well put, though his actions were wild, rash and foolish' (xvii.578). By and large, Don Quixote appears sane when he speaks and utterly mad when he acts, and this kind of compartmentalization of thought and action, in so far as it appears to convert the knight's lunacy into mere incompetence, may be said to encourage symbolic readings where the madman can be transformed into a heroic failure, his madness becoming a metaphor for the irrationality of spirit in refusing to succumb to a heartless world; otherwise his incompetence can be turned into a moral error, like pride or ambition, in contrast with the healthy common sense of Sancho.

The paradox of the mad knight's occasional interludes of sanity therefore raises possibilities of symbolism which might (as Don Quixote constantly exhorts Sancho) 'restrain the natural impulses' of the ironic author. Indeed, we have seen how much of what Don Quixote believes and says uncannily recalls themes central to the culture of the age: his belief in divine intervention in human affairs, his reverence for authority and for the wisdom of books, his scholastic mentality, his aspiration to the glories of heroism, his cultivation of the Christian virtues, the analogy between his courtly devotion to an ideal lady and the mystic's love of God. Through Don Quixote, Cervantes seems to have decanted ideas, values and attitudes that express the ideological essence of the cultural tradition he has inherited. But this is precisely the nub of the mad/sane paradox: the vehicle of this ideology is a thoroughgoing lunatic, and the reader, when he happens to be in sympathy or agreement with the knight, will find himself suddenly slipping into madness once again. However deeply we might hope to identify with the old *hidalgo*, his madness will inevitably introduce a warp in the pattern of our sympathies.

In fact, the mad warp in the narrative is aggravated by an additional twist to the mad/sane paradox. Don Quixote's eloquent, measured speeches are often fissured by internal dissonances of tone or style which vitiate the superficial impression of rational control, while conversely, his normally impetuous actions sometimes appear to be shot through with hints of a canny self-interest. The former phenomenon, termed 'stylistic gaffes' by one critic,[9] can be explained simply as Don Quixote's deafness to his own lapses of tone and decorum as well as to other people's. We have already seen the way he remains quite innocent of the carnal implications of the story of the young widow and the friar which he uses to explain his platonic love for Dulcinea; he is also insensitive to the absurdity of the image of the princess Dulcinea winnowing 'grains of oriental pearl'; in his speech on the Golden Age, rather too much emphasis is placed on the perils that threaten the virtue of maidens, with the result that the lucidity of the speech as a whole is cast in doubt: 'But now, in this detestable age of ours no maiden is safe even though she is hidden in the centre of another Cretan labyrinth; for even there, through some chink or through the air, by dint of its accursed persistence, the plague of love gets in and brings them to ruin despite their seclusion' (I.xi.86).

These discrepancies in the knight's speech are related to ironies in his behaviour. Don Quixote occasionally acts in ways which belie one's expectations of the disinterested courtesy which he aims to emulate. For example, it is rather surprising to find the knight, who is usually so chivalrous and even punctilious, forcing Sancho to sit down to a meal with him and the goatherds in order to demonstrate his magnanimity by bestowing such a privilege upon his squire (I.xi.85). Similarly, he grabs hold of Maritornes in the dormitory and forces her to listen to his rejection of her alleged advances (I.xvi.122). On another occasion he too readily agrees with Sancho that he should defeat the giant oppressing Micomicona before going to see Dulcinea, even though the latter would appear to have been his most pressing desire (I.xxxi.272). Again, in the middle of the absurd ructions at the inn, Don Quixote feels unable to help Maritornes against genuine aggressors until he has obtained permission from Princess Micomicona to embark on a different adventure (I.xliv.400). When he arrives at El Toboso with Sancho to seek out Dulcinea's palace, he agrees, at Sancho's bidding, to retire to a wood and allow his squire to seek out Dulcinea's house the next day, after their joint efforts that evening have proved fruitless (II.ix.600). Later, he justifies his abandonment of Sancho to the angry villagers of the braying contest by saying that it was the prudent retreat of a valiant man, examples of which abound in the history books (II.xxviii.652). On all these occasions it is difficult to know what his true motives are; behind the madness there appears at times to be an element of self-interest or calculation which contrasts strikingly with the lapses of tone and decorum at other times. The overall effect is to blur any clear distinction between lucid thought and mad action, producing the impression of a continuum between the two which is subsumed in an unwaning lunacy.

The reader's experience of seeing perfectly respectable ideas and values veer unexpectedly in and out of a laughable madness is both unsettling and intriguing. In the first place, the symbolic dualism of Quixote and Sancho cannot be retained as a serious principle of order in the narrative because of the ironies that tend to cut across the entire range of Don Quixote's thoughts and activities. The cultural shock produced by the mirage of sanity playing over the knight's lunacy is a new, and sinister, development of the *admiratio* produced by that teasing *ingeniosidad* of Don Quixote's. In addition to this, the effect of the stylistic gaffes and behavioural quirks that complicate the mad/sane paradox itself is to make Don Quixote unpredictable for the reader so that, in the last resort, attempts to organize the narrative into a symbolic order must confront the question of the specific springs of the knight's actions: Don Quixote is clearly unhinged, but what is it that moves him exactly? Cervantes's irony, since it suggests symbolic interpretations only to frustrate them, succeeds in shaping a literary character who seems to exist irreplaceably on his own enigmatic terms, and who thereby eschews literary classification according to type or anti-type. Strangely enough, it is in this deepening of irony beyond coherent symbolization that the seeds of the order needed to limit the power and freedom of the ironic author are to be found. By seeking to create *admiratio* through the individualization of Don Quixote, Cervantes fosters curiosity about the knight's unique motivation, and thus opens the way to the development of character and the emergence of plot.

CHAPTER FIVE

From Romance to the Novel

(i) *The Emergence of Character*

The view that the *Quixote* was conceived whole and written to a predetermined plan has been largely discredited by now. It seems certain that the length of the original *Quixote* covered only about the first twelve of the present chapters, which would suggest that Cervantes had initially set out to write a short parody of the Spanish romances no longer than one of his exemplary *novellas*. From internal bibliographical evidence R.M. Flores has reconstructed the various phases in the composition of *Don Quixote* Part I, and has produced a fascinating account of Cervantes at work: introducing fresh material, interpolating stories, rearranging episodes, noticing new possibilities, and changing direction accordingly.[1] A picture emerges of Cervantes as a writer who was not afraid to follow a creative hunch or elaborate an interesting new idea even if it meant going back and re-working earlier passages.

What needs to be done now is to relate this experimental, tentative method of composition to those theoretical issues of narrative art debated by Renaissance aestheticians which Cervantes himself discussed in his works. As regards verisimilitude and the marvellous, we have seen how they are reconciled in a strikingly novel way in the madness of Don Quixote. The other major issue of Renaissance literary theory was the question of combining narrative unity with variety. Indeed, one of the criticisms levelled at the Spanish romances concerned their lack of structural coherence. I have already discussed the results in the later books of the *Amadis*, and particularly in the *Esplandian*, of Montalvo's disruption of the crisis-structure inherited from the French romances. The romances of the sub-Arthurian genre are composed of endlessly extensible sequences of episodic adventures with few motivating themes beyond the hero's eventual marriage to his one sweetheart and his progressive acquisition of territory. Criticizing this obvious flaw in the romances, as the Canon of Toledo does in the *Quixote* itself, was one thing, finding a remedy for it quite another. The episodic principle proved difficult to supersede because Renaissance literary theory was rather vague when it came to Aristotle's ideas about probability and necessity; narrative unity tended to be conceived in terms of a harmonious web-like structure of complementary themes and sub-themes, or as a well-proportioned edifice in which episodes were the basic building-blocks of the narrative.

Flores's investigations show that Cervantes followed two directions in the process of expansion. In the early phases he simply added adventures until he realized that the material was susceptible of larger treatment. This decision to extend the parody, in Flores's view, explains the division of Part I into books—a feature of the romances of chivalry—as well as the development of the burlesque narrator-historian Cide Hamete.[2] Cervantes's expansion also involved the interpolation of extraneous tales. The Marcela story and the *Tale of Foolish Curiosity* were inserted first, followed in later stages by the five other interpolated stories of Part I.[3] In short, the Quixote–Panza line is extended on a horizontal axis in a sequence of single adventures much like the episodic action of the Spanish romances; while the other line of expansion is vertical, so to speak, involving the intercalation of ready-made love-stories into the narrative for the sake of variety.

These stories, however, are of the same genre as Cervantes's Italianate *novellas*: they have highly-organized plots which rely on coincidences, *deux ex machina* devices, and spectacular forms of *peripeteia* and *anagnorisis* for their articulation. In effect, their style and form display a close kinship with the narrative mode of chivalric romance.[4] It is ironical, of course, that these interpolations — Cervantes's first response to the emerging problem of unity and variety created by his own decision to expand the original skit on the romances — should have the effect of reintroducing the other major aesthetic problem of reconciling verisimilitude with the marvellous, which Don

Quixote's madness seemed set to resolve. Cervantes reacts to these periodic revivals of the romance ethos in his parody by adopting a kind of Ariostean ambivalence to them; the paradoxes and ironies that result from the uneasy contact between the world of high romance and the mercilessly parodic environment Don Quixote inhabits are subtly cultivated in a spirit not far removed from Cervantes's arch, frivolous treatment of the narrative subterfuges of Spanish romance authors.[5] Various intriguing gradations of fiction are created and then implicitly played off against each other. The *Tale of Foolish Curiosity*, for instance, is presented straightforwardly as a fictional story read by the priest to the company assembled in the inn. This provides an opportunity for literary discussion, some of whose participants like Dorothea and Cardenio are themselves involved in a type of plot which is indistinguishable from that in the fictional story. Quite apart from her 'real' situation, Dorothea is pretending to Don Quixote that she is a princess of romance because she is colluding with the priest and barber in an absurd travesty of a chivalric plot designed to entice the madman back home. At this point in the narrative, one romantic tale is followed by yet another romantic tale through an incredible series of coincidental arrivals at the inn which begins to link the characters involved in the separate romantic plots in an amazing labyrinth of relationships.

This interweaving of plot and episode suggests that in search of variety Cervantes was experimenting with a species of *entrelacement* so typical of medieval and Renaissance romances. And yet, the progressive concentration of romance denouements in the one inn seems equally calculated to produce a rather dizzying effect upon the reader, an effect which is accentuated by having as the next sudden arrival at the inn the barber whose basin Don Quixote had seized in the belief that it was the helmet of Mambrino. To the various strands of fiction and reality that have already been spun into a complex enough web of romantic stories, Cervantes deliberately adds the vexed question of the basin-helmet, an issue which by this stage of the *Quixote* has come to epitomize the fundamental incompatibility between the madman's romance ideals and ordinary perceptions. That is to say, at the height of this mounting sequence of interlaced romantic tales Cervantes suddenly reverts to Don Quixote, his chief vehicle of parody, and thus starkly highlights the difference that exists between the idealized world of romance and the domain of common-sense experience. As if to flaunt the romance attributes of the interpolated tales, he piles up their providential denouements in the inn until the overloaded narrative collapses into a quixotic farce, thereby creating the impression that such marvellously optimistic endings, when set in the context of the madman's perversely idealizing attitude to the everyday world, turn out to be little more convincing than the multiple misunderstandings that took place earlier in that same inn over Maritornes's assignation with the mule-driver.

Cervantes's sly shuffling of narrative styles and categories of fiction, his Ariostean transitions across the bounds of artifice and plausibility, reflect the creative uncertainties of an experimental writer taking the measure of his manifold fictions. Fearing that an unrelieved succession of parodic adventures may pall on the reader, he seeks to widen his range of characters, yet in doing so he retreats into a kind of literary conservatism, for when the new characters are not hoaxing the madman they tend to fall into plots that belong to some well-tried sub-genre of Renaissance romance. It would seem, therefore, that in Part I Cervantes clearly escapes the narrative processes of romance only when he attacks them head-on through Don Quixote, otherwise he organizes stories, quite understandably, in a conventional mode. Cervantes is as yet feeling his way along the uncharted territory between the romance author, who plays God with his characters, and the realist author, who seeks to conceal his manipulations by pretending that his characters are autonomous and that the action develops from inherent probability.

Nevertheless, all the interpolated tales in Part I, including the stories of Marcela and Leandra, are invariably likened in some way or other by Cervantes to the fantasies of the romances of chivalry.[7] That is to say, in the last resort, for all the variety the interpolated tales introduce into the linear narrative, Cervantes respects the rationale of his novel, based as it is on a parody of romance story-telling. However much Cervantes may seek to vary the main episodic action by digressing into a form of romance, he will sooner or later have to bring his mad protagonist back to due prominence, and the unity–variety problem will accordingly reappear.[8]

There is, none the less, a principle of variation inherent in the linear axis of Don Quixote's adventures. It emerges also from Cervantes's decision to expand the narrative. For if the comic basis of the novel is to be sustained, the knight's madness must become supple enough to survive the repeated onslaughts of reality without appearing tedious. In the earliest adventures we find Cervantes seeking to modulate the madness so as to guard against an all too easy collapse of the *hidalgo*'s illusions. Don Quixote is at first nourished in his ideas by fortunate coincidences (e.g. the blowing of a swineherd's horn as he approaches the inn which he takes to be a castle) or by the good humour of the innkeeper and the prostitutes. His adventures with the disrupters of his vigil or the liberation of the boy Andrew can likewise be counted fortuitous successes. But if Don Quixote's madness is not actually to flout plausibility and appear to get away with restoring romance, he will sooner or later suffer a reverse, and he would then either have to abandon his illusions or attempt to justify them. Once endowed with the ability to justify reversals he will have become something more than a parodic stooge, he will be seen to possess a degree of ingenuity and wit capable of eliciting admiration from the reader rather than straightforwardly dismissive laughter. It is the possibility of alternating laughter with *admiratio* that permits Cervantes to develop his comic idea beyond the length of a short skit on the romances of chivalry. The more he extends the narrative, all the more will he have to enrich Don Quixote's ingenuity and resourcefulness. In short, as the parody flourishes it stimulates the development of character.

Cervantes's handling of Don Quixote's early humiliations and setbacks shows the expansion of the parody germinating character, as it were. Don Quixote falls from his horse as he prepares to attack the merchants of Toledo and is then beaten up by a muleteer. When he recovers, he first attempts to safeguard his self-esteem by recalling some passage from the books of chivalry which he can imitate in order to smooth over the defeat. This, as yet, is a form of escapist delusion where Don Quixote tries actually to dissolve his identity into that of romance heroes such as the knight Baldwin or the Moor

Abindarraez. When his neighbour Pedro Alonzo happens to pass that way, such tactics become less feasible, although Don Quixote counters Alonzo's factual reminder of his true identity with absurd, solipsistic bluster (viz. the 'I know who I am' speech; I.v.54). However, on arriving at the village he is forced to come out of this defensive, head-in-the-sand attitude and offer a more convincing chivalric rationalization; he blames his horse and calls for Urganda the Unknown to come and minister to his wounds. Here at least is a more sophisticated excuse since it represents a balance between some cognizance of what actually happened and a stubborn persistence in the world of chivalry.

Don Quixote's second reverse, the burning of his library by the priest and the barber, marks an important advance in the development of face-saving ingenuity. When his housekeeper explains to him that it was an enchanter who spirited the books away, she provides not just any excuse but a specifically chivalric one which the knight can elaborate upon and fit conveniently into his own obsessions by assuming it is the sage Freston, the magician-narrator of *Sir Belianis of Greece*, who has made his books vanish. Two very important escalating factors are involved here: the as yet embryonic but fertile concept of enchantment, and the use of sane characters to foster Don Quixote's illusions, knowingly or otherwise, by providing him with excuses that will conform with the world of romance. A plausible framework is found for Don Quixote's ingenuity to weave unsuspected ironic patterns between the polarized realities of his actual existence and the romances of chivalry, and so keep his chivalric enterprise afloat.

Cervantes then introduces Sancho as a regular interlocutor who can act both as receptive audience and as a foil. These new arrangements are seen at work in the adventure of the windmills where Don Quixote announces his interpretation of reality, Sancho contradicts that, and the knight rides into the attack in order to justify his assertions. When he is defeated he can no longer defensively withdraw into solipsism because he has to confront Sancho. Instead, he mitigates his ignominy by having recourse to some impressive chivalric explanation. A process is set in train in which Sancho acts increasingly as an ironic counter-weight to Don Quixote. The squire passes comments and criticisms on the madman's behaviour until at last he begins to exercise a degree of power over his master in the fulling-mills episode. As Sancho's ironic mentality blossoms, their relationship turns into a form of changing power-struggle between master and servant which may engender subsidiary themes but which remains the main narrative thread of the novel.[9] The advantage Sancho gained at the fulling-mills is somewhat offset by Don Quixote's winning of Mambrino's helmet, and particularly by the ensuing speech on the career of the knight errant, which stirs the squire to renewed enthusiasm for the material benefits of chivalry and puts him in thrall to his master's effusive imagination. Once again, as a counterbalance to the peasant's ironic cunning Cervantes enhances Don Quixote's ingenuity, and from there he will gradually develop this tendency into the all-important mad/sane paradox.

Sancho provides a spur to the madman's ingenuity, but Cervantes also hits on a structural device which will test Don Quixote's ingenuity in another way. I shall call this device ironic recurrence. It first occurs when the boy Andrew, whom Quixote had saved from his cruel master in Chapter iv, suddenly reappears in Chapter xxxi and complains that Don Quixote's interventions on his behalf had no effect whatsoever and, worse still, earned him a more severe punishment. The madman must now face up to the adverse consequences of a chivalrous act which at the time had appeared to be entirely successful. This is rather different from a straightforward defeat as in the adventures of the windmills or of the flocks of sheep. It forces upon Don Quixote's own consciousness the fact that he has been the victim of a deception perpetrated by John Haldudo; and Quixote now sees himself drawn willy-nilly into the equivocal relations of human society. For the first time the madman feels himself to be impotent and without redress in the face of human malice. When this is compounded by Andrew's curse against knights errant, we are afforded a glimpse into the state of the knight's emotions; we are told that he was 'very much abashed' (p. 276). This ironic recurrence creates an element of self-consciousness in the knight and allows some display of feeling beyond stereotypes of the romance hero or anti-hero. We see Don Quixote reacting to a particular circumstance and not to a conventional, set-piece occasion. The madman is thus individualized, and there are already intimations of an inner, psychological dimension to his character.

At this juncture the main action is submerged by the successive interpolated stories which are not directly related to Don Quixote. The central narrative thread is taken up after the Doña Clara story with a second example of the principle of ironic recurrence when the barber returns to reclaim his basin. Again, Don Quixote has to face the consequences of his impetuous chivalric actions in the context of society at large; a mock-trial is mounted, which degenerates into a farcical brawl. A third ironic recurrence follows immediately when one of the troopers, recognizing Don Quixote as the man who set the galley-slaves free, attempts to arrest him. Don Quixote justifies his liberation of the galley-slaves by haughtily lecturing the trooper on the rights of a knight errant, who is above the laws of man by virtue of his divine calling (I.xlv.409-10). Eventually the troopers are persuaded by the priest's explanation of Don Quixote's madness to let him go.

This last ironic recurrence has an effect *opposite* to the earlier ones. In the previous two examples Don Quixote was forced to countenance the treachery and perversity of the human world—John Haldudo's deceitfulness or the barber's refusal to yield to chivalric reality—but here he is allowed to get away with the idea that his actions are exempt from the ordinary constraints of society; he can therefore draw back from the entanglements of social intercourse, albeit thanks to the protective tolerance of the other characters. In this respect Cervantes's ironic treatment of the knight is ambiguous. On the one hand, Cervantes creates irony by impelling Don Quixote towards a confrontation with the real world, but on the other, the madman is occasionally allowed to extricate himself from social reality through some form of ingenious rationalization or through the indulgence of others, this too producing irony.

From the point of view of the development of character and plot, Cervantes's two-way irony has both advantages and limitations. In its positive aspect it enables Cervantes to move towards plot by portraying the mutable relations between the different characters, and giving the reader some insight into the motives and intentions which inform their behaviour. But on the two occasions when character interaction is at its most intense, namely the Maritornes imbroglio in Chapter xvi and the Camp of Agramante episode in Chapter xlv, the narrative soon tumbles into slapstick and farce. The reason for this is that, in spite of the mad/sane paradox and other subtleties, Cervantes ultimately makes an exception of Don Quixote among the sane characters. The knight is allowed to disentangle himself from any situation which will force him radically to question his chivalric premisses or to reveal his motives; for in order to keep the parody going, Cervantes must eschew the serious motivational conflicts of plot, either by reverting to episodic action or by careering forward into farce. Cervantes's expansion of his parody may germinate character and, to some extent, plot, but already one can see in Part I how the fact that Don Quixote is mad is beginning to act as an inhibiting factor in this development. On the other hand, since the 'sane' social world itself seems capable of functioning only on the basis of romance-style plots, Cervantes would appear to have been faced at this stage with the alternative of either traditional romance plotting or repeating single comic episodes involving the mad knight.

Nevertheless, in Part I Cervantes does succeed in producing the semblance of a coherent relationship between two characters who become prey to an unforeseeable destiny. The relationship between Don Quixote and Sancho alone evolves beyond the alternative of parody or romance plotting because none of the other characters in Part I respects the madman enough to allow him any proper consideration. To the priest and barber, to Dorothea and Don Ferdinand, or to Maritornes and the innkeeper for that matter, Don Quixote is little more than a fool to be mocked or baited. Only the gullible Sancho bridges the gap between madness and society because he does not quite realize the extent of the knight's lunacy. Through fear of his master's displeasure or occasional admiration for his superior intelligence, Sancho is sufficiently in awe of the mad knight to entertain serious relations with him. It is Sancho's genuine anxiety at Don Quixote's reactions in the fulling-mills episode or upon his return from his embassy to Dulcinea that leads him into the calculated irony and duplicity which so deeply complicates their relationship by establishing an argument between them upon whose outcome depends the fate of the hero. In this argument one finds the makings of a rudimentary plot which will be more fully developed in Part II.

(ii) *Character and the Elements of Plot*

Most critics have observed a qualitative difference between the first and second parts of the *Quixote*. Part II has been considered generally more complex and organic than Part I, and several reasons have been advanced for this development. The most popular seems to be the view that Don Quixote enters into a more social world, leaving the arid byways of La Mancha and accepting the hospitality of various characters.[10] There is also the argument that the knight is not so much mad in Part II as vulnerable to the deceptions of others.[11] A further explanation is that Don Quixote is guided more by Part I, the published 'history' of his exploits, than by the ideology of chivalry.[12]

Don Quixote does indeed spend time under more people's roofs than in Part I, but he also spends a considerable time on the road. Even though there is an appreciable decrease in the number of isolated 'cross-roads' adventures, the episodic principle is by no means abandoned. The narrative is still constructed from single adventures sewn together, mostly sequentially, except for the alternation of episodes between the account of Sancho's governorship and Don Quixote's misfortunes at the ducal palace. I would also dissent from the view that Don Quixote is credulous rather than mad. The two terms are not in any way opposed. An essential aspect of Don Quixote's madness is his credulity—his blind belief in the books of chivalry—and, in any case, he has been gulled by others at least since Part I Chapter iii when the innkeeper pretends to knight him after his vigil at the inn.

The most convincing explanation is Salvador de Madariaga's view that Don Quixote is assailed by doubts as to the validity of his enterprise.[13] Don Quixote, as we have seen, does succumb to misgivings about his chivalric project, and in so far as this produces a greater complexity of character it enhances the impression of narrative substance. These doubts, however, do not take the form of an empirical undermining of the knight's romance beliefs; he is still steadfastly guided by chivalry. The key to the change lies in complexity of character, but the knight's doubts do not by themselves account for the new sense of order in the novel, they must also be related to other developments in characterization which contribute to the inner logic which the Quixote–Sancho relationship is evolving.

By the end of Part I Sancho is coming to enjoy a certain degree of influence over Don Quixote, and this breeds enough confidence in his own hold upon reality to enable him to persist in arguing with his caged master about the enchantment of which the latter claims to be victim. In spite of Don Quixote's repeated attempts in Part I to put distance between himself and his irritatingly ignorant squire, in Part II Sancho has become an antagonist with whom the knight will have to contend on an increasingly equal footing. Taking up the thread of their relationship, which had been dropped when he introduced the multiple interpolations of Part I, Cervantes sends his characters off to El Toboso in search of an audience with Dulcinea. Although such a move is a logical consequence of the situation reached by Quixote and Sancho after the squire's alleged visit to Dulcinea, it is fraught with innumerable dangers for the author and reveals immense creative audacity: Dulcinea does not exist at all except in Don Quixote's imagination and Sancho has lied through his teeth to his master about having seen her. For Cervantes to make the characters visit the non-existent Dulcinea is to invite a crisis and work himself into a very tight corner indeed. The novel seems bent on a course which can only lead to the madman's discovering the gaping emptiness of his chivalric dream, not to mention the low mendacity of his trusted servant.

Still, out of this distinctly perverse and unpromising beginning the energy to launch Part II is drawn. Cervantes allows Sancho to aggravate his deception of the knight by persuading him that a repellent peasant girl on an ass is Dulcinea enchanted. Sancho wounds the knight to the quick, but the notion of enchantment ensures that Don Quixote's illusions are not altogether destroyed. It is at this point, when he is cheated out of his most fervent aspirations, that Don Quixote's character attains unequivocal pathos. In contrast to the false and mocking rhetoric of Sancho, and the gross exclamations of the peasant girl, Don Quixote is dumbfounded and pensive for a good while, opening his mouth only to utter words of such noble cadence and conceptual elegance that all traces of authorial mockery melt away: 'Rise, Sancho . . . for I see that Fortune, unsatisfied with the ill already done me, has closed all roads by which any comfort may come to this wretched soul I bear in my body . . . ' (II.x.530).[14] Even so, Sancho gloatingly teases his stricken master when he tries to help the putative Dulcinea back on to her ass. The mad knight says nothing and merely follows the receding trio of peasants with his eyes, turning to Sancho only when they are no longer visible, to utter: 'Do you see now what a spite the enchanters have against me, Sancho? See to what extremes the malice and hatred they bear me extend, for they have sought to deprive me of the happiness I should have enjoyed in seeing my mistress in her true person' (p. 531).

Dulcinea's enchantment represents the climactic turning-point in the novel because it produces the definitive detachment of the protagonist's feelings from the external action, creating the space for an inner life which puts the knight beyond the reach of other characters. Quixote's new blindness to romance reality causes him intimate distress: 'And to think that I did not see all this, Sancho! . . . Now I say once more—and I will repeat it a thousand times—I am the most unfortunate of men' (p. 532). There is a critical difference here between Sancho's deception and, say, Dorothea's make-believe involving the princess Micomicona in Part I. Micomicona is a positive, welcome confirmation of Don Quixote's prejudices, but the enchanted Dulcinea not only disappoints his most fundamental hope, it suggests that he has been cut off from access to a romance reality which others, ironically, can perceive. Whereas in Part I he felt a welcome sense of positive irony when he found himself dining in humdrum circumstances with Princess Micomicona and other noble persons, now he is born to the bitter experience of negative irony: he knows from Sancho that the romance world is visible but cannot for the life of him see it for himself. This terrible alienation internalizes his own relations with romance.[15] No longer confident that he can interpret the everyday world in chivalric terms, he must instead seek his own private ways of re-establishing contact with it, regardless of other people's actions.

The next chapter shows Don Quixote crestfallen and brooding: 'Very much downcast Don Quixote went on his way, pondering on the evil trick the enchanters had played on him in turning his lady Dulcinea into the foul shape of a village girl, and he could think of no remedy he could take to restore her to her original state' (II.xi.532). Here, then, is the new motive that will drive Don Quixote in Part II: he realizes he can do little to change the world without previously transforming his lady, the source of all his chivalric energy, back to her pristine glory. This single objective will override all others. As a result, he is less affected by events around him, as if he had discovered a private responsibility to himself and to his lady that took precedence over any other consideration or distraction.

Don Quixote's new inwardness confers upon him a certain immunity to mockery or irony, even when it emanates from the author himself. Let us take for example the passage that runs on from the above quotation: 'These thoughts took him so much out of himself that he gave Rocinante the reins without noticing it. And his horse, feeling the liberty he was given, lingered at each step to browse the green grass, which grew thickly in those fields.' Even though the irony is clearly aimed at Don Quixote, it fails to engulf him, serving rather to deepen the impression of his morbid self-absorption, and even to enhance his moral standing in the reader's eyes. In other words, the madman's interiority tends to mitigate the contradiction between his buffoonery and his ingenuity, and enables him to attract more sympathy from the reader which, in turn, is a stimulus to further character-development. The pointed contrast between the sad, inward-looking knight and the mocking, deceitful world will carry a suggestion of a troubled inner life flowing beneath the surface events of the story. His successes will be tempered by an undertow of sadness, whereas his failures will become less damaging to his dignity.

After the enchantment of Dulcinea, Sancho's behaviour is also carefully modulated by Cervantes. In Sancho there had always been a credulous side, laced with greed, that kept him loyal to his mad master, and a more fractious, sceptical side that threatened to disrupt the partnership. Towards the end of

Part I the conflict within Sancho's character came to be contained, if not reconciled, by his growing ironic attitude towards Don Quixote. But having now gained unprecedented control over his master's chivalric vocation, his power is great enough in fact to destroy the knight if he so wished.

Dulcinea's enchantment injects tension and suspense into the lives of the protagonists, for there is no small piquancy in a relationship where the intricate chivalric world envisaged by Don Quixote's bookish imagination hangs by a slender thread held in the uncouth hands of his squire. Clearly Don Quixote's position at this juncture is precarious, and profoundly ironic: the enchantment of Dulcinea has sunk him in a pool of intimate fears and forebodings which, on the one hand, partly abstracts him from the external action, but which on the other, makes him more vulnerable than ever before to Sancho's scheming. Thus, although the episodic principle is not abandoned in Part II, and even though Don Quixote's madness still prevents him from engaging in sustained social relations with sane characters, the enchantment of Dulcinea locks master and servant into a self-contained, evolving conflict of motives, a capsule of plot, as it were, which provides the episodic narrative with an element of organic necessity.

Indeed, the new situation produces a critical shift of narrative interest from action to character. In romance, adventures symbolically defined the moral quality of the hero, but now in the *Quixote*, the character of the hero is increasingly disconnected from the outcome of his actions. Given his sense of alienation, Don Quixote is led to seek value and meaning within himself, he becomes more individual. In Part I the madman's morale was directly correlated with the vicissitudes of his adventures, but in Part II adventures are ambiguous, and the knight has to evaluate their worth or interpret their significance himself. His encounter with the Knight of the Mirrors, for instance, appears to be a resounding victory. When Sancho insists that the defeated knight is in fact Sampson Carrasco, Don Quixote replies that if enchanters had previously blinded him to Dulcinea's beauty it is not surprising that, foreseeing his victory, they should also have created the delusion that the Knight of the Mirrors was Carrasco in order to rob him of the glory he deserves: 'Even so, however, I am consoled; for, after all, whatever shape he may have taken, I have vanquished my enemy' (II.xvi.563). Despite the confusion of appearances, it is the intrinsic value of his victory that counts. Similarly, the adventure with the lions is reckoned a success by Don Quixote, but once again only in an inward sense. Although the beasts refuse to respond, Don Quixote insists that he has displayed great courage and this in itself constitutes a moral victory over the enchanters: 'What do you think of that, Sancho? . . . Do any enchantments prevail against true valour? The enchanters may indeed be able to rob me of good fortune; but of resolution and courage, that is impossible' (II.xvii.577).

Both adventures demonstrate Don Quixote's own awareness of the duality in his career between the public sphere, where his actions may have a controversial impact, and an interior, private sphere where their true chivalric value resides. His address to Don Diego de Miranda acknowledges this double dimension in an unprecedented way: 'No doubt . . . your worship considers me both foolish and mad. And it would be no marvel if you did, for my deeds testify no less. But, for all that, I wish your worship to take note that I am not so mad or so lacking as I must have seemed to you' (II.xvii.578). Bereft of Dulcinea, his confidence is easily shaken, and he can become surprisingly self-conscious, wrily sensitive to the absurd figure he cuts in the eyes of a fellow *hidalgo* like Don Diego.

Dulcinea is clearly never far from his thoughts. The earthenware pots from El Toboso outside Don Diego's house remind him of his lady who is sadly transformed, and he laments his fate out loud 'regardless of what he said or before whom he said it' (II.xviii.580). So great is his anguish that he is carried away, oblivious of his surroundings and circumstances, utterly absorbed by his own inner grief.

However, Don Quixote's sojourn in the house of Don Diego is a gratifying respite from the mockery that bedevils his relations with other people. It marks the high point of the mad/sane paradox: Don Diego and his family treat the knight with unwonted kindness and respect, listening to his lucid arguments without trace of malicious intent. This is the closest Don Quixote comes to establishing serious social intercourse with sane characters other than Sancho, and it can be taken as a measure of the mad knight's evolution as a character. The hectoring fool of Part I is left far behind as Don Quixote settles down to civilized discussion with his hosts. Nevertheless, the maturing of the knight's character cannot disguise his madness for too long, and inevitably, Don Quixote and Sancho return to the open road.

Another measure of the extent to which Don Quixote's character has been elaborated beyond the confines of romance is the Cave of Montesinos vision where the reader is given direct access to the knight's consciousness. This brings Don Quixote very close to the condition of a modern character, for as Robert Scholes and Robert Kellogg have observed, one of the major distinctions between the modern and the ancient conceptions of character is the question of interiority; the modern writer attempts to reveal that part of a person's mind which is hidden from himself.[16] Don Quixote's account of his dream-vision in Montesinos' Cave lays bare unconscious areas of his psyche, and the reader is allowed some insight into the emotional disarray caused by his alienation from the world of chivalry. There are strong elements of wish-fulfilment in his recognition by Montesinos, contrasted with recurring images of loss and frustration as evidenced in the behaviour of Durandarte or Belerma. But although much of the vision is burlesqued through internal ironies which escape Don Quixote's notice, the knight is not humiliated. For example, his meeting with the enchanted Dulcinea, in spite of the anticlimactic banality of her handmaid's request for six *reales*, retains an element of sobering pathos, given the reader's appreciation of Don Quixote's touching *naïveté* in having so profoundly absorbed Sancho's cruel lie. No amount of burlesque can fully travesty or negate the sincerity of the madman's feelings for Dulcinea, nor blind the reader to the inherent poignancy of the situation. Paradoxically, the burlesque elements enhance the moral stature of the madman, particularly when Sancho learns of the apparition of Dulcinea, privately scoffs at his master, and then attempts to persuade him to deny the truth of this supreme experience.

The Cave episode, furthermore, serves to knit the Quixote–Sancho relationship more closely together. Not only does it reinforce Don Quixote's determination to disenchant

Dulcinea, it correspondingly increases Sancho's anxiety to prevent his master from discovering his deception. Despite its controversial nature it is a positive experience from the knight's point of view; he is able to wrest some of the initiative from Sancho, who is consequently forced into an awkward, defensive posture, arguing against the reality of the experience yet unwilling to press his arguments too far for fear of exposing his original lie. As Sancho's lie acquires an impetus of its own, a new tactical formula is found which insures Don Quixote against the total destruction of his illusions by his squire; the argument about the validity of the Cave vision is added to the problem of the enchanted Dulcinea, and both will crop up continually in the novel, mostly as a private reference between knight and servant when everything otherwise is parody and burlesque. As far as other characters are concerned, the adventures that follow, such as the encounter with Master Peter's prophesying ape or, much later, the ride on Clavileño, are nothing more than tricks and nonsense, but for Don Quixote and Sancho there is a great deal at stake, since these episodes may have a critical bearing on the one unresolved issue between them which will determine the innermost direction and quality of their lives.

In Part II, then, there is a change of emphasis from action to character, accompanied by a closer interdependence of the main characters. These developments make for variety within the linear sequence of adventures, but these variations possess a kind of organic necessity: they grow from within the evolving logic of the characters' previous experience. In this sense they adumbrate the cause-and-effect structure of realist plots, and begin to uncover new areas of narrative interest such as the moral evaluation of ambiguous experience, internal conscious-ness, and even unconscious motivation.

The interaction between Quixote and Sancho continues beyond their arrival at the Duke's castle until the scene of the chivalresque pageant where a servant dressed up as Merlin predicts that Dulcinea will be disenchanted if Sancho inflicts 3,300 lashes on himself (II.xxxv.700-1). Merlin's prediction represents the absolute climax of Don Quixote's fortunes and the peak of his development as a character. Though it supplies Don Quixote with what he wants—a concrete remedy for

Dulcinea's enchantment—the actual method of disenchantment confirms his dependence on Sancho, a humiliation which
is compounded later when the squire is taken off to govern an
island leaving his master behind in the castle empty-handed.
At the high point of his career Don Quixote is robbed of the
prize which must follow his reception to a great lord's castle
according to the anticipated pattern laid down by the books
and recapitulated in his speech in Part I Chapter xxi. It is his
ignoble squire who is undeservedly honoured. Don Quixote's
fortunes have now been reversed and his external chivalric
career, which had shown such promise of late, has fallen away
to nothing.

At the Duke's castle the relationship between Don Quixote
and Sancho Panza, which holds the life-blood of the novel, at
last arrives at its logical climax. Within the bounds of their
eccentric relationship, each character attains to a decisive
destiny: Sancho gains his promised island while the knight
becomes abjectly dependent on his squire for a release from the
dead-end in which he languishes. This overturning of their
positions is the ultimate and most damaging travesty of
chivalric romance. What is in essence an aristocratic mode of
literature, incarnate in Don Quixote, has suffered a rude
democratization at the hands of the peasant Sancho, whose bad
faith, duplicity, and ironic vigour—all of them, as we have seen,
traditional enemies of the romance hero—have succeeded in
bringing low the heroic ideals of the knight errant.

Merlin's prescription for the disenchantment of Dulcinea by
Sancho transforms the relationship between knight and squire.
In the first place, it robs Don Quixote of the one motivating
force which had sustained him so well in Part II precisely
because it disengaged him from the vicissitudes of the episodic
action. After Merlin's prophecy, the knight is forced to look
outwards to a trivial mechanical solution to his problems; his
ability to pursue his chivalric vision is seriously impaired,
leaving him in a position of virtual impotence before the
cruelties of the other characters. With the initiative now
decisively on Sancho's side, his power to destroy Don Quixote
has been fully restored; the knight can do little but wait until
the squire consents to flagellate himself, but equally, Sancho
can at any time refuse this absurd self-laceration and let the cat

out of the bag about Dulcinea. There are few resources left by this stage in Don Quixote as a character to forestall or counteract such a disastrous eventuality.

Not surprisingly, Cervantes separates the two companions at this juncture; Sancho is sent off to Barataria and Don Quixote remains at the palace. The narrative divides into a Sancho-strand and a Quixote-strand which are interlaced in alternate, self-contained chapters. But the bifurcation of the novel, due partly to the necessity of protecting Don Quixote's illusions from Sancho's ironic knowledge, obviously disrupts the course of their relationship and occasions a relapse into the narrative practices of romance. The interweaving of the respective Quixote and Sancho chapters is symptomatic of romance, as is the series of letters between the principal characters—Sancho, Don Quixote, the Duke, the Duchess, and even Sancho's wife—which is reminiscent of the exchange of letters and messages between the main characters in the *Amadis* Book IV which served to connect the different focal points of the action.[17]

It is significant that at this stage, namely at the beginning of Chapter xliv, Cervantes, for the first time in the entire novel, stands back from the narrative to comment seriously upon the creative and aesthetic problems he has been facing during its composition. He writes that Cide Hamete regrets 'having undertaken so dry and cramped a story; since he seemed always to be restricted to Don Quixote and Sancho, not daring to launch out into digressions and episodes that would have yielded both pleasure and profit. He said that to have his mind, his hand and his pen always confined to a single subject and to so scanty a list of characters was an unbearable hardship, in no way fruitful for the author; and that to avoid this inconvenience in the first place he had resorted to short tales like *The Foolish Curiosity* and *The Captive Captain*, which are, in a sense, separate from the story, though the rest of the tales concern the adventures which befell Don Quixote himself and could not well be omitted' (II.xliv.746).

Many of the contemporary aesthetic problems about unity and variety, the difference between historical and poetic truth, or between verisimilitude and the marvellous, are alluded to in this authorial aside. Cervantes calls the story 'dry and cramped' specifically because he feels that he has had to concentrate upon Don Quixote and Sancho Panza, not 'daring' to extend beyond them to other digressions and episodes. Here Cervantes clearly expresses his intention of developing the relationship between the characters, avoiding as much 'vertical' interpolation as possible. But the effort of concentrating on a single subject proves almost unbearable; not only does it require speaking through only a handful of characters, it is especially unrewarding because the benefits of such labours may well not redound to the credit of the author.

The passage turns into a rather piquant protest by Cervantes against the very effectiveness of those techniques of character-autonomy and authorial self-effacement which he has been pioneering in Part II in order to enhance the unity and plausibility of the narrative; the more successful these techniques become the more 'independent' will the characters appear, with the dismaying result that the writer's talents will be eclipsed. The temptation the author faces then is to remind the reader of his artistic skill, to lay bare the artfulness and ingenuity that go into creating narrative fiction. Cervantes confesses to having perhaps succumbed too readily to this tendency in Part I with the interpolated tales. He implies that this flaunting of inventiveness can only be taken so far because, if excessive, it will become self-defeating and will detract from the coherence of the main narrative. Therefore, even in Part I, he attempted to adhere to the discipline of presenting incidents as necessary and true by virtue of their relevance to Don Quixote's experience ('adventures which befell Don Quixote himself, and could not well be omitted').

Cervantes goes on to say that in Part II he had tried to reinforce this principle of narrative unity and poetic truth by cutting down on digressions and other matters which did not spring naturally from the main action. Because of this tightened discipline, and the even greater unobtrusiveness of the author which it entails, he openly requests the reader not to underestimate his artistry, and asks that he should be praised not so much for what he has written but for his restraint in not having indulged his imagination and skills more freely:

So he decided not to insert any tales, either detached or connected, in this second part, but to include some similar episodes arising out of the actual happenings themselves; and even these should be sparing and no longer than their bare narration required. So, being confined and enclosed within the narrow limits of the story, though he has the skill, the knowledge and the capacity for dealing with the whole universe, he begs that his pains shall not be under-valued, and that he shall be praised not for what he writes, but for what he has refrained from writing.

Cervantes's professed dedication to self-restraint explicitly runs counter to Renaissance ideas on the art of narrative, according to which abundance and variety were signs of imaginative vigour, and the ability to encompass 'the whole universe' in the microcosm of a work of art was the supreme goal of the artist.

Such expansive and heroic ideals lay behind attempts to revive the epic of Antiquity during the Renaissance, but even in the theories of Tasso and the neo-Aristotelians, the view that topical variety and a wide-ranging imagination were indispensable aesthetic values remained a fundamental assumption.[18] Unity and verisimilitude were fairly elastic standards used to check tendencies to structural chaos or rein in the impulse to over-indulge in fantasy, but they were not intended to limit the poet's ability to display his manifold skills nor hamper his freedom to traverse as wide and varied a terrain as his imagination and learning would allow. What is new is Cervantes's avowed concern to find narrative unity and a form of poetic truth by deliberately confining himself to evolving a chain of relations between only a few characters, a chain whose linkages would be determined ultimately by a logic of relevance to the experience of the characters.

There is more involved here than Cervantes's parodic lip-service to historical verisimilitude. A curious note of plaintiveness can be detected in his admission that this cleaving to the 'truth' is often an uncomfortable struggle with recalcitrant material, especially thankless for being necessarily so self-concealing. The passage represents a serious declaration of aesthetic purpose. It is Cervantes's most direct statement of his wish to attain to a form of poetic truth, not by extending the freedom of his imagination but by submitting it to the wearisome discipline of relating the action to the experience of his characters. This self-effacement in the pursuit of a sense of objectivity in fiction represents Cervantes's decisive advance, within the context of Renaissance narrative, towards the realism of the modern novel.

(iii) *Sancho's Triumph and Its Aftermath*

At the isle of Barataria Sancho's character is given a new lease of life by the use of a device analogous to the mad/sane paradox which had served so well to develop the character of Don Quixote. Exploiting the ambiguity in Sancho between credulous bumpkin and cunning peasant, Cervantes strikes a fresh source of *admiratio* for the reader: the surprise of discovering a peasant who is able to govern wisely despite his lowly birth and deficient education. The powerful attraction of this paradox exercises a distinct pull away from the by now routine baiting of Don Quixote at the Duke's castle. In this new role, Sancho threatens to eclipse the mad knight; his success as governor represents, as it were, a capital transfer of wit from bankrupt master to *arriviste* servant.

This, of course, is as it should be, following the logic of their relationship: Sancho's ironic awareness has undermined the basis of Don Quixote's authority, and he has come to enjoy an ascendancy which he appears quite competent to maintain. Sancho's triumph over Don Quixote possesses a double aspect: his governorship of the 'island' of Barataria is a great victory within the terms of Don Quixote's romance madness, but a conclusive victory over the mad knight must clearly involve a total repudiation of the quixotic madness itself: Sancho's final awakening to ordinary reality.

Nevertheless, while he is governor, Sancho is intriguingly poised between the crazy, quixotic world and the real world; for a short spell, he takes the place of a real Duke in one of his real dominions and rules over real subjects successfully. Even though Sancho's reward issues from the literary matrix of Don Quixote's madness, his purely symbolic usurpation of his master's feudal authority is mischievously extended by Cervantes and allowed to impinge seriously on the real world, where the peasant is able to exercise the power of a genuine aristocrat.

The political implications of Sancho's governorship have not been lost on critics. Political government is, after all, a subsidiary but none the less recurrent theme in the *Quixote*, following naturally from the knight's very endeavour to reform the world. It is overtly touched on in his Golden Age speech (I.xi), in his discourse on Arms and Letters (I.xxxvii-xxxviii), and in his advice to Sancho on the art of government (II.xlii-xliii). José Antonio Maravall has argued that Don Quixote's conception of authority is based on medieval notions of military prowess and moral leadership which were by that time obsolete and ineffectual.[19] By contrast, Sancho's governorship is taken to signify Cervantes's qualified acceptance of a Renaissance view of political authority derived from the *lumen rationis* to which any man, however humble, can lay claim. Agustín Redondo, furthermore, finds a cultural model for the Barataria episode in the festival of Carnival.[20] Demonstrating Sancho's literary affinities with the representative Carnival-figure of popular tradition, he concludes that since Carnival permitted a symbolic overturning of power-relations in society, Cervantes is using Sancho here to criticize the ruling classes under the mantle of comedy.

These interpretations accord with the logic of Sancho's triumph over his mad master. Nevertheless, Carnival is an agreed social ritual, whereas Barataria is a powerful man's hoax on an unsuspecting peasant.[21] Thus, in so far as Sancho's exercise of aristocratic authority has some impact on the real world, Cervantes's relieving him of it also carries political implications. Had Sancho simply been driven from office by force, the question of his moral right to govern by comparison with the Duke's would have become unavoidable; but, equally, if he had been allowed to rule for much longer Cervantes's original purpose of parodying the romances of chivalry could have spilled over into a much less innocuous subversion of certain rather more tangible forms of authority. One is led to contemplate once again the mystery of Cervantes's intentions: was Sancho endowed with the ability to govern wisely for the purely innocent aesthetic purpose of creating *admiratio*, or could there have been a political motive behind the literary device? If the latter were the case its significance is by no means clear, for the phenomenon of a peasant governor may well suggest advanced Renaissance ideals of government, but his loss of office is no less susceptible of reactionary interpretation.

Cervantes circumvents thorny issues of political morality by a sleight of hand that combines a show of force with a further development of Sancho's character. The peasant governor is subjected to a violent attack by unknown assailants. His lack of courage and military aptitude are thereby exposed, and this persuades him to relinquish the governorship and return to his normal station in life, a decision which is presented as a further sign of Sancho's good sense. The Duke's violent and arbitrary re-possession of authority is thus converted rather artfully into a pretext for Sancho's ultimate awakening to reality from the quixotic delusion of Barataria. After all but a flicker of the peasant's *lumen rationis*, it would seem that the medieval notions of military prowess and natural hierarchy are pressed by Cervantes into the service of fiction as justifications for Sancho's sudden demotion.

Still, inasmuch as Sancho's power is the end-result of Don Quixote's mad enterprise, it makes perfect sense to represent his giving it up as a release from illusion and an acceptance of actual social realities. When compared to Don Quixote's wrong-headed persistence in chivalry, the peasant's self-knowledge will inevitably enhance his status as a more mature character. In renouncing his governorship Sancho has won through to a fuller perception of the nature of his circumstances, whereas Don Quixote is still pining for the miraculous outcome of his servant's self-flagellation.

Cervantes's treatment of Don Quixote while Sancho is away is indecisive. With his chivalric career in suspension there remain signs of inner distress which are emphasized to produce pathos. On the other hand, since his helplessness is a consequence of his madness, he is remorselessly mocked. Cervantes vacillates between empathy and parody but understandably fails to achieve a synthesis of the two attitudes.

Almost immediately after Sancho's departure Don Quixote is inconsolably dispirited. When the Duchess notices his melancholy appearance and asks if he is sad because of Sancho's absence, he replies:

> It is true, my lady . . . that I grieve for Sancho's absence. But that is not the principal cause of my seeming sad; nor the reason why of the many offers your Excellency makes me I can only accept the goodwill with which they are made. For the rest I entreat your Excellency to

give me leave to wait upon myself within my own apartment.
(II.xliv.748)

The main cause of Don Quixote's sadness is not his squire's absence but, by implication, the condition of his lady Dulcinea. An element of compassion for Don Quixote's plight is further evinced in the lamentations over his laddered stockings, which become a token of material indigence and spiritual desolation (pp.749-50). But the good knight's lamentations are taken up by Cide Hamete, and soon undermined by parodic exaggeration. This renewal of parody is reinforced by the appearance of Altisidora singing a burlesque serenade to the forlorn lover.

When our attention is next drawn to the troubled Don Quixote in Chapter xlvi, it is to witness a new humiliation at the hands of the Duke and Duchess. The knight asks for a lute to be delivered to his room, and when night falls he sits by his window and sings a song reminding Altisidora of his loyalty to Dulcinea. The song itself invites sympathy for Don Quixote; it is coherently composed, with none of those comical lapses of taste which marred his earlier poem to Dulcinea (I.xxvi.216). But while the knight gives voice to his sentiments, the languorous, romantic atmosphere of music and love in a nocturnal garden is shattered by an infernal clanging of bells. A sack full of cats is dropped from the floor above, several of which get into Don Quixote's room and scratch the unfortunate *hidalgo* severely in the face. The outcome of the joke exceeds even the Duke and Duchess's intentions: 'The noble pair left him to rest and went away concerned at the unfortunate result of their joke, for they had not thought the adventure would have proved so tiresome and costly to Don Quixote' (II.xlvi.764).

The regrets of the Duke and Duchess over this practical joke turned sour reflect the ambivalence of Cervantes's attitude towards Don Quixote at this point. Much has been done to evoke the melancholy dignity of the character, only to have it suddenly overwhelmed by renewed comic ferocity. It is as if Cervantes could not give rein to the more sober, suffering side of Don Quixote without pulling him up short and castigating his chivalric madness. A new and ominous element has appeared for the first time in the whole of Part II: the grieving knight is subjected to the sort of pitiless physical brutality from which he had been largely spared since going up into the Sierra Morena in Part I Chapter xxiii. In the Sierra Morena Cervantes had inaugurated a shift from sequential adventures to a more subtly modulated treatment of the madness based progressively on the interlocking relationship between Don Quixote and Sancho. Now, only three chapters after master and servant are parted, Cervantes again has recourse to farcical knockabout as a laughter-raising expedient. Henceforward, the knight's inner life will be increasingly masked from view as he once more becomes a mere figure of fun, a butt of cruelty and mockery.

The separation of Quixote and Sancho allows comparisons to be drawn between them: Sancho's self-confidence makes him a source of *admiratio* in his own right, whereas Don Quixote is crestfallen and buffeted by a resumption of violent parody.[22] This disparity could be said to reflect their respective destinies: the sane Sancho gains the upper hand over the mad Quixote, whose chivalric mania is shown to be fruitless even on its own terms. Yet now that the principal narrative argument has been successfully resolved, a difficult problem arises. If Sancho were to return to serve Don Quixote as his squire, the entire movement and rationale of the satire on chivalric romance would be put into reverse, for the relationship would be resumed under the old dispensation of Don Quixote's ostensible authority over Sancho. How then is Cervantes to reunite the protagonists when the servant not only has the knowledge to destroy his master's illusions about romance but is alleged to have a firmer grip on reality to boot? Sancho's experience at Barataria would seem to call for Don Quixote's return to his senses, for there is little prospect of raising the knight to a degree of self-knowledge comparable to Sancho's other than by delivering him from his mania for chivalric romance. But if Don Quixote does not emerge from his madness, Sancho would have to be relegated to his former position of subservience to the madman by a direct intervention of the author in the narrative, a show of literary force that would parallel the Duke's snatching back control of Barataria from Sancho.

The ex-governor's fall into a deep pit on his way back to the

Duke's castle performs just such a narrative function (II.lv.823). This episode is the only one in the novel that produces such a strong impression of having been introduced for symbolic reasons alone.[23] Although an entirely fortuitous event, it is interpreted by Sancho as a punishment for his 'follies and fantasies', and compared unfavourably to Don Quixote's experience in the Cave of Montesinos where the knight was granted 'beautiful and delightful visions', whereas now Sancho fears he will see nothing but 'toads and snakes' (p. 823). Regardless of the power conferred upon him by Merlin's prophecy, not to mention his own success as governor, Sancho is prepared to fly in the face of all experience and concede the transparently absurd argument over the Montesinos vision to his crazy master. Finally, the fact that Sancho should be delivered from his plight by Don Quixote himself, who happens quite by chance to be out exercising Rocinante that morning, strongly suggests that the whole point of the episode is to re-establish in symbolic terms the squire's former dependence upon the madman.

Sancho's fall and rescue by Don Quixote shows Cervantes, the self-effacing, proto-realist novelist, reverting to the old manipulative ways of a romance author. But ironically, a measure of Cervantes's success at elaborating independent characters can be had by examining the problems he encounters when he reclaims the creative freedom to shape the narrative at will. The mood and character of the *Quixote* undergo a distinct change, of which the most obvious sign is the reappearance of interpolated episodes that have no direct bearing on the fortunes of the central characters. Throughout most of Part II until they arrive at the Duke's castle there is only one similar tale, Basilio's, and then Don Quixote is instrumental in deciding its outcome. At the Duke's castle there is the Tosilos story, which turns out to be one of a number of practical jokes played on Don Quixote by the Duke. However, in the Roque Guinart and Claudia Jeronima interpolations, and in the Ana Felix story, Don Quixote remains on the sidelines.

The knight's passivity in these circumstances betokens a kind of impotence rather than greater lucidity;[24] it is an index of his loss of vitality as a character, which can be attributed directly to his creator's arbitrary intrusions into the narrative. For if the tales of Part I were interpolated at a time when Cervantes had not yet realized the potential of his central characters, these other interpolations come when the Quixote–Panza relationship has already been fulfilled at Barataria.[25] At this point in the novel Cervantes is keeping that relationship artificially alive—after Sancho's experience of governorship there is no reason why Don Quixote should not be delivered from his absurd madness. In this regard the entire section which deals with the journey to Barcelona and back appears to be no more than a digression, since it serves merely to delay the natural outcome of Don Quixote's enterprise: the inevitable realization that it was futile from the start.

Don Quixote's seemingly impromptu decision to go to Barcelona instead of Saragossa could be taken as a sign of his autonomy as a character. There is, however, a detail that suggests the opposite, that the character is in fact being unfairly manipulated by the author: the Barcelona digression begins and ends with a scene at an inn. In the first inn (II.lix), Don Quixote meets two gentlemen reading an alleged history of his exploits by Alonso Fernández de Avellaneda, a plagiarist of Cervantes's *Quixote* Part I. So outraged is Don Quixote at Avellaneda's impertinence that he decides to go to Barcelona in order to prove the falsity of the rival history. In the second inn (II.lxxii), he comes across Don Alvaro Tarfe, a character from that 'apocryphal' history, who is made to admit the authenticity of the Cervantes version.

On both occasions Cervantes makes a point of explaining that the mad knight did not mistake the inns for castles (p. 848, and p. 924, respectively). These are the only two instances in the whole of the *Quixote* where any overt indication is given that the knight's madness may have receded. Their connection with the attack on Avellaneda is not fortuitous; for in using his character to condemn the plagiarism, Cervantes must contend with the awkward difficulty that the intrinsic *raison d'être* of Don Quixote is no other than his lunatic inability to tell fact from fiction. Clearly if he now wishes his character to say that the Avellaneda *Quixote* is fiction while the Cervantes version is fact, some authoritative assurance would have to be given to the reader that the knight's intractable confusion on this very issue has somehow been momentarily clarified. This puts Cervantes in a position of considerable disingenuousness; for in appearing to exalt Don Quixote's independence of character he is actually compromising that independence by reducing the mad knight to being a vehicle of his own vengeful pique against a rival.[26] Not only does Cervantes regress to the condition of a romance author after Barataria, his *trompe l'œil* manipulations at this point evince little of the playful Ariostean spirit of Part I; he is closer instead to the furtive chicanery of Montalvo, whose tortuous stratagems were designed to dissemble rather than disclose the true motives of the author.

It may be argued, of course, that the journey to Barcelona was necessary to maintain the leisurely narrative rhythm of the novel and provide a slow winding-down of the action that would reflect the decline in Don Quixote's morale prior to the recovery of his wits. Even if the Barcelona detour had been included for this reason alone rather than to spite Avellaneda, it would still have created considerable problems as regards the treatment of Don Quixote at least. For by prolonging his madness so far beyond Sancho's triumph at Barataria, Cervantes is committing himself to continuing the parody of the mad knight when there is little reason any longer for doing so. Although the absurd madness has been attacked from every conceivable angle by now, whenever Cervantes compensates for this exhaustion of parody by resorting to the paradox of Quixote's flashes of wisdom or to reminders of his inner distress, the effect created is one of gratuitous cruelty, as if the author had been needlessly tormenting a helpless victim. The situation calls to mind the question Thomas Mann asked himself of the *Quixote*: 'Does not all this cruelty look like self-flagellation, self-revilement, castigation?'[27] The charge of cruelty is, I believe, valid only during the Barcelona digression. The notion of Cervantes's self-punishment, however, is particularly apt when we consider that by choosing to extend Don Quixote's madness, Cervantes tightens the inherent contradiction between parody and sympathy into a kind of self-defeating double-bind: the more the knight is mocked for his madness the more will he be seen to suffer, and such suffering will cry out for some deliverance, but however much goodwill the knight may inspire, so long as his chivalric obsession endures, he will necessarily invite ridicule. Indeed, the motif of Sancho's self-flagellation is a fitting symbol of Cervantes's creative predicament. For this trite motif is all that is left now to hold Quixote and Sancho together. It goads the pair through the journey to Barcelona and locks them into a dialectic of mutual degradation as the knight squanders his moral capital on ever more desperate appeals to his increasingly cynical squire to flog himself.

(iv) *Pathos and Parody*

Interpolated episodes apart, a sense of *déjà vu* pervades the Barcelona digression. Except for the scene of his final defeat at the hands of the Knight of the White Moon, there is little about Don Quixote which gives rise either to *admiratio* or to laughter; he is very much a spent force by this stage. With Sancho, as we shall presently see, it is a rather different matter, but even so, his master's continuing madness will prevent him too from achieving his full potential as a character. Since the central relationship can no longer make any significant headway, the novel settles into unmotivated episodic action characterized by the use of recycled ideas and scenes of gratuitous cruelty to the madman.

The episode of the counterfeit Arcadia serves very little purpose other than to introduce the horrible trampling of the old gentleman by a herd of bulls. When they arrive in Barcelona Don Quixote and Sancho are invited by Don Antonio Moreno to stay at his house, much as Don Diego de Miranda had done earlier in Part II. But unlike Don Diego, their new host emulates the Duke in choosing to play malicious tricks on the mad knight. These are either appallingly childish, such as pinning a notice of his identity on Don Quixote's back so as to invite the populace to jeer at the bewildered knight in the street, or, as in the case of the Enchanted Head, clearly modelled on Master Peter's prophesying ape. Don Quixote's sojourn in Barcelona is otherwise occupied with sight-seeing. He visits a printing-press and is taken on a trip aboard a galley where he witnesses the denouement of Ana Felix's story.

At this point Cervantes introduces the scene which contains a mechanism that will eventually release the knight from his lunacy. Sampson Carrasco again appears, disguised this time as the Knight of the White Moon, and defeats Don Quixote in a chivalric duel. As a penalty for his defeat, the mad knight has to promise to return home and give up arms for a year. There is an impressive narrative economy in this device; it performs the indispensable function of compelling Don Quixote to return to his village. But as it observes also the conventions of chivalric practice to the letter, it spares the knight the trauma of a sudden, humiliating collapse of his illusions. In fact, it enhances his dignity, for even in defeat Don Quixote refuses to renounce the primacy of Dulcinea's beauty in the world:

Then, battered and stunned, without lifting his vizor Don Quixote proclaimed, in a low and feeble voice, as if he were speaking from inside a tomb: 'Dulcinea del Toboso is the most beautiful woman in the world, and I am the most unfortunate knight on earth; nor is it just that my weakness should discredit that truth. Drive your lance home, knight, and rid me of life, since you have robbed me of honour.'

(II.lxiv.890)

The madman's profession of loyalty to his lady is accompanied by a simile whose poignancy transforms it into an emblem of his long and troubled passion: the prostrate knight speaks without raising his vizor, his words rising from within his shuttered helmet as from the depths of a tomb. The image elegantly captures the tragic blindness induced by his chivalric madness: Don Quixote remains stubbornly impervious to the claims of a degraded reality even in the face of death itself.

The poetic force released by this one image gives some inkling of the vitality that is stored up in the figure of Quixote. So successful has Cervantes been in arousing sympathy for the knight that he has contrived a situation whereby the character's nobility lies in his loyalty to ideas which render him a fool. This paradox will remain attractive and intriguing so long as the knight's loyalty is seen to have some point, but once it becomes footling even on its own terms, as the flagellation of Sancho theme makes it, then a glaring disproportion arises between the increasing triteness of the surface incidents and the latent moral grandeur of the stricken hero.

It comes therefore as no surprise that the homeward journey is again marked by repetitious devices and the remodelling of former incidents. Tosilos reappears (II.lxvi.899), and reveals that he has after all been punished, a result which parallels the fate of the boy Andrew (I.xxxi). Don Quixote is again needlessly trampled, this time by hogs (II.lxviii.906-7). There is another interlude at the Duke's castle, the sole point of which is to parody the already ridiculous remedy for breaking the spell on Dulcinea. Now it is the counterfeit damsel Altisidora who must be restored to health by the pinching and pricking of the luckless Sancho (II.lxix.911). In the next chapter (II.lxx), Don Quixote is made to repulse the importunate advances of Altisidora yet again, thus reiterating his earlier rebuff in Chapter xliv, and bringing to mind his rejection of Maritornes in the early stages of Part I.

Cervantes's handling of Sancho is also beset with difficulties. For a while after Barataria Sancho accepts a position of subservience to Don Quixote. The expropriated governor, for example, tells the Morisco Ricote that all he has gained from his experience is 'the knowledge that I'm no good at governing anything but a herd of cattle' (II.liv.821). Later, when he describes how he fell into the pit to the Duke and Duchess, he says that 'if Heaven hadn't sent me my master Don Quixote, I should have been there till the end of the world' (II.lv.828). He then expresses relief that he can once more 'pass into the service of my master Don Quixote'.

Nevertheless, not too long after these benign professions of humility and self-denial, Sancho begins unequivocally to reassert his will to power, as it were.[28] The first questions he puts to the Enchanted Head betray his ambitions: 'Shall I ever get another governorship? Shall I quit this hungry squire's life? Shall I see my wife and children again?' (II.lxii.874). A little later the narrator observes that 'although he loathed being a governor as has been said, he still longed to rule again and be obeyed; for such are the evil effects of authority, even of mock authority' (II.lxiii.879). Sancho even dares to usurp Don Quixote's authority when he is asked by two labourers to settle a dispute: 'It's my job to settle this question and give a decision on the whole case, as it is only a few days since I gave up being a governor and a judge, as all the world knows' (II.lxvi.898). Significantly, Don Quixote here is too troubled to bother with the labourers' problems, 'for I am not fit to give crumbs to the cat, my wits are so shaken and shattered'. Sancho is now back on top gubernatorial form and cleverly resolves the labourers' dispute. Once again we are reminded that the squire possesses the necessary qualities for leadership and authority, which revival of Sancho's acuity and self-confidence contrasts with the deflated spirits of his master. It is as if Cervantes had found it necessary to fall back on Sancho's recently discovered capacity to cause *admiratio* and had virtually given up on the mad knight as a source of wit and comic energy. In fact, Cervantes, in spite of some attempts to curtail Sancho's assertiveness, does allow himself to hint at the actual shift in literary interest and imaginative resources from master to servant without altogether upsetting the formal structure of their relationship. It is interesting to look at this phenomenon more closely as it manifests itself in the text.

One of the signs of Sancho's independence of Don Quixote's authority is the condescension with which he begins to treat the knight, as when he exclaims to the maidens of the counterfeit Arcadia that nobody could tell that his master was a madman after hearing him speak so wisely. Don Quixote is insulted: 'Who set you meddling with my affairs, and enquiring whether I am a man of sense or crazy? Be quiet! Say no more, but saddle Rocinante, if he is unsaddled' (II.lviii.845). But condescension is soon replaced by sheer effrontery whenever the knight attempts to consolidate his crumbling authority over his squire. At one point, Don Quixote's authority disintegrates altogether when he threatens to beat Sancho with his own hands in order to hasten the disenchantment of Dulcinea. Sancho jumps on his master, wrestles him to the ground, and places his foot on his chest. Don Quixote exclaims: 'What, traitor? . . . Do you rebel against your *master and natural lord?* Do you presume against your bread-giver?' (my emphasis). But Sancho is confident enough to bring into the open his real attitude to the knight, an attitude that had been incubating since the fulling-mills episode in Part I. In that earlier episode there had been talk of Don Quixote's being Sancho's 'master and natural lord' (p. 160); however, Sancho now does not bother to disguise his feelings with irony, he plainly states: 'I depose no King, I make no King . . . but help myself who am my own lord. Promise to let me alone, your worship, and not try and whip me for the present, and I'll let you go free' (II.lx.855-6).

After this crystal-clear assertion of the sovereignty of his individual will, Sancho begins covertly but unequivocally to extricate himself from the trammels of Don Quixote's chivalric lunacy. It is possible to plot the emergence of a curt, ironical indifference on Sancho's part to the enduring preoccupations of his deluded master. Still, before proceeding with our examination, it is as well to mention Salvador de Madariaga's influential account of the 'quixotification' and 'rise' of Sancho in relation to the knight.[29] Sancho is said to become 'quixotified' because the hitherto materialistic peasant is gradually drawn to less material satisfactions, for instance his pride in having become famous as a result of the publication of Part I. In Part II Sancho feels himself increasingly to be the equal of Don Quixote as his vanity and self-importance infuse in his spirit fantastical aspirations that are analogous to his master's. Thus, according to Madariaga, the fortunes of master and servant are neatly inter-crossed; the squire's ascent from 'reality' to 'illusion' intersects the knight's descent from 'illusion' to 'reality'.

But Don Quixote does not in fact descend from illusion to reality at all, instead he remains hopelessly engrossed in his chivalric obsession. Similarly, it can be shown that Sancho does not succumb to illusion, much less any illusion that in any way resembles his master's and could therefore be termed quixotic. It is exactly the reverse; Sancho's ironic dismissal of his master's ideals becomes so decisive that towards the end he reveals himself to be more emphatically materialistic and self-interested than ever he was before. Madariaga explains Sancho's rising confidence as the result of the self-importance he feels when he is charged by Merlin with the disenchantment of Dulcinea, or when he is said to possess the virtue of 'resurrecting' Altisidora. However, in neither of these cases is Sancho taken in; his confidence is based on far more concrete grounds than mere vanity or self-congratulation. We shall see Sancho become progressively dismissive of all the major aspects of Don Quixote's madness. He will dissociate himself from the notion of enchantment, from the utopian ideals of pastoral, from his master's pedagogical pretensions, and from the rhetoric and conventions of courtly love-service.

When they encounter the lackey Tosilos once again, Don

Quixote refuses to believe that it is the same person who he assumed had been allowed to marry the duenna Rodríguez's daughter in Chapter lvi. He rationalizes this anomaly, as one would expect, by calling it an enchantment. Sancho will have none of that and insists that it really is Tosilos. Adding insult to injury, the squire has the gall to accept the lackey's offer of food and drink. Sancho, moreover, readily agrees with Tosilos that the knight is mad: 'Plainly I see it, and plainly I tell him; but what's the use? Particularly now that he's done for, for he's been conquered by the Knight of the White Moon' (II.lxvi.900). He has not, in fact, confronted Don Quixote openly about the madness but he tells Tosilos otherwise presumably to excuse himself for the embarrassment of continuing to serve an obvious lunatic. As further evidence of his rejection of the notion of enchantment, he replies to Don Quixote's request that he start whipping himself: 'To tell you the truth, I can't persuade myself that the flogging of my posterior has anything to do with the disenchanting of the enchanted. For you might as well say: If your head aches, anoint your knees' (II.lxvii.901).

A little later Don Quixote begins to entertain ideas of creating a pastoral idyll. Sancho humours him in this but is not above a touch of malice when he suggests that Sampson Carrasco and the barber might wish to become shepherds too, 'but God grant it mayn't come into the priest's head to enter the fold as well—he's so gay and fond of his amusements' (II.lxvii.902). The knight, however, is impervious to Sancho's raillery, and he continues to extol the delights of pastoral. The squire plays his master along with growing relish yet it takes just one ironic remark to puncture the illusoriness of the idyllic dream: Sancho voices the fear that his pretty daughter Sanchica might fall prey to the base desires of the other shepherds—'I wouldn't like her to go for wool and come back shorn'—and, following this piquant popular saying, he unleashes a string of other proverbs until Don Quixote has to ask him to desist. In reply Sancho impudently points out that the knight often resorts to proverbs himself and should not therefore be calling the kettle black: 'You scold me for quoting proverbs, and string them together in pairs yourself' (II.lxvii.904).

In the next chapter, when the two of them are trampled by a herd of hogs, Sancho reacts with unwonted belligerence and asks his master for his sword to avenge himself by killing some of the beasts. Don Quixote launches instead into a lament: 'Let them be, friend . . . for this outrage is the penalty for my sin, and it is Heaven's just chastisement on a conquered knight errant, that jackals shall devour him, wasps sting him and hogs trample him down' (II.lxviii.907). Sancho replies sardonically: 'And it's Heaven's chastisement too, I suppose . . . that flies shall sting the squires of vanquished knights errant, that lice shall eat them and hunger assail them.' Thus is Don Quixote's pious chivalric claptrap about 'Heaven's chastisement' angrily deflated by Sancho's hard-nosed cynicism, to which is added an outright rejection of any sense of shared fate between knight and squire: 'But what have the Panzas to do with the Quixotes?' By way of consolation Don Quixote proposes to vent his sorrows in a madrigal. Sancho is unyielding: 'To my mind . . . thoughts that yield to verse can't be very troublesome. Rhyme it as much as you please, your worship, and I'll sleep as long as I can.' The knight proceeds regardless to sing a song of love and weep over Dulcinea, but his squire has already cruelly exposed the amorous plaint for the arbitrary, mannered convention it is.

Sancho's rejection of the forms of chivalry and courtly love is also evident in his reaction to Altisidora's renewed mockery of Don Quixote. When the damsel spitefully taunts the knight for having believed that she could truly have died of unrequited love for him, Sancho remarks: 'That I can well believe, . . . for this dying for love's a joke. They may talk about it, but as for doing it—believe it, Judas!' (II.lxx.919). Later he says of Altisidora: 'Maidens who have work to do spend more thought on finishing their jobs than on thinking of their loves.' And when Altisidora leaves the room after having crudely insulted Don Quixote yet again, Sancho rebukes her for having taken advantage of a kind-hearted soul like his master, and makes it quite clear that, not being mad like Don Quixote, he would not himself stand for any courtly love nonsense from her.

Having now expressed his utter indifference to Don Quixote's chivalric concerns in a variety of small but maliciously telling ways, Sancho begins to turn his master's perverse obstinacy in delusion to his own material advantage.

It starts with his complaining that he has not been given the six smocks promised by Altisidora for having 'resurrected' her. 'And I won't believe that Heaven has endowed me with the virtue I have for me to communicate it to others free, gratis and for nothing' (II.lxxi.921). Don Quixote then offers to pay Sancho if he whips himself for the sake of Dulcinea, 'and Sancho opened his eyes and ears a foot wider at this offer'. Having settled a price to his taste, he consents and remarks: 'I shall go home rich and contented, though soundly whipped.'[30] Don Quixote is overwhelmed: 'O blessed Sancho! O kindly Sancho! . . . How deeply we shall be bound to serve you, Dulcinea and I, all the days of our lives that Heaven shall grant us.' The formal relations between master and servant are all but inverted in this pathetic outburst of gratitude: to all intents and purposes the would-be hero of romance and his peerless lady are now in thrall to a money-grubbing yokel.

The motif of self-flagellation culminates, therefore, in a transaction which exposes the real significance of Merlin's prophecy and takes the logic of Sancho's triumph at Barataria to its ultimate and all too explicit consequences. None the less, all the signs are that Cervantes is playing it for laughs, at least as far as Sancho is concerned. For even though he has become openly mercenary, Sancho still delights in teasing and deceiving the demented knight. No sooner does he start to lash himself than it occurs to him to whip tree-trunks instead, 'uttering such deep groans from time to time that with each one it sounded as if his spirit were being torn from his body' (p. 923). And yet, amusing though Sancho's cunning ruse may be, Cervantes has Quixote respond to it in a manner that transforms the scene into a bleak tableau of moral cruelty.

Moved to pity by his squire's ostensible suffering, the lunatic suggests Sancho stop flogging himself until they get back to their village, but the roguish servant magnanimously insists that he prefers to get it over with there and then. After beating the trees a while longer he lets out a great howl of pain which makes Don Quixote exclaim: 'Heaven forbid, Sancho my friend, that you should lose your life for my pleasure, for it must serve to support your wife and children. Let Dulcinea await another opportunity and I will contain myself within the bounds of proximate hope until you gain new strength to

conclude this matter to everyone's satisfaction.' Scenting total
victory, Sancho now milks his master for all he is worth. He
asks to borrow Don Quixote's cloak to throw over his shoulders
so as not to catch cold, 'which is a danger your new flagellants
run'. Don Quixote, remaining only in his doublet, duly covers
Sancho, 'who slept till the sun woke him'.

Such exploitation of the knight's generosity makes this the
one scene in the novel which offers concrete support to the myth
of Quixote as Christian saint, a variant of the Romantic
interpretation favoured most notably by Miguel de Unamuno
and W.H. Auden. Indeed, it is as though Cervantes had chosen
to crucify Don Quixote upon the contradiction between
sympathy and parody. For when the mockery of the madman's
obsession with Dulcinea has reached a point of utter
heartlessness, the deluded knight offers to put the squire's
welfare before his most cherished hope of disenchanting his
lady.

Nevertheless, for all the sympathy that could be wrung from
the moral sacrifice of the madman, Don Quixote does not attain
to a condition of unqualified pathos even here. The persistence
of the knight's ludicrous madness would appear to call for a
compensatory lurch into parody, producing yet another twist of
Cervantes's creative double-bind. When knight and squire
arrive next day at the inn which marks the end of the Barcelona
digression, Don Quixote's crazed fascination with derring-do
makes him a laughing-stock once more. Seeing the paintings of
Dido and Helen of Troy, he boasts that had he been fortunate
enough to have been a contemporary of theirs he would have
averted the burning of Troy and the destruction of Carthage by
the simple expedient of killing Paris.

It is only after the Barcelona digression is over, when Sancho
has fraudulently completed the number of lashes prescribed by
Merlin, that Cervantes proceeds to relieve the knight of the
madness that has come to torment him. As they approach their
village, Don Quixote scrutinizes every woman that happens to
pass their way to see if it is Dulcinea transfigured into her true
form. As the terrible truth insinuates itself upon him, he seizes
on chance happenings as signs of ill omen. A hare chased by
hounds takes refuge under Sancho's ass and the knight's
composure cracks: '*Malum signum! Malum signum!* A hare flies;

the hounds pursue her; Dulcinea will not appear!' The fractured syntax and stunned reiteration breach Don Quixote's reserve to betray once more the depth of his inward suffering; briefly, he regains some of his emotional complexity, like an ember flaring up one last time before it finally goes out.

Sancho, for his part, affirmed now in his supremacy, permits himself a gesture of compassion for the doom-laden knight by taking it upon himself to break the influence of the omens.[31] In spite of this, his first words to his wife reveal a gross insensitivity to the plight of his former master: 'I bring money—and that's what counts—gained by my own industry and at no cost to anyone' (II.lxxiii.932). His wife's reply is suitable hard-headed, exhibiting a studied indifference to ethical considera-tions: 'Bring your money, good husband . . . I don't care where you gained it, for however you got it you won't have started up a new custom in the world.' Like so much else in the novel, indeed like Don Quixote's suffering itself, Teresa Panza's words reverberate with moral suggestion. When set against the broken figure of Quixote, they give an impression of cynical rationalization, if not of gloating triumph, impressions which go a long way in these final chapters towards inspiring the Romantic myth of an idealistic madman brought low by the material ambitions of moral inferiors. The parodic buffoon of Part I, having been succeeded in Part II by a more complex figure—alternately sympathetic and ridiculous—now reaches a point where his sufferings enable him to outface derision, turning parody into callous abuse.

Don Quixote's actual transition to self-knowledge comes suddenly by way of a mysterious illness that affords only a fleeting interval of lucid calm and recognition at the threshold of death itself. For sanity and death are, after all, two sides of the same coin as far as the mad hero is concerned: one of the signs by which his companions 'concluded that he was dying was the ease with which he changed from mad to sane' (II.lxxiv.936). As the madness lifts so is the punishing contradiction between pathos and parody dissolved; the old *hidalgo*'s last hours are so peculiarly moving because the reader is at last able to release those reserves of sympathy for the grieving knight which had been repressed so long as his obsession with chivalric romance held sway over his imagination and reduced him repeatedly to a mere object of ridicule.

When considered in its entirety the form of the *Quixote* reflects those working-methods in Part I that bibliographical investigations have recently brought to light. Just as it is no longer reasonable to suppose that Cervantes was following a preconceived plan of composition, so too does it appear unnecessary to postulate the existence of a set of fixed intentions that uniformly motivated Cervantes throughout both Parts of the *Quixote*. It would seem rather that the narrative passes through phases that correspond to the artistic decisions Cervantes made in the course of writing.

To speak of phases in the *Quixote* is neither to rob it of continuity and momentum nor yet to detract from its remarkable comic energy. It is rather an attempt to describe the novel in terms that will convey the sense of a unique process of discovery in which a narrative artist like Cervantes, after placing his imagination in the very eye of the literary controversies of his age, was possessed of sufficient confidence in his own inventiveness to strike out beyond contemporary limits of theory and genre, beyond the strict parody of romance even, towards a new mode of writing fiction.

The motor of change is precisely the source of comedy in the novel, namely Don Quixote's madness. In so far as it is a vehicle of parody of the Spanish romances it remains within the ambit of contemporary literary practice, but what transforms Don Quixote's chivalric mania into a powerful spearhead of innovation is Cervantes's decision to extend the narrative beyond the length of a *novella*. Thenceforward, the madness cannot simply remain a device to make the reader laugh, time and again, at the ridiculous romances; it will increasingly command attention in its own right and, in effect, becomes a mantle of comedy behind which Cervantes conceals his witty lunges at the reader's common sense. Cultivation of the admirable as well as the laughable aspects of the madness inspires a succession of new ideas: the development of Sancho's ironic mentality, the mad/sane paradox, the Aldonza/Dulcinea issue, the knight's inward grief, Sancho's governorship, and so on—all of them flourishes of *invención* aimed at outwitting expectations of Don Quixote's disillusionment. The resultant oscillations between laughter and *admiratio* sharpen into a species of contradiction, in which parody vies with pathos and the most intricate thought or feeling can slip into the crudest slapstick.

Cervantes's inventiveness thrives on the effects this dialectic engenders, supreme amongst them being the irony of the suffering buffoon whose very lunacies invest him with the virtues of the hero he so much wants to become. The double-edged thrust of Quixote's career remains creative for as long as the action possesses direction and some element of inner logic, but after Merlin's prophecy, the alternation between pathos and parody is overextended, threatening the novel with the stigma of gratuitous cruelty. None the less, it is a sign of Cervantes's sureness of touch that even after he allows himself to be blown off course by his anger over Avellaneda's plagiarism he can still turn his abuse of Quixote's independence to good account. Although the journey to Barcelona is an entirely otiose interpolation, Cervantes eventually cuts his losses, as it were, and impales the pathetic madman upon the crucial contradiction of his comic existence, while Sancho is made to shoulder the blame for the appearance of cruelty. Thus it is that Cervantes's original desire to parody a sub-genre of Arthurian romance should have acquired such moral and even spiritual resonance. For the purely aesthetic, not to say technical, opposition between two types of literary response—laughter and *admiratio*—as it is drawn out by the nugatory wrangles of Quixote and Sancho, gathers about it the attributes of an intensifying conflict whose outcome insinuates itself upon the imagination as a paradigm of some universal experience.

The *Quixote*, therefore, operates on two levels. First, it is a straight satire of a chivalric *historia*, but it unfolds on quite another, autonomous plane where the madman and his squire will pursue their footling destinies through various ingenious complications of character and situation. According to Cervantes, a simple reader will confine himself to the more obvious comic turns in the novel, but the more discerning reader will, he hopes, come to admire the imaginative order that sustains the comedy. Indeed, Cervantes eventually becomes the victim of his own success at producing *admiratio* from Quixote's absurd madness. The countervailing *invención* is so highly developed that it proceeds to outstrip the parodic *raison d'être* of the *historia* until the evolution of Don Quixote's character is blocked by the very fact that he is mad.

The reason for this blockage, quite simply, is that there can be no half-measures about the knight's madness; any incident or experience, however trivial, which were to give him the slightest inkling of his fundamental error in believing that the romances were true would bring him to his senses in a flash. Given the origins of the madness in literary satire, there can be no genuine process of self-questioning or introspective doubt; Don Quixote's character can evolve only within the latitude allowed him by the gap between his unshakable romance logic and his actions. And so, if the demented knight is seen to suffer, the nature of that suffering cannot be explored beyond a certain point.

Don Quixote's madness, then, replaces the supernatural marvels of romance; but it ultimately inhibits the development of character, and therefore precludes the creation of an organic plot that could conceal Cervantes's hand altogether. The book, as a result, hovers between romance and a kind of realism, self-consciously retaining the narrative equivocations of Renaissance comic romance, while reflecting much of the substance of lived experience that characterizes the modern novel.

CONCLUSION

Don Quixote's place in literary history has generally been discussed in terms of its significance for the development of literary realism. There has often been implicit in such discussions the notion that modern narrative fiction, in so far as it seeks to render lived experience, is somehow more convincing than the marvellous heroics of medieval romance. This largely tacit bias in favour of realism among Cervantists has served to obscure the extent to which Arthurian romance was not simply an escapist literature but could represent instead a serious, and sometimes profound, view of the world. Cervantes parodied its late, degenerate manifestations at a time when it had indeed become a stagnant form that could no longer address itself convincingly to the problems of the day.

However, in the twelfth century, French writers like Chrétien de Troyes who set about reworking the Breton stories created a new relationship between the imagination and reality which enabled successive generations to cast experience in alluring and significant forms. The imaginative power of Celtic myth was harnessed by the intellectual structure of Christian Platonism, a combination that allowed Chrétien considerable freedom to deploy his imagination in the interpretation of reality. Creative freedom of this order is largely due to the nature of a writer's authority, and Chrétien's authority is considerable, for he can draw upon compelling resources: his subject-matter still enjoys the prestige of legend, while he assumes for himself a measure of divine inspiration akin to that of an epic narrator. Chrétien's particular authoritativeness, in effect, consists in his presenting himself to his audience as a man with the special insight and skill to interpret a superior past for the improvement of the degenerate present.

Nevertheless, even in Chrétien's own work, the legacy of Celtic myth is not perfectly assimilated to Christian ideology. In thirteenth-century prose romances, there emerges an

ambivalence towards the Arthurian world. Although celebrated still for its chivalry and courtly love, Arthurian romance
is brought increasingly under the compass of a stricter
Christian outlook: military adventure becomes further
spiritualized, sexual love profane, and Lancelot's adultery a sin
that spells disaster for the Kingdom of Logres. This *double esprit*,
as it has been called, reflects the beginnings of a rift between the
enduring mythic potency of the Celtic legends and the doctrinal
authority of the Church. Chrétien had been able to call upon
both equally to bolster his own narrative persuasiveness, but in
later prose romances the two sources of authority are set in
opposition to each other. The supremacy of the Church's truth
over the rival attractions of myth gradually converts Celtic
folk-motifs into vehicles of traditional doctrine. Allegorized
folklore yields in turn to allegorized fantasy through what I
have called the didactic alibi.

In the first instance, the subordination of the narrative
imagination to the external authority of the Church *increases* an
author's freedom. However, it is a freedom that is enjoyed at
the cost of diminishing the value of fiction; it contributes to the
decline in the authority of the imagination, a decline
accelerated by attempts to justify romance by identifying it
with history. A conflict ensues between the illusion of
historicity and those marvels of Arthurian romance inherited
from myth or simply invented by the author. In Montalvo's
revision of *Amadis of Gaul*, and especially in his own sequel
Esplandian, the conflict between historicity and the marvellous
produces a crisis of authority within the text itself as the author
progressively doubts the validity of his inventions and resorts to
a variety of ploys to authenticate his fiction.

The concepts of verisimilitude and narrative unity were
evolved by sixteenth-century neo-Aristotelian theorists in
order to defend literary art from charges of falsehood and
fantasy. Verisimilitude, however, like the late romance illusion
of historicity itself, tended to justify fiction in terms of natural or
historical plausibility. Neo-Classical notions of unity remained
vague because no clear principle of organic necessity had been
successfully formulated. Such difficulties were due to the
'rhetoricizing' of aesthetics under the influence of the Council
of Trent: the inner priorities of the artist's imagination were

given less weight than the effects of art upon the public.

If Renaissance aesthetics further drained fiction of value by regarding it primarily as a medium of moral improvement, the literary imagination in Cervantes's time came under pressure from a new quarter. One can sense it in Cervantes's references to the gulf between the cultivated minority and the general public, in his concern about the popularity of his works, or in his criticism of dramatists like Lope de Vega whom he accused of pandering to the philistine tastes of his audiences with plays that had no regard for serious artistic values.[1] In short, the force of rank commercialism, intensified by the spread of the printing-press, was added to the pressures of didacticism and historicity inherited from the Middle Ages. A writer like Cervantes found himself caught in something of a cleft stick: wishing on the one hand to edify the public, but acutely conscious, on the other, that the public itself cared very little about edification or the rules of art.

The conflicting pulls of aesthetic principle and commercial expediency influence the ambivalent attitudes towards the reader that characterize the prologues to the *Quixote* and the *Exemplary Novels*. Cervantes's comments on aesthetic questions may be couched for the most part in the language of neo-Aristotelian doctrine, but it is in certain untheoretical moments of actual creation that one comes closest to his feelings about the status and possibilities of the art of fiction. In fact, the most disreputable of Cervantes's fictional narrators, Lieutenant Campuzano of the *Deceitful Marriage* and *The Colloquy of the Dogs*, affords us a particularly revealing insight into Cervantes's approach to fictional truth and literary rules.

Having failed to persuade Peralta that the outrageously improbable *Colloquy of the Dogs* is a faithful record of a real experience, Campuzano urges his friend to read it anyway, if only for the pleasure he might derive from finding out what was said by the dogs. The swindler Campuzano thereby releases fictional truth from direct dependency upon experience, let alone verisimilitude or historicity, associating it instead with mere pleasure. Nevertheless, when the Licentiate Peralta finishes reading the *Colloquy*, he encourages Campuzano to write a second. The latter is delighted with this response and agrees, 'without entering into further arguments over whether or no the dogs actually spoke'. Peralta replies: 'Lieutenant, let us not go back to that dispute. I appreciate the artifice of the *Colloquy* and its invention, and that is sufficient. Let us go to the Espolón to refresh the eyes of the body, since I have already refreshed the eyes of the mind.' The Spanish verb used by Peralta is *recrear*, which signifies either to refresh or to re-create. The value of fiction, then, is indistinguishable from its capacity to delight; it consists in seeing things afresh with the mind's eye.

A direct analogy can be drawn between the Campuzano–Peralta relationship and Cervantes's attitude to the reader of the *Quixote*. Just as Peralta forgets his scruples about the authenticity of the talking dogs once he has appreciated the *invención* of the *Colloquy*, so too does Cervantes in the 1605 Prologue urge the reader to go beyond the *historia* and admire the *invención* of the *Quixote*. Peralta's quaint notion of 'refreshing the mind's eye' restores to the creative imagination a measure of intrinsic worth which makes up for the lost authority of the romance author. And so, like the trickster Campuzano, Cervantes refrains from claiming any *a priori* authority over his reader. If anything, he portrays himself as being entirely subject to the reader's judgement: the reader is deemed to be as absolute a master of his opinions as the king is of his taxes. It follows that if the author wishes to earn admiration for his fiction he must in some way win this self-sufficient reader over to his own way of seeing things. As in the case of Campuzano and the sceptical Peralta, the truth of the *Quixote* depends upon the emergence—in and through the reading of the story—of an unsuspected rapport, a bond of friendship, as it were, between Cervantes and the initially king-like reader.

When at the end of his novel Cervantes draws a distinction between his 'genuine' Don Quixote and the plagiarized Quixote of Avellaneda, the touchstone of truth is just such an imaginative bond between author, reader, and fictional creation. In the first place, Cervantes speaks of himself and the protagonist of his novel as having been destined for each other:

For me alone was Don Quixote born and I for him. His was the power of action; mine of writing. Only we two are one, despite that fictitious and Tordillescan scribe [i.e. Avellaneda] who has dared, and may dare again, to pen the deeds of my valorous knight with his coarse and

ill-trimmed ostrich feather. This is no weight for his shoulders, no task
for his frozen intellect.   (II.lxxiv.940)

Moreover, this unique bond between creator and creature has
been confirmed by 'the delight and approval' the knight's
adventures 'have won from all to whose notice they have come,
both here and abroad'.

As Henry James observed, 'art derives a considerable part of
its beneficial exercise from flying in the face of presumptions'.[2]
The bond that unites Cervantes, Don Quixote, and the reader
is the final reward of Cervantes's ironic tactic of flying in the
face of the reader's presumptions. For only after the reader has
had his presumptions—be they about verisimilitude, moral
utility, or pleasure—unsettled in some way, can he enjoy the
're-creation' of the mind's eye wherein fiction finds its truth and
justification.

The *Quixote* is, above all, a satire against the romances of
chivalry. But a major ingredient of the novel is the comic thrust
directed against the reader's own tastes and values. This is part
and parcel of the satirist's task, in so far as his attacking a
popular target must involve poking fun at the prejudices of his
audience, making them laugh at themselves to some extent.
There would be little point otherwise in mocking something
that was already the object of universal derision. Therefore, the
peculiar comic power of the *Quixote* cannot be explained wholly
in terms of its attack upon a literary genre that was
intellectually discredited and had already lost much of its
general appeal; it stems from Cervantes having discovered
more sensitive targets lying within the declared zone of
hostilities.

We have seen that, in spite of the absurdities of the Spanish
books of chivalry, Arthurian romance as such was far from
ridiculous. As Cervantes extends and deepens his satire, he
makes contact with this core of serious ideals and values that is
embodied in Arthurian romance and which forms part of the
legacy of medieval Europe. The fact that it is a lunatic who is
the champion of these ideals creates strange ironic effects: the
ideals themselves are touched by the craziness of the madman,
while the latter's madness is in turn dignified by the nobility of
its ancient influences. Thus, in having made Don Quixote
admirable as well as risible, Cervantes may have 'killed the

king' more effectively than he had anticipated. For the reader's laughter is hollowed out as he senses that Don Quixote and his ridiculous antics may be compromising a whole structure of authority and value that rests, no less than the madman's, upon a belief in the truth of certain books.

The paradoxical, double-edged quality of Don Quixote's folly was already appreciated in the seventeenth century—well before it was solemnized by the Romantics in the nineteenth. Cervantes's novel won the highest praise from Charles de Saint-Évremond (1613-1703), one of the most renowned sceptics and *libertins* of the age, who confessed that of all the books he had ever read *Don Quixote* was the one he would most like to have written: 'I admire how, through the mouth of the greatest fool in the world, Cervantes has found the means of showing himself to be the most knowing and most acute man one could imagine.'[3] Clearly, Saint-Évremond saw that Don Quixote is not simply a stooge who is forever being castigated for his folly, but that he is just as much a vehicle of Cervantes's wit.

Nevertheless, the writers who first used the deluded knight as a model for their own literary satires stressed the negative side of the quixotic madness, using it simply as the butt of their attack. Thus Charles Sorel, wishing to ridicule the pastoral romance in his *Le Berger extravagant* (1627-8), has his hero lose his wits and attempt to live a pastoral idyll in Paris.[4] Marivaux's first novel *Pharsamon*, composed in 1712, parodies the preciosities of the sentimental romances: the hero's head is turned by a beautiful girl, and he conducts his courtship in the high-flown style of the romances until he is cured thanks to the good offices of an older lady who has her own designs on him.[5] By utilizing only the negative side of the madness, these satirists blunted the edge of the Spanish original, failing to capture that pointed ambivalence Saint-Évremond so admired.

The positive side of the Quixote paradox was most fruitfully developed by Henry Fielding. His early play *Don Quixote in England* employs the figure of Quixote as a device to condemn social evils. In the novel *Joseph Andrews* (1742), whose title-page proclaims it to have been 'written in the manner of Cervantes', the Quixote-figure is not an object of ridicule but the bearer of the author's own values. Quixote's madness is replaced by the naive, and therefore endearingly comic, Christian idealism of Parson Adams, which becomes a vehicle of satire against the hypocrisies and affectations of those around him.

This device is elaborated further in *Tom Jones* (1749), where the hero is another innocent who shows up the corruption of society. In this novel, Fielding's triumph was to have related the Quixote-theme to the unfolding of the action: not being mad, Tom can learn from experience, and his life is duly modulated by vicissitudes designed to teach him the consequences of bad behaviour and the benefits of virtue. Fielding was thus able to create the kind of causal interplay between character and incident which forms the basis of plot, and which was denied to Cervantes—except for the relations of Quixote with Sancho—by the unwaning lunacy of his knight errant.

Even so, the aesthetic purpose that informs the plot of *Tom Jones* is close to that of Cervantes in the *Quixote*; it is to create *admiratio* without recourse to the supernatural. After rehearsing the traditional Aristotelian distinctions between probability and possibility, Fielding argues that, unlike historians who can write about anything so long as it is in the public records, novelists ('we who deal in private Character') must keep within the bounds of probability both in the action and in character-drawing.[6] This is a stricter rule than either Aristotle's 'probable impossibility' or Tasso's 'legitimate marvellous', which admitted an element of the supernatural. It is more in line with Cervantes's comments in Part II Chapter xliv on authorial self-effacement and character-autonomy. Moreover, having ruled out the supernatural and the impossible as sources of wonderment, Fielding, like Cervantes, advocates in their stead a tactic of surprise:

Within these few Restrictions [i.e. probability of action and character], I think, every Writer may be permitted to deal as much in the Wonderful as he pleases; nay, if thus he keeps within the Rules of Credibility, the more he can surprise the Reader, the more he will engage his Attention, and the more he will charm him.[7]

The critical difference between *Don Quixote* and *Tom Jones*, however, is that in the former surprise lay mostly in the ambiguous characters of the knight and squire, whereas Fielding, unimpeded by madness, was able to extend it to the entire structure of the action. The plot of *Tom Jones* is, in consequence, fundamentally ironic, not just because the action as a whole turns upon the final discovery of the hero's parentage, but also because in this larger structural irony there is subsumed a host of smaller ironies and reversals of expectation along the way. As a result, the effect upon the reader is unsettling and divisive. In the words of one critic, 'we have a sense of duality not only in the book itself but in our own response to it. . . . Our responses to the book are, we may say, part of the reason for Fielding's laughter, a laughter in which we share. We are, in short, never quite ignorant nor yet entirely omniscient.'[8]

The modern novel could, therefore, be said to owe its fundamental drive to comic satire. The novel's potential for criticism, no less than its ability to lay bare new areas of experience, depending as they do on shaking the reader out of his normal frame of mind, can be traced back to Cervantes's and Fielding's interest in narrative surprise. As both writers were all too aware, it was no longer feasible to disregard empirical probability in fiction; but even while bending to the claims of observable reality, an ironic tactic of 'killing' the king-like presumption of the reader can compensate the novelist for the lost authority of the epic or romance author, restoring to the modern narrative artist the freedom to impress his own imagination upon experience.

A good part of the critical controversy which currently surrounds the *Quixote* is the outcome of the various attempts to explain the complex paradoxical and ironic effects of the novel either by reducing their impact or by accentuating them in an unwarrantedly modern way.

Don Quixote is regarded by some critics as a didactic work, Cervantes's comic intention, beyond the satire on chivalric romance, being the chastisement of Don Quixote's over-reaching pride and folly. Such critics underestimate Don Quixote's sympathetic moral nobility, and, more seriously, overlook Cervantes's very acute understanding of the import of the knight's idealizing madness. There is, after all, as little reason to denounce the mad *hidalgo*'s quest for chivalric glory as there would be to castigate the concern of Chrétien de Troyes's knights for honour and renown. In Don Quixote's case the ends are entirely blameless but the means are clearly insufficient, since they are based on a single intellectual mistake which amounts to madness. Incompetence is not in itself a moral issue; a lack of awareness of one's own incompetence may well be, but Cervantes has pre-empted the possibility of moral judgement on Don Quixote by making him not bad but simply mad. Critics who favour this didactic approach tend to look for signs of Don Quixote's growing sanity or moral responsibility (the two are often identified)—as if the mad knight's virtue must be measured by his readiness to accept the evidence of his senses.

Romantic critics, on the other hand, overlook the fact that Cervantes's mockery of the madman persists right to the end of the novel. They underplay the force of opposition to Don Quixote in order to make his madness respectable. But for all that Don Quixote's madness contains significant vestiges of the Platonic idealism intrinsic to Arthurian romance, it is quite inescapably absurd because based on the crass error of believing that the fictional romances are literally true. Romantic critics aspire to a consistent reading of the novel on the basis of some symbolic scheme in which Don Quixote represents 'idealism' and other characters represent 'realism'. But Don Quixote's behaviour and his relations with Sancho are so full of subtle twists and turns that they preclude coherent symbolization. Indeed, it is this idiosyncrasy which carries the narrative beyond neat symbolic antinomies towards a form of characterization that heralds the modern novel.

There does, nevertheless, exist in the text an objective basis for the reader's identification with the madman, even though Romantic critics have grossly exaggerated it. The irony produced by this identification cannot be straightforwardly universalized into a conflict between two equally tenable points of view. It is generated by the irrefrangible nature of Don Quixote's madness in the teeth of common sense and experience. Only as a consequence of this lunatic imperviousness, in so far as his madness leads the knight actually to suffer, can the reader begin to appreciate the irony of such a radical dislocation of ends and means, feeling and form. From this textually-specific level, it is legitimate to progress towards larger, but necessarily partial, analogies generated by a character who is divided against himself for reasons which lie beyond his insanely limited purview.

The third major critical tendency, the Perspectivist, explains the paradoxes of the *Quixote* by exaggerating them in yet another way. Perspectivist critics relate the ironies created by Don Quixote's madness within his fictional world to the comic play of the unreliable narrators or to the self-referential features of the multi-layered text. All these ironies are then taken together as evidence of Cervantes's moral and even epistemological relativism. However, these two aspects of the novel need to be distinguished. As we have seen, the multiple narrators and self-referential devices are *primarily* Cervantes's parody of the subterfuges employed by Spanish romance authors to validate literary truth in terms of historical veracity. On the other hand, the ironies created by Don Quixote's dealings with other characters have little to do with Perspectivism and everything with leg-pulling, deception, and conflicts of interest between individuals. As for the con-tradiction which emerges between Don Quixote as fool and as a figure of pathos, the Perspectivists actually diminish its poignancy by regarding the madness as little more than one of several points of view in a reality presumed to be as baffling as a hall of mirrors. To suggest that Cervantes may have held such a view about the nature of reality is, I believe, an anachronism.

But even though one might argue that Romantic and Perspectivist interpretations are based on demonstrable distortions of the text, there is little doubt that they testify to the fact that *Don Quixote* touches a chord in the imagination of the modern reader. The novel's capacity to inspire such diverse interpretations is of interest in itself to the literary critic, and I have already put forward some reasons for its enduring appeal. However in the final analysis, one need not have recourse to ideas borrowed from Romanticism, Existentialism, or some form of philosophical relativism to account for the 'modernity' of Cervantes's novel; its effects can be explained in terms of traditional Aristotelian poetics.

Don Quixote, as we have seen, everywhere bears the marks of literary experiment, and it is by a singular stroke of genius that Cervantes created an unprecedented phenomenon: he produced the essential features of a tragic action within an envelope of total lunacy. To start with, Don Quixote's madness accords perfectly with Aristotle's definition of the Ridiculous: 'a mistake or deformity not productive of pain or harm to others'.[9] But as Cervantes prolongs the madness in order to elicit *admiratio*, that mistake of believing literally in the romances *does* begin to cause pain and harm, if not to others, certainly to Quixote himself. The absurd mistake therefore assumes the character of *hamartia*, the tragic error that impels the hero towards his fate.[10] Driven by the fastidious romance logic of his madness, the knight goes to El Toboso to witness the transformation of Aldonza into Dulcinea. It is here that he makes the inevitable discovery—tragic in his terms—that Dulcinea's peerless beauty has been corrupted into a frightful hideousness. Now the crazy chivalric optimism of Part I gives way to deepening misery. When this peripety or reversal of fortune is added to the discovery of Dulcinea's enchantment, and to the suffering that follows, one has the three parts of a complex tragic plot described by Aristotle.[11] But although the persistence of Don Quixote's madness—a truly undeserved misfortune as it turns out—may elicit pity in the classic way, it is a pity which, given the satiric origins of the chivalric mania, cannot cut loose from mockery and farce, and so prevents the kind of identification with the hero which could arouse fear.[12]

The intrinsically absurd but none the less absolute character of the madness blocks the release of the full tragic emotions; catharsis becomes impossible because Quixote's knot of fate cannot plausibly be unravelled on its own terms. To have the lunatic commit a genuine tragic deed such as murder would immediately wreck the delicate interplay between chivalric ideals and common sense which forms the basis of the entire narrative. Whatever fear might be caused by such a tragic action would, in any case, be felt at the expense of pity, for Don Quixote's madness would then appear to be not just unsympathetic but also arbitrary and dangerous, and therefore downright ugly.

Lacking any possibility of a proper denouement, Don Quixote can expect only deliverance, which duly comes in an inevitably abrupt and miraculous form; without this sudden cure his madness could have endured indefinitely. For this very reason, the quixotic blend of the tragic and the ridiculous precipitates in the long run a species of unappeasable terror. In spite of his countless vicissitudes, there is a dreadful immobility about Don Quixote's fate; beyond laughter, and farce, and the brilliant flourishes of wit, the general comic atmosphere of the book finally crystallizes into a timeless, tragic moment, in which a man is caught forever, condemned to make a fool of himself with no hope even of knowing why.

The knight's stubborn, helpless blindness—too unyielding to be merely comic and yet far too banal to be properly tragic—gives Don Quixote that ambivalence which has proved so fascinating to the modern imagination. Moreover, if this is true of the protagonist, it may also explain the attraction of the work as a whole. For in the long, complex transformation of medieval romance into the novel, *Don Quixote* stands as a readily accessible half-way house, from where the modern reader can contemplate the heroic age that has been left behind, while savouring the expectancy of what he has since come to know.

NOTES

PREFACE

1. Unless otherwise stated, all quotations from *Don Quixote* in subsequent chapters are taken from the English translation by J. M. Cohen (Penguin, Harmondsworth, 1950. Copyright © J. M. Cohen, 1950. Reprinted by permission of Penguin Books Ltd). Chapter- and page-references to this edition are given in the text. Quotations from the Spanish are taken from *Don Quijote de la Mancha*, ed. Martín de Riquer (Juventud, Barcelona, 1968).

2. See A. D. Deyermond, 'The Lost Genre of Medieval Spanish Literature', *HR* xliii (1975), 231-59.

3. 'The Art of Fiction' in *The House of Fiction: Essays on the Novel by Henry James*, ed. Leon Edel (London, 1957), p. 29.

4. Ibid., p. 35.

CHAPTER ONE

1 See W. P. Ker, *Epic and Romance* (London, 1931), pp. 349-50, and John Stevens, *Medieval Romance* (London, 1973), p. 15.

2 Jean Frappier, *Chrétien de Troyes: L'Homme et l'œuvre* (Paris, 1957), p. 12.

3 Huizinga, *The Waning of the Middle Ages*, trans. F. Hopman (Penguin, Harmondsworth, 1955), p. 66.

4 Marc Bloch, *Feudal Society*, trans. L. A. Manyon (London, 1962), p. 83.

5 See M.-D. Chenu, O.P., *Nature, Man and Society in the Twelfth Century*, ed. and trans. J. Taylor and L. K. Little (Chicago, 1968), pp. 23-5.

6 Ibid., pp. 34-7 and 46-8.

7 Ibid., pp. 62-3.

8 Foucault, *The Order of Things* (London, 1970; paperback, 1974), p. 17.

9 Example used by Foucault, p. 27.

10 See Chenu, op. cit., p. 116.

11 See Jean Pépin, *Dante et la tradition de l'allégorie* (Montreal, 1970), pp. 45-51, and A. C. Charity, *Events and Their After-Life* (Cambridge, 1966), pp. 1-9.

12 See Chenu, op. cit., pp. 139-40.

13 Sidney Painter, *French Chivalry* (Ithaca, New York, 1957; Cornell Paperbacks, 1964), pp. 28-37.

14 Ibid., pp. 113-14.

15 See Winthrop Wetherbee, *Platonism and Poetry in the Twelfth Century: The Literary Influence of the School of Chartres* (Princeton, NJ, 1972), pp. 224-5.

16 Frappier, *Chrétien de Troyes*, pp. 23-61.

17 Ker, p. 349.

18 Quotations from the works of Chrétien refer to the English translation by W. W. Comfort, *Arthurian Romances* (London, New York, 1941, 1975). Comfort does not include a translation of *Perceval*. Line-references relate to the Old French texts edited from the Guiot Copy and published in the series *Les Classiques Français du Moyen Age* under the direction of Mario Roques (Paris, 1952, 1957, 1958, 1960, 1972-3).

19 These page-references are to the modern French translation of *Perceval* by Jean Pierre Foucher and André Ortais (Paris, 1974). Line-references to the *Classiques Français* edition of the *Conte du Graal* by Félix Lecoy (Paris, 1972-3).

20 Norris J. Lacy, *The Craft of Chrétien de Troyes: An Essay on Narrative Art* (Leiden, 1980), pp. 23-7, notes the fact that 'the play on perception, understanding, and illusion is a primary source of drama in Chrétien's romances' but adds that it has 'occasioned brief commentary' and that 'its precise function . . . has not been adequately defined'. He does not himself enlarge upon this theme nor does he relate it to contemporary interest in Platonism.

21 David J. Shirt, '*Cligés*—A Twelfth-Century Matrimonial

Case-Book?', *FMLS* xviii (1982), 75-89, argues that Chrétien was defending the Church's teaching on consent in marriage. Alis's treachery, amongst other things, puts him in breach of canon law whereas Fenice's secret love for and eventual marriage to Cligés is not adulterous but signifies a true and legitimate relationship.

22 The translation is from L. T. Topsfield, *Chrétien de Troyes: A Study of the Arthurian Romances* (Cambridge, 1981), pp. 76-7.

23 Topsfield, pp. 77-8, believes that the repetition of 'nothing' indicates Chrétien's satirizing of a contemporary philosophical preoccupation with the 'reality' of nothingness which some twelfth-century troubadours had adopted in order to celebrate the delights of fantasizing about their ladies: 'Jaufre Rudel, about 1147, had found "wondrous joy" in the dream illusion of possessing his lady.'

24 See Lucienne Carasso-Bulow, *The Merveilleux in Chrétien de Troyes' Romances* (Geneva, 1976), pp. 35-6.

25 Fourquet, 'Le Rapport entre l'œuvre et la source chez Chrétien de Troyes et le problème des sources bretonnes', *RPh* ix (1955-6), 298-312. See also Carasso-Bulow, op. cit., pp. 126-7.

26 Lacy, *The Craft of Chrétien*, p. 4, notes that *Yvain*, *Lancelot*, and *Perceval* 'all provide illustrations of the deleterious effects of a slavish adherence to a learned code of chivalry, when that code and the values attached to it are taken as an end, as their own justification'.

27 John Stevens, *Medieval Romance*, pp. 100-1, divides the marvellous into three categories: the 'mysterious', i.e. unmotivated occurrences; the 'magical', i.e. the marvellous controlled by man such as magic rings and ointments; and the 'miraculous', i.e. the marvellous controlled by God. He does not, however, make a distinction between those marvels emanating from a good source and those from an evil one.

28 See W. A. Nitze, '"*Sans* et *matière* " dans Chrétien de Troyes', *Romania*, xliv (1915-17), 14-36; Faith Lyons, '*Entencion* in Chrétien's *Lancelot*', *SP* li (1954), 425-30; Jean Frappier, *Chrétien de Troyes*, p. 62.

29 Recent studies of irony stress its negative qualities. Wayne Booth, *A Rhetoric of Irony* (Chicago, 1974), p. 240, talks about

the 'negation that begins all the ironic play: "this affirmation must be rejected", leaving the possibility . . . that since the universe . . . is inherently absurd, all statements are subject to ironic undermining'. D. C. Muecke, *The Compass of Irony* (London, 1969), p. 122, observes that the contradictions revealed by irony 'have forced men into a realization of their essential and terrifying loneliness in relation to others or to the universe at large'. In the medieval world, however, irony can be positive because human expectations may be contradicted by Providence. Chrétien is expert in this kind of irony.

30 The grateful lion is generally considered to have been modelled on the old motif of Androcles and his lion, but modified here by the introduction of the serpent; cf. Frappier, *Étude sur Yvain ou le Chevalier au Lion de Chrétien de Troyes* (Paris, 1969), pp. 108-9. W. W. Ryding, 'Narrative Structure, Free Association, and Chrétien's Lion', *Symposium*, xxiii (1969), 160-3, believes the serpent to be derived from Petrus Alfonsus' *Disciplina Clericalis* which was translated into French at about the time Chrétien must have been working on *Yvain*. The serpent is also clearly a symbol of evil in the Christian tradition.

31 Harris, 'The Rôle of the Lion in Chrétien de Troyes' *Yvain*', *PMLA* lxiv (1949), 1143-63; Haidu, *Lion-Queue-Coupée: l'écart symbolique chez Chrétien de Troyes* (Geneva, 1972), pp. 71-82.

32 Other symbolic functions have been ascribed to the lion. D. M. Murtaugh, '*Oïr et entandre*: Figuralism and Narrative Structure in Chrétien's *Yvain*', *RR* lxiv (1973), 161-74, sees it as a figure of Yvain's unfulfilled nobility; Norris J. Lacy, 'Yvain's Evolution and the Rôle of the Lion', *RN* xii (1970), 198-202, as symbolizing spiritual chivalry—superior to the worldly chivalry of Gauvain—towards which Yvain must evolve. Without excluding either of these views, I see the lion as a more contextually productive symbol, even while representing both Providence and the spiritual potentiality of Yvain's experience. Robert Guiette has argued against rigidity in the interpretation of Chrétien's symbols in two excellent essays:'Symbolisme et sénéfiance au Moyen Âge' and 'Lecteur de roman, lecteur de symbole', collected in 'Questions de Littérature', *Romanica Gandensia*, viii (Ghent, 1960), pp. 33-51, and pp. 51-60, respectively.

33 C. R. B. Combellack, 'Yvain's Guilt', *SP* lxviii (1971),

10-25, argues against Alfred Adler, 'Sovereignty in Chrétien's *Yvain*', *PMLA* xlii (1947), 281-305, and Julian Harris, op. cit., that there is no sin of pride attached to Yvain's decision to part from Laudine to seek adventures; he was simply doing his chivalric duty and is praised for it by Arthur and Gauvain. Combellack, however, minimizes the significance of Yvain's failure to return to Laudine within the year. The extremity of Yvain's reaction to Laudine's rejection suggests that his broken promise was a very grave and disabling infringement of the chivalric code.

34 Frappier, *Étude*, p. 69, n. 1, claims that Chrétien was the inventor of the love-madness theme in Arthurian romance, and of the figure of the hermit who gives succour to the knight. Neither exists in the Welsh 'mabinogi' of *Owein*.

35 Zaddy, 'The Structure of Chrétien's *"Yvain"*', *MLR* lxv (1970), 523-40 (pp. 538-9).

36 Frappier, *Étude*, pp. 153-4, explains Laudine's behaviour exclusively in psychological terms, seeing her as proud, impetuous, and temperamental. But surely she is doing no more than observing the chivalric code to the letter. After all, her fidelity to the laws of chivalry is precisely what enabled her to overcome psychology and marry Yvain in the first place, even after he had killed her husband Esclados. When her maidservant Lunete undertook to 'prove' to her 'that he who defeated your lord is better than he was himself', she did so by pointing to the verdict of armed combat, which in terms of courtly chivalry reveals the true qualities of a knight (see the Comfort translation, pp. 202-5, and n. 42 below).

37 The fact that the romance has *two* objectives—Yvain's regaining of glory as much as his restoration to favour with Laudine—explains why some major adventures like the Pesme Avanture or the climactic duel with Gauvain remain unknown to Laudine. Critics like Zaddy and Combellack, while rightly criticizing the 'expiation of guilt' school of thought, still interpret the romance as a love-story, and regard reunion with Laudine as Yvain's supreme goal. Thus they are hard put to it to explain the relevance of any adventure that is not obviously connected with the love-theme, nor can they account for the structural significance of Yvain's amnesia. Those adventures that are unknown to Laudine concern Yvain exclusively; they

refer symbolically to the separate though related issue of his chivalric honour.

38 See Frappier, *Étude*, pp. 63-4. *Entrelacement* is not to be found in the *chansons de geste*, in Wace, or in the Matter of Rome. It would appear to spring from the subject-matter of Chrétien's romances—the abiding concern to represent dualities of love and glory, folly and good sense, and the final achievement of an equilibrium between them.

39 Reto R. Bezzola, *Le Sens de l'aventure et de l'amour (Chrétien de Troyes)* (Paris, 1947), p. 47, refers to the symbolic value of the hero's incognito in *Perceval* and *Lancelot*. Similarly, Yvain's surrogate identity here can be seen to symbolize the incompleteness of his identity before his achievement of glory and his reunion with Laudine. Frappier, *Étude*, p. 64, claims that this device of incognito or surrogate identity is original to Chrétien. It will become a recurrent feature of Arthurian romance (viz. Amadis of Gaul's surrogate name Beltenebros, assumed after his despair in the wilderness when repudiated by Oriana).

40 E. Peter Nolan, 'Mythopoetic Evolution: Chrétien de Troyes' *Erec et Enide*, *Cligès* and *Yvain*', *Symposium*, xxv (1971), 139-61, (p. 155). Topsfield, p. 205, finds the ending 'unconvincing' and wonders whether Chrétien 'did not see in this conclusion the patching together of a story which on its higher level of meaning had transcended its narrative framework'.

41 Frappier, *Étude*, p. 157, n. 1.

42 According to R. Howard Bloch, *Medieval French Literature and Law* (Berkeley and Los Angeles, 1977), p. 18, 'the judicial duel belongs to the series of ordeals common to any primitive sense of justice in which legal process remains indistinguishable from divine process, human will from godly will, positive law from divine law'. Analogously, Yvain's victory in combat represents the objective will of God which, as in his earlier victory over Laudine's first husband Esclados, must override the individualistic psychological impulses of Laudine (see also n. 36 above).

43 See Northrop Frye, *The Secular Scripture* (Cambridge, Mass., and London, 1976), p. 107: 'There is often a god behind the

action of a romance who expresses his will by some kind of oracle or prophecy. . . . A god of this type is clearly a projection of the author himself, and as such, he is placed outside the action.'

44 See Frye, ibid., p. 54.

45 Auerbach, *Mimesis*, trans. W. R. Trask (Princeton, NJ, 1953), p. 140.

46 Gillian Beer, *The Romance* (London, 1970), p. 3.

47 Frye, op. cit., p. 49, identifies four levels in romance: the heavenly, the Edenic, the everyday, and the demonic. Nevertheless, the fundamental distinction is surely between the everyday and the supernatural.

48 For the origin of the Celtic Other World and its relationship with the human world, see Topsfield, pp. 15-16.

49 See Auerbach, p. 134: 'The values [of courtly chivalry] . . . are all directed toward a personal and absolute ideal—absolute both in reference to ideal realization and in reference to the absence of any earthly and practical purpose.'

50 For a review of the question of the dating of Chrétien's romances, see Frappier, *Chrétien de Troyes*, p. 12, and *Étude*, pp. 11-17.

51 Topsfield, p. 165, constantly stresses the analogy between temporal and spiritual chivalry in Chrétien but remarks of Lancelot that the source of his virtue and courage cannot lie in religious faith but in courtly love or *Fin' Amors*. He refers to this romance's 'auras of Celtic and Christian meaning' but refrains from integrating them (pp. 173-4). It seems clear that Chrétien's *Lancelot* presents a *prima facie* contradiction between *caritas* and *Fin' Amors* which is a stumbling-block for any attempt to establish a continuum between the two forms of love.

52 Frappier, *Étude*, p. 17.

53 See David J. Shirt, ' "Le Chevalier de la Charrette": A World Upside-Down?', *MLR* lxxvi (1981), 811-22.

54 Topsfield, p. 174, suggests that Chrétien realized with *Lancelot* that 'the problems of profane love are not to be cured in the context of worldly values. There is no impregnable wholeness of the spirit, no lasting peace of mind, no absolutely pure and complete love to be found in the world of Lancelot and

Guinevere'. These observations reinforce the view that the Platonism inherent in *Fin' Amors* cannot finally be accommodated within an orthodox Christian notion of *caritas*. As Topsfield says, 'the problems which persist in *Lancelot* can be resolved only in the symbol of the Grail'.

CHAPTER TWO

1 Vinaver, *The Rise of Romance* (Oxford, 1971), p. 103.

2 See Fanni Bogdanow, *The Romance of the Grail* (Manchester, 1966), pp. 2-8.

3 See Bogdanow, op. cit., pp. 197-200.

4 See Jean Frappier, 'The Vulgate Cycle' in *Arthurian Literature in the Middle Ages*, ed. R. S. Loomis (Oxford, 1959), p. 304.

5 Ibid., p. 311.

6 Bogdanow, p. 215.

7 See Eugène Vinaver, 'A la recherche d'une poétique médiévale', *Cahiers de civilisation médiévale, Université de Poitiers*, ii (1959), 1-16, and *The Rise of Romance*, pp. 53-67.

8 *Entrelacement* was first identified by Ferdinand Lot in his *Étude sur le Lancelot en Prose* (Paris 1918, 1954), pp. 17-28.

9 R. S. Loomis, *The Development of Arthurian Romance* (New York, 1970), p. 95. For an account of how *entrelacement* advances the moral significance of the action see Rosemond Tuve, *Allegorical Imagery: Some Medieval Books and their Posterity* (Princeton, NJ, 1966), p.364.

10 Guiette, 'Symbolisme et sénéfiance', p. 48.

11 According to Chenu, p. 144, symbolism starts from experience, constituting it in images or metaphors 'which mediate mystery to us', whereas allegory 'starts with critical analysis and from it derives abstract thoughts which it ultimately employs in a didactic presentation. In the final stage, explanation submerges signification'. The same point is made by Bezzola, *Le Sens de l'aventure et de l'amour*, p. 8, and Huizinga, p. 197.

12 In the *Queste* the marvellous or mysterious adventures

undergone by the knights possess an allegorical meaning which is subsequently explained to them by a monk or a fairy-like maiden. See, for example, *The Quest of the Holy Grail*, trans. P. M. Matarasso (Penguin, Harmondsworth, 1969), pp. 58-60, 63-5, 195-9, 218-20.

13 *The Quest of the Holy Grail*, p. 284.

14 For an interesting discussion of the problem of interpreting history in terms of allegory, see Gabriel Josipovici, *The World and the Book* (London, 1971), pp. 136-44.

15 See Walter J. Ong, S.J., 'A Dialectic of Aural and Objective Correlatives' in *The Barbarian Within* (New York, 1962), pp. 26-40 (p. 28).

16 *The Death of King Arthur*, trans. James Cable (Penguin, Harmondsworth, 1971) p. 235.

17 See María Rosa Lida de Malkiel, 'Arthurian Literature in Spain and Portugal' in Loomis, *Arthurian Literature*, pp. 406-18.

18 See Lida de Malkiel, op. cit., p. 406, and Harvey L. Sharrer, *A Critical Bibliography of Hispanic Arthurian Material I* (London, 1977).

19 See Grace S. Williams, 'The *Amadís* Question', *RHisp* xxi (1909), 1-167 (pp. 39-146); E. B. Place, 'Fictional Evolution: The Old French Romances and the Primitive "Amadís" Reworked by Montalvo', *PMLA* lxxi (1956), 521-9.

20 Bohigas Balaguer, 'La novela caballeresca, sentimental y de aventuras', *Historia general de las literaturas hispánicas*, ii (Barcelona, 1951), p. 222.

21 Michels, 'Deux traces du *Chevalier de la Charrette* observées dans l'*Amadís de Gaula*', *BHisp* xxxvii (1935), 478-80 (p. 478).

22 See Sir Henry Thomas, *Spanish and Portuguese Romances of Chivalry* (Cambridge, 1920), pp. 41-63; E. B. Place, '¿Montalvo, autor o refundidor del *Amadís* IV y V?' in *Homenaje a A. Rodríguez-Moñino*, ii (Madrid, 1966) 77-80; A. Rodríguez-Moñino, 'El primer manuscrito del *Amadís de Gaula*', *BRAE* xxxvi (1956), 199-216; M. R. Lida de Malkiel, 'El desenlace del *Amadís* primitivo', *RPh* vi (1953), 283-9.

23 See Samuel Gili Gaya 'Las sergas de Esplandián como crítica de la caballería bretona', *BBMP* xxiii (1947), 103-11, and José Amezcua, 'La oposición de Montalvo al mundo del *Amadís de Gaula*', *NRFH* xxi (1968), 320-37.

24 Thomas, p. 46.

25 Williams, 'The *Amadís* Question', p. 127; A. Durán, *Estructura y técnicas de la novela sentimental y caballeresca* (Madrid, 1973), pp. 133-4.

26 Menéndez y Pelayo, *Orígenes de la novela*, i (Madrid, 1962), p. 357.

27 All quotations from *Amadis of Gaul* are taken from the English translation by Edwin B. Place and Herbert C. Behm (University Press of Kentucky, Lexington, 1974).

28 Frida Weber de Kurlat, 'Estructura novelesca del *Amadís de Gaula*', *Revista de literaturas modernas*, v (1967), 29-54, shows that Montalvo's organization of the narrative is 'external' and 'explicit', creating a 'quantitative crescendo' (pp. 51-3).

29 Pierce, *Amadís de Gaula*, Twayne World Authors Series (Boston, 1976), pp. 46-56.

30 Weber de Kurlat, pp. 44-7.

31 Pierce, pp. 56-72.

32 Ibid., p. 56.

33 See the Place and Behm translation, pp. 17-20.

34 This subterfuge is very ancient. William Nelson, *Fact or Fiction: The Dilemma of the Renaissance Storyteller* (Cambridge, Mass., 1973), pp. 17-19, gives examples from Antiquity and from third-century Christian apocryphal texts.

35 For discussion of the directness of the narrator of epic, see Erich Auerbach, *Mimesis*, pp. 3-23, and Marthe Robert, *L'Ancien et le nouveau* (Paris, 1963), p. 98. This directness excludes the possibility of irony in the narration of the story according to Robert Scholes and Robert Kellogg, *The Nature of Narrative* (New York, 1966), p. 55.

36 See Place, 'Fictional Evolution', p. 528.

37 My colleague Roger Walker has pointed out to me that there is only one previous instance of this device in Spanish romance. It occurs in the Epilogue to *Oliveros de Castilla* published in 1499. This was a translation of the French *Le Livre d'Olivier de Castille et d'Artus Dalgarbe* published in 1482. There is no Epilogue, however, in the French original.

38 See Pierce, p. 54.

39 Translations of the *Sergas de Esplandián* are my own from the

edition by Pascual de Gayangos, *BAE* xl (Madrid, 1857), pp. 403-561.

40 Scholes and Kellogg, p. 244, observe that 'we do not find in Greek romance the author–narrator claiming to have been an eyewitness to or participant in the events he is narrating, and founding his authority on his own testimony'.

41 See p. 54 above.

42 F. G. Olmedo, S. J., *El Amadís y el Quijote* (Madrid, 1947), p. 26, sees the whole passage as Montalvo's joke on readers who took chivalric fictions seriously, and Lida de Malkiel, 'Dos huellas del *Esplandián* en el *Quijote* y el *Persiles*', *RPh* ix (1955), 156-62 (pp. 157-8) regards it as evincing the author's humorous attitude towards his characters. However, neither critic attempts to situate Chapters 98 and 99 in the process of Montalvo's revision of the *Amadis* and, as a result, they fail to explain why Montalvo's 'humour' should suddenly appear only towards the end of the *Esplandian*.

43 See Lida de Malkiel, 'El desenlace del *Amadís* primitivo'.

44 Lida de Malkiel, 'Dos huellas del *Esplandián*', p. 157, considers these chapters to be an anticipation of *Don Quixote* inasmuch as Montalvo seems to manipulate different planes of fiction and reality. She looks at these chapters in retrospect, as it were, from the heights of *Don Quixote*, but from the perspective of medieval romance itself they appear to be more like a last resort in the process of textual authentication rather than evidence of comic irony.

45 A measure of the contemporary popularity of the *Esplandian* can be had from the fact that the present Golden State of the USA was named California by Cortés after the island in Montalvo's romance. The fictitious California was situated 'on the right hand of the Indies and very near to the Earthly Paradise'. It was inhabited by a warrior race of women who killed all men except the few needed for the procreation of females. See Thomas, op. cit., p. 82.

46 For further discussion of this conflict see William Nelson, op. cit., pp. 38-55; Scholes and Kellogg, op. cit., pp. 250-3.

47 *Amadis of Gaul* became famous throughout Europe as much as a guide to courtly manners as for its literary qualities. See

E. B. Place, 'El *Amadís* de Montalvo como manual de cortesanía en Francia', *RFE* xxxviii (1954), 151-69.

48 See Thomas for an extensive account of the development of the Spanish romances and their dissemination in Europe.

49 Thomas, pp. 68-75, shows how the authors of these works styled themselves 'proof-correctors' or 'translators', and even when they wished to criticize a rival they would still keep up this pose, as if they dared not dispel the illusion that the wise magician was the real author of the 'history'.

50 See Martín de Riquer, 'Cervantes y la caballeresca' in *Suma cervantina*, edd. J. B. Avalle-Arce and E. C. Riley (London, 1973), pp. 273-92; E. Glaser, 'Nuevos datos sobre la crítica de los libros de caballerías en los siglos XVI y XVII', *Anuario de estudios medievales*, iii (Barcelona, 1966), 393-410; Menéndez y Pelayo, op. cit., i, 440-7.

CHAPTER THREE

1 See C. P. Brand, *Ariosto* (Edinburgh, 1974), pp. 46-56.

2 Brand, op. cit., p. 48, points out that the oral tradition of the romances was still strong in Renaissance Italy.

3 Quotations in English are from *Orlando Furioso*, trans. Guido Waldman (Oxford, 1974).

4 See Robert Durling, *The Figure of the Poet in Renaissance Epic* (Cambridge, Mass., 1965), pp. 175-6.

5 Weinberg, *A History of Literary Criticism in the Italian Renaissance* (Chicago, London, 1961), ii, pp. 797-813. Horace was also an authority, but neo-Aristotelians found parallels with Aristotle and 'transferred the Horatian precepts to the Aristotelian text' (Weinberg, p. 807).

6 See *Aristotle on the Art of Poetry*, trans. Ingram Bywater (Oxford, 1920), p. 37: 'Tragedy is essentially an imitation not of persons but of action and life, of happiness and misery. All human happiness or misery takes the form of action; the end for which we live is a certain kind of activity, not a quality.'

7 As E. C. Riley, *Cervantes's Theory of the Novel* (Oxford, 1962), p. 198, has observed, the problem of idealization was 'really

more crucial to the novel than that posed by fantasy. This problem springs from the potential discrepancy between the ideal and the possible—a discrepancy that was simply disregarded in the concept of verisimilitude inherited from Antiquity'.

8 See Weinberg, ii, pp. 803-4.

9 See Weinberg, ii, p. 804, and William Nelson, pp. 60-2.

10 Weinberg, ii, pp. 805-6, describes the 'rhetoricizing of poetic doctrine'.

11 Durling, p. 9.

12 See C. P. Brand, *Torquato Tasso* (Cambridge, 1965), pp. 60-3.

13 See Weinberg's account of this long-running theoretical dispute, ii, pp. 954-1073. See also Brand, *Ariosto*, p. 185.

14 Torquato Tasso, *Prose*, ed. E. Mazzali (Milan, 1959), p. 573. Quoted in English by Brand, *Tasso*, p.62.

15 Tasso's theories have been explained and thoroughly discussed by Cervantes scholars; see Riley, *Cervantes's Theory*, *passim*, and Alban K. Forcione, *Cervantes, Aristotle and the 'Persiles'* (Princeton, NJ, 1970), pp. 27-48.

16 See E. C. Riley, 'Aspectos del concepto de *Admiratio* en la teoría literaria del Siglo de Oro', *Homenaje a Dámaso Alonso*, iii (Madrid, 1963), pp. 173-82.

17 See Brand, *Ariosto*, pp. 189-90.

18 See Riley, *Cervantes's Theory*, pp. 3-5.

19 See refs. in n. 15 above.

20 Spitzer, 'On the Significance of *Don Quijote*' in *Cervantes: A Collection of Critical Essays*, ed. Lowry Nelson, Jr. (Englewood Cliffs, NJ, 1969), pp. 82-97 (p. 95).

21 From the nineteenth century to our day Cervantes critics were inclined to the view that Cervantes's work developed from 'idealism' to 'realism' largely on the supposition that, the *Quixote* being his most influential achievement, it must also represent the ultimate stage of his artistic evolution. The trouble with this view was that it was hard put to it to explain the significance of the highly idealistic *Persiles* which came out after Cervantes's death; see Mack Singleton, 'The *Persiles* Mystery' in *Cervantes Across the Centuries*, edd. A. Flores and M.

J. Benardete (New York, 1947). Ruth El Saffar, *Novel to Romance* (Baltimore and London, 1974), has reversed the old view and argues that the development is from 'realism' to 'idealism'. But in doing so, she has to make a qualitative distinction between *Quixote* Part I ('realistic') and Part II ('idealistic') (pp. 3-13). The problem is of the Cervantists' own making, arising from a preoccupation with the notion of an author's 'development'. For a review of the traditional arguments see El Saffar, op. cit., pp. 169-77.

22   See Alban K. Forcione, *Cervantes' Christian Romance: A Study of 'Persiles y Sigismunda'* (Princeton, NJ, 1972).

23   The literary experimentation of the *Persiles* is further accentuated when we consider that Cervantes himself in the Dedication of the *Exemplary Novels* (1613) boasted that it 'dared to compete with Heliodorus'. Heliodorus' *Ethiopic History* had been rediscovered at about the same time as Aristotle's *Poetics*; it was translated into Spanish in 1587, and was particularly favoured in the first decades of the seventeenth century as a model of the epic in prose. In writing the *Persiles* Cervantes was, once again, attempting to innovate.

24   See Robert J. Clements and Joseph Gibaldi, *Anatomy of the Novella: The European Tale Collection from Boccaccio and Chaucer to Cervantes* (New York, 1977).

25   For two excellent discussions of these twinned tales, see L. J. Woodward, 'El casamiento engañoso y el coloquio de los perros', *BHS* xxxvi (1959), 80-7; and Ruth El Saffar, *'El casamiento engañoso' and 'El coloquio de los perros'*, Critical Guides to Spanish Texts, 17 (London, 1976).

26   D. C. Muecke, *Irony* (London, 1970), pp. 14-15, defines *eironeia*, as first recorded by Plato in the *Republic*, as 'a smooth, low-down way of taking people in'. For Theophrastus an *eiron* was 'evasive and non-committal, concealing his enmities, pretending friendship, misrepresenting his acts, never giving a straight answer'.

27   My translation.

28   Eleanor S. O'Kane, *Refranes y frases proverbiales españoles de la Edad Media*, Anejo II, *BRAE* (Madrid, 1959), gives two examples of this proverb: 'So mi manto al rey mato' from *Seniloquium*, 441 (1450-1500), Biblioteca Nacional, MS 19.343;

'Debajo de mi manto al rey mato' from A. Galante, 'Proverbes judéo-espagnoles', *RHisp* ix (1902). A. A. Parker, *The Humour of Spanish Proverbs*, Diamante Series, xiii (London, 1963), p. 16, gives the following meanings: 'the assertion of independence', 'the refusal to cringe', 'every man is his own master'.

29 Cervantes nowhere uses the word *ironía* in the *Quixote* to describe an attitude that, I will argue, pervades the entire novel. Muecke, *Irony*, pp. 15-17, notes that 'the word "irony" does not appear in English until 1502 and did not come into general use until the early eighteenth century'. This may well have been the case in Spain; I know of no study of the history of the word irony in the Spanish language. The absence of a term for the literary attitude we now call 'ironical' might explain why Cervantes's declaration of ironic intent is expressed in the form of a proverb which vividly captures the basic relations intrinsic to all irony.

30 For a similar interpretation of this passage, see Américo Castro, 'Los prólogos al Quijote' in *Hacia Cervantes*, 3rd rev. edn. (Madrid, 1967), pp. 270-1.

31 Forcione, *Cervantes, Aristotle and the 'Persiles'*, p. 46, points out that the neo-Aristotelians' 'interpretation of mimesis could not overcome a realist or naturalist tendency and an orientation toward external or objective truth rather than a more abstract truth. The result was that Renaissance mimetic theories succumbed to one of the "troublesome implications of the mirror", its function as a literal reflector'.

32 In the original Spanish the contrast is clearer: 'Procurad también que, leyendo vuestra historia, el melancólico se mueva a risa, el risueño la acreciente, el simple no se enfade, el discreto *se admire* de *la invención*, el grave no *la* desprecie, ni el prudente deje de alabar*la*.' The two object pronouns I have emphasized refer to 'la invención' rather than to 'la historia', and so the sentence divides into two classes of reader: one whose reaction will be 'risa', and another who should respond with varying degrees of *admiratio*, as my emphasis shows. *Admiratio* and laughter are again referred to by Cervantes in Part II, xliv, p. 748, this time as alternatives. This alternation has received little attention, although, as I will argue in Chapter 5, it is a decisive factor in the novel.

33 *Discreción* involved intelligence but referred more particu-

larly to powers of discernment, discrimination, and perspicacity. Cervantes's repeated allusion to two classes of reader is evidence of his fascination with the problem that also exercised Tasso of making art acceptable to the *vulgo* as well as to *discretos*. It is interesting to compare these allusions in the Prologue with the Canon of Toledo's Tasso-like exasperation with the obtuse vulgarity of the public in I.xlvii; see p. 78 above. The Canon's views have been taken by most scholars, except Forcione, *Cervantes, Aristotle and the 'Persiles'*, pp. 91-130, to be a reliable expression of Cervantes's own opinions, but the Prologue, which was most likely written *after* the Canon's speech, presents the *Quixote* itself as a work capable of bridging the gap between high and low art.

34 See Roger Scruton, *Art and Imagination* (London, 1974), pp. 205-6: 'In understanding a piece of literature as a representation we may suspend our judgement of its literal truth; we appreciate it not as a means of conveying information, but rather as a vehicle of thought in whatever form.' He likens literature to painting in which representation is 'partly dependent upon the author's intentions'. Richard Wollheim, *Art and its Objects* (Penguin, Harmondsworth, 1970), pp. 117-18, distinguishes between appreciation of beauty in ordinary reality and in art, for in the latter one is constrained by the authority of 'the artist who has made or moulded the work of art according to his own inner demands. It is the imprint of these demands upon the work that we must respect, if we are to retain the aesthetic attitude.'

35 After demonstrating Cervantes's misgivings about neo-Aristotelian theory, Forcione, *Cervantes, Aristotle and the 'Persiles'*, pp. 343-5, pictures him as being in two minds about aesthetic issues: 'reason–emotion, edification–pleasure, *culto–vulgo*, the verisimilar–the marvellous, unity–variety, Tasso–Ariosto' (p. 343). This ambivalence is seen as reflecting 'the birth-struggle of the modern novel, a drama of disengagement as the new literary form breaks free from the strictures which ages had created' (p. 344). I believe the birth was smoother and more fun for Cervantes once he hit on a narrative formula which allowed him to outwit his readers. Forcione's position leads back to the Perspectivism of Ortega y Gasset and Leo Spitzer: 'What is true? What is false? Cervantes' works are

full of characters who are preoccupied with truth' (p. 340; see also n. 47 below).

36 Modern critics of a Perspectivist inclination sometimes write as if Cervantes himself had been seriously tied up in this contradiction. Thus, many narrative jokes have been solemnized and, ironically, the *Quixote* itself read as if it laboured under the confusions between fiction and reality it had set out to satirize. See, for instance, Mia I. Gerhardt, *Don Quijote: la vie et les livres* (Amsterdam, 1955); Richard L. Predmore, *El mundo del 'Quijote'* (Madrid, 1958); René Girard, *Mensonge romantique et vérité romanesque* (Paris, 1961); Angel del Río, 'El equívoco del *Quijote*', *HR* xxvii (1959), 200-21; Bruce W. Wardropper, '*Don Quixote*: Story or History?', *MPh* lxiii (1965), 1-11.

37 For a comprehensive survey of these two highly influential schools of modern *Quixote* criticism, see Anthony Close, *The Romantic Approach to 'Don Quixote'* (Cambridge, 1978).

38 See A. A. Parker, 'El concepto de la verdad en *Don Quijote*', *RFE* xxxii (1948), 287-304; Oscar Mandel, 'The Function of the Norm in *Don Quixote*', *MPh* lv (1957), 154-63; A. J. Close, 'Don Quixote's Love for Dulcinea: A Study of Cervantine Irony', *BHS* l (1973), 237-55, and 'Don Quixote's Sophistry and Wisdom', *BHS* lv (1978), 103-13.

39 See J. J. Allen, *Don Quixote: Hero or Fool? Part Two* (Gainesville, Florida, 1979), p. 110, who differentiates critics that basically identify with the madman from those that see him merely as the butt of satire. Allen pinpoints the insufficiency of each attitude: 'The "hard" critics do not satisfy us when they interpret Part II. The "soft" critics do not satisfy us when they interpret Part I. Both interpretations are static at precisely the point where the novel is dynamic.'

40 See, respectively, Mark Van Doren, *Don Quixote's Profession* (New York, 1958); Luis Rosales, *Cervantes y la Libertad* (2 vols., Madrid, 1960); Salvador de Madariaga, *Guía del lector del 'Quijote'*, 3rd edn. (Buenos Aires, 1947) translated into English as *Don Quixote: An Introductory Essay in Psychology* (Oxford, 1935; in paperback, 1961); W. H. Auden, 'The Ironic Hero: Some Reflections on Don Quixote' in *Cervantes: A Collection of Critical Essays*, pp. 73-81.

41 Miguel de Unamuno, *Vida de Don Quijote y Sancho* [1905]

11th edn. (Madrid, 1958). For a representative account of Don Quixote's progressive sanity see Avalle-Arce and Riley, pp. 47-79.

42 Nevertheless, Otis H. Green, 'El Ingenioso Hidalgo' in *The Literary Mind of Medieval and Renaissance Spain* (Lexington, 1970), pp. 171-84, has shown that Don Quixote's mad humours conform to the theories expounded by Huarte de San Juan in his *Examen de Ingenios* (1575). *Don Quixote*, however, is clearly not intended as a study of madness as such.

43 The distinction between Aldonza and Dulcinea which the madman makes here has been generally overlooked. Dulcinea is usually considered to be a fully realized ideal in Don Quixote's imagination from the start (cf. Unamuno, p. 25), and an ideal which is destined to be eroded by experience (cf. Madariaga, pp. 134-41). But the madman, in fact, wishes to set in train a *process* of transforming Aldonza into Dulcinea, a tricky business which, even in Don Quixote's view, is vulnerable to setbacks and misunderstandings. Without this sense of process, many of the intricate comic ironies that characterize the theme of Dulcinea in the novel are lost.

44 This, of course, is Platonism gone mad, although the belief that the world would degenerate unless sustained by chivalric practice is wholly orthodox. In *Yvain*, Chrétien presupposes that such a degeneration has taken place and purports to write the romance in order to encourage a return to old standards and values. See Chapter 1, p. 10.

45 If a distinction between surface appearance (Aldonza) and ideal potentiality (Dulcinea) is not made, the madman would appear at times to be lying. Thus Close, 'Don Quixote's Love for Dulcinea', p. 248, logically regards this speech as 'the only place in which he admits the gap between reality and his idealization of it. He is brought to this admission because his image of Dulcinea partly involves the deliberate falsification of fact. He may indeed see windmills as giants, he *knows* in some sense that Dulcinea is not a princess'. On this basis the madman's love for Dulcinea does seem to be a 'comic sham'. But I feel there is no need to impute bad faith to the madman. Quixote always insists that Aldonza is the princess Dulcinea but he freely admits that this truth is, as yet, not immediately obvious to everyone; it is his chivalric duty to make it so.

46 Modern criticism has tended to produce an exaggerated voluntarism in Don Quixote derived either from Unamuno's 'admirable Knight of Faith' (p. 35), or from Américo Castro's proto-existentialist hero, who stubbornly wills his own form of being regardless of circumstances ('La estructura del "Quijote"' in *Hacia Cervantes*, p. 322). But Quixote's attitude is for the most part exploratory and open to correction if need be.

47. This last statement is the germ that has allowed the growth of a very influential Perspectivist school of *Quixote* criticism. Ortega y Gasset, *Meditaciones del Quijote* (Madrid, 1914), freely read the novel in a manner that was rather too congenial to his own philosophy of Perspectivism. Leo Spitzer, in a famous essay, 'Perspectivismo lingüístico en el "Quijote"' in *Lingüística e historia literaria* (Madrid, 1955), pp. 161-225, found evidence of Perspectivism in Cervantes's language and style. Many critics have since approached the *Quixote* as if Cervantes had been a Perspectivist himself, even though there is no textual evidence at all to suggest that either Cervantes or Don Quixote subscribed to epistemological pluralism. Cognitive mix-ups are simply evidence of Cervantes's comic play with the knight's demented Platonism.

48 For a discussion of positive irony, see Chapter 1, pp. 16–17.

49 Spitzer, 'Perspectivismo lingüístico', pp. 195-9, makes much of Sancho's neologism *baciyelmo* ('basin-helmet'; I.xliv.403), seeing it as an occasion where Cervantes 'liberates himself from the limitations of language' in order to express the fragmentation of reality into two equally valid perspectives. It seems clear from the text, however, that *baciyelmo* is an example of Sancho's defensive irony, representing a compromise between his need to defer to his mad master and his reluctance to abandon common sense altogether.

50 Don Quixote may be more circumspect but he is no saner. Knud Togeby, *La estructura del Quijote*, ed. and trans. A. Rodríguez Almodóvar (Seville, 1977), pp. 113-14, Rosales, ii, p. 65, Avalle-Arce and Riley, p. 67, argue that Don Quixote sees things as they really are in Part II, and this is adduced as evidence of his progress towards sanity. But even in Part I the mad knight accepted ordinary appearances, he merely believed them to have degenerated from their true romance character.

51 Stevens, p. 20.

52 Rosales, ii, pp. 93-101. Since Rosales believes that in Part II the madman begins to recognize ordinary appearances (see n. 50 above), he seeks to explain the persistence of the obsession with Dulcinea, quite logically, as willed self-deception. But in his bid to reconcile logic with Unamuno, Rosales produces a reading in which Don Quixote's alleged self-deception converts him into a Christ-figure and even ennobles Sancho, the original deceiver, who is now said to serve his master like a Simon of Cyrene (p. 187). Thus, allegedly forgetting Aldonza, the knight is presumed to collude with Sancho in creating a 'myth' of Dulcinea. So, from the chivalric caricature she was in Part I, Dulcinea is transformed by Quixote's 'creative faith' into the 'ideal symbol of the beloved' in Part II.

53 See Gerald Brenan, 'Cervantes' in *Cervantes: A Collection of Critical Essays*, pp. 22-6.

54 See Helena Percas de Ponseti, *Cervantes y su concepto del Arte* (2 vols., Madrid, 1975), pp. 448-583, for a very full account of the romance sources of the Montesinos Cave episode. Lida de Malkiel, 'Dos huellas del *Esplandián*', noted similarities with Chapters 98 and 99 of Montalvo's romance. There is, in addition, an ironically inverted analogy between the two episodes. Montalvo interrupted his romance world and introduced us into the real world of his own experience just as Don Quixote here interrupts the real world in order to plunge into the world of romance. Moreover, Montalvo used the real world to bolster the credibility of his romance whereas Don Quixote resorts to an oneiric experience of romance to enhance his own credibility in the real world.

55 See Avalle-Arce and Riley, p. 67.

56 See Madariaga, p. 218; Avalle-Arce and Riley, p. 57, n. 22.

57 Madariaga formulated the very influential interpretation that Don Quixote is dogged by an 'internal enemy' of self-doubt consisting in his intimate awareness that his whole chivalric enterprise was illusory (p.134). The 'internal enemy' idea has become enshrined in critical orthodoxy: Don Quixote's career is almost invariably seen as a piecemeal surrender to empirical facts.

58 See Allen, *Don Quixote: Hero or Fool? Part Two*, pp. 34-5.

59 Those 'hard' critics like Parker, Mandel, Close and P. E.

Russell, '*Don Quixote* as a Funny Book', *MLR* lxiv (1969), 312-26, who rightly counter the sentimental solemnities of the Romantics and the Perspectivists by stressing the function of ordinary reality as a corrective to Don Quixote's folly, in turn overlook the operation of the madness as a device that upsets the reader's expectations. This countervailing thrust is, I believe, an indispensable source of comic vitality in the novel.

CHAPTER FOUR

1 See Chapter 1, p. 5.

2 Spitzer, 'Perspectivismo lingüístico', p. 173, drew attention to the analogy between the sacrament of baptism and the chivalric practice of giving a new name to a novice knight. In both cases, the new name would denote an essential truth.

3 Bertrand Russell, *History of Western Philosophy*, 2nd edn. (London, 1961), p. 428, refers to the defects of the scholastic method: 'Indifference to facts and science, belief in reasoning in matters which only observation can decide, and an undue emphasis on verbal distinctions and subtleties.'

4 Scholastic realism represented one aspect of the medieval dispute over universals which was a consequence of Aristotelian refinement of Plato's theory of forms. Proper names, such as 'Quixote' or 'Dulcinea', say, designate particular entities, but words such as 'knight' or 'beauty' designate whole groups or species of particulars, and are therefore 'universal'. The question then arises whether these universals refer to real things or are merely words. If universals are real, it becomes difficult to distinguish the universal essence of beauty from the individuated essence of Dulcinea's particular beauty. See Russell, op. cit., pp. 141-3, 175-7, 210-1, 428-30, 458.

5 For similar approaches to this scene, see Spitzer, 'Perspectivismo lingüístico', p. 194, and Close, 'Don Quixote's Sophistry', pp. 104-6.

6 See Chapter 1, pp. 15–16.

7 I make a distinction here between the ironic author and

Cervantes's narrative personae, either as alleged editor of the novel, Cide Hamete, or any of the other narrative intermediaries. The functions of these narrative personae have been widely studied. See, for instance, Riley, *Cervantes's Theory*, pp. 205-12; Wardropper, '*Don Quixote*: Story or History?'; George Haley, 'The Narrator in *Don Quijote*: Maese Pedro's Puppet Show', *MLN* lxxx (1965), 145-65; Ruth El Saffar, 'The Function of the Fictional Narrator in *Don Quijote*', *MLN* lxxxiii (1968), 164-77; Allen, *Don Quixote: Hero or Fool? Part Two*, pp. 3-15.

8 'He used to say that the Cid Ruy Diaz must have been a very good knight, but that he could not be compared to the Knight of the Burning Sword, who with a single backstroke had cleft a pair of fierce and monstrous giants in two. And he had an even better opinion of Bernardo del Carpio for slaying the enchanted Roland at Roncesvalles, by making use of Hercules' trick when he throttled the Tital Antaeus in his arms. He spoke very well of the giant Morgante; for, though one of that giant brood who are all proud and insolent, he alone was affable and well-mannered. But he admired most of all Reynald of Montalban, particularly when he saw him sally forth from his castle and rob everyone he met, and when in heathen lands overseas he stole that idol of Mahomet, which history says was of pure gold. But he would have given his housekeeper and his niece into the bargain, to deal the traitor Galaon a good kicking' (p. 32).

9 See Close, 'Don Quixote's Love for Dulcinea', p. 253.

CHAPTER FIVE

1 Flores, 'Cervantes at Work: The Writing of *Don Quixote*, Part I', *JHP* iii (1979), 135-60.

2 Ibid., pp. 139-42.

3 Ibid., pp. 142-5.

4 Thomas Mann, 'Voyage with Don Quixote' in *Cervantes: A Collection of Critical Essays*, pp. 49-72, found Cervantes's mixture of romance and anti-romance parody rather perplexing: 'I cannot but shake my head over the single tales scattered

through it, so extravagantly sentimental they are, so precisely in the style and taste of the very productions that the poet had set himself to mock. . . . In those idylls he resigns his earlier role, as though to say that if the age wanted that sort of thing he could give it them, yes, even be a master at it' (p. 56).

5 For a fuller discussion of the effects of interpolation, see my article 'Romance and Realism in the Interpolated Stories of the *Quixote*', *Cervantes*, ii (1982), 43-67.

6 Northrop Frye, pp. 46-7, writes that in realistic fiction the author 'tries to conceal his design, pretending that things are happening out of inherent probability'.

7 Javier Herrero, 'Arcadia's Inferno: Cervantes' Attack on Pastoral', *BHS* lv (1978), 289-99, detects elements of parody in Cervantes's treatment of the Marcela and the Leandra stories.

8 See Flores, op. cit., p. 156: 'There cannot be any doubt that the interpolation of the speech on Arms and Letters and the sandwiching of the episode of the wineskins in *El curioso impertinente*, balanced once again the narrative by giving Don Quixote and Sancho some badly needed limelight exposure.'

9 Sancho's development is usually discussed in terms of Madariaga's notion of 'quixotification', pp. 165-76. The full implications of his growing sense of irony have become obscured by Madariaga's Romantic hypothesis. See, for instance, Fernando Sainz, 'Don Quijote educador de Sancho', *Hispania*, xxxiv (1951), 363-5; Victor Oelschläger, 'Sancho's Zest for the Quest', *Hispania*, xxxv (1952), 18-24; John A. Moore, 'The Idealism of Sancho Panza', *Hispania*, xli (1958), 73-6; Dorothy Tharpe, 'The "Education" of Sancho Seen in his Personal References', *MLJ* xlv (1961), 244-48; R. M. Flores, 'Sancho's Fabrications: A Mirror of the Development of his Imagination', *HR* xxxviii (1970), 174-82.

10 See Joaquín Casalduero, *Sentido y forma del 'Quijote'* (Madrid, 1949), p. 211; Knud Togeby, p. 100; Michael Bell, 'The Structure of *Don Quixote*', *Essays in Criticism*, xviii (1968), 241-57 (p. 252); Avalle-Arce and Riley, p. 68.

11 See Rosales, ii, p. 65 and *passim*; Avalle-Arce and Riley, pp. 67-8.

12 See Aubrey F. G. Bell, *Cervantes* (Norman, Oklahoma, 1947), p. 97; A. Castro, 'Cervantes y Pirandello' in *Hacia*

Cervantes, pp. 477-85; Casalduero, op. cit., p. 210; Michael Bell, op. cit., pp. 242-4.

13 Madariaga, pp. 125-41, 176-91, 215-32.

14 Eric Auerbach, p. 340-1, gives a superb rhetorical analysis of the sentence Don Quixote addresses to Dulcinea which follows directly upon the one I have quoted. Calling it 'a very beautiful sentence', Auerbach observes that 'Cervantes is very fond of such rhythmically and pictorially rich, such beautifully articulated and musical bravura pieces of chivalric rhetoric (which are nevertheless rooted in the tradition of antiquity).'

15 Auerbach, ibid., p. 340, observes that the travesty of Dulcinea would be expected to 'bring on a terrible crisis' that could lead either to 'a much deeper insanity' in Don Quixote or an 'instantaneous liberation from his idée fixe', and argues that since neither appears to occur, the scene is reduced to 'merry play' that avoids tragic complications. However, a terrible crisis *does* ensue—but within the terms of Quixote's chivalric madness. Cervantes's genius can be appreciated precisely in his ability to create a full-scale tragic crisis in the madman's life without producing a cure that would bring the novel to an end. The whole point of the *Quixote* is surely to keep up the madness in spite of the reader's, indeed of Auerbach's, expectations. The result is the creation of an unprecedented mixture of the tragic and the ridiculous, namely the 'quixotic'. Auerbach himself recognizes this quality in the novel: 'Don Quijote's feelings are genuine and profound. Dulcinea is really the mistress of his thoughts; he is truly filled with the spirit of a mission which he regards as man's highest duty. . . . It may be absurd, fantastic, grotesque; but it is still ideal, unconditional, heroic' (p. 343). However, he goes on to attribute this perception to the Romantic period which 'withstands all attempts on the part of philological criticism to show that Cervantes's intention was not to produce such an impression'. He believes that the novel 'remains pure farce', yet he acknowledges that there is a difficulty 'which lies in the fact that in Don Quijote's idée fixe we have a combination of the noble, immaculate, and redeeming with absolute nonsense'. In an otherwise splendid essay, Auerbach fails to get to grips with this fundamental contradiction between the noble and the nonsensical.

16 Scholes and Kellogg, p. 176.

17 See Chapters 89-108, pp. 345-450.

18 See Riley, *Cervantes's Theory*, p. 117.

19 Maravall, *Utopía y contrautopía en el Quijote* (Santiago de Compostela, 1976).

20 Redondo, 'Tradición carnavalesca y creación literaria: Del personaje de Sancho Panza al episodio de la ínsula Barataria en el "Quijote"', *BHisp* lxxx (1978), 39-70.

21 Francisco Márquez Villanueva, 'La locura emblemática en la segunda parte del *Quijote*' in *Cervantes and the Renaissance*, ed. M. D. McGaha (Easton, Pennsylvania, 1980), 85-112 (p. 107), argues that the paradoxical madness of Don Quixote transcends the allegorical and moral purpose of the motifs of Carnival, wise buffoonery, or Ship of Fools that characterized the literature of folly in the Middle Ages and the Renaissance.

22 E. Moreno Báez, 'Arquitectura del *Quijote*', *RFE* xxxii (1948), 269-85, remarked of Don Quixote's treatment at the Duke's castle that the excessive number of practical jokes actually becomes rather tedious (pp. 274-5). I would add that this is due to causes more profound than mere numerical excess.

23 A point made by Avalle-Arce and Riley, p. 71.

24 Martín de Riquer, *Aproximación al Quijote* (Barcelona, 1967), pp. 162-8, notes this strange passivity in Don Quixote and interprets it as a sign that the end is nigh.

25 However, see Williamson, pp. 58-67, for a discussion of how the interpolated stories in Part II are in turn influenced by Cervantes's fuller realization of the Quixote–Panza relationship.

26 Riley, *Cervantes's Theory*, p. 216, sees in Cervantes's treatment of Avellaneda's *Quixote* an element of 'tit for tat' which entailed 'the sacrifice of some logic and verisimilitude'.

27 Thomas Mann, p. 57.

28 The view that Sancho's renunciation of his governorship is a sign of self-discovery or *desengaño* has become widespread. It has most recently been expressed by J. J. Allen, *Don Quixote: Hero or Fool? Part Two*, pp. 32-4.

29 Madariaga, pp. 165-76.

30 Gethin Hughes, 'The Cave of Montesinos: Don Quixote's

interpretation and Dulcinea's disenchantment', *BHS* liv (1977), 107-13, analyses the deleterious effects of money on Don Quixote's career.

31 For a fuller analysis of this episode see E. C. Riley, 'Symbolism in *Don Quixote*, Part II, Chaper 73', *JHP* iii (1979), 161-74.

CONCLUSION

1 See Riley, *Cervantes's Theory*, pp. 107-15, for a discussion of Cervantes's attitude to the public.

2 Henry James, 'The Art of Fiction' in Edel, p. 36.

3 See Maurice Bardon, *'Don Quichotte' en France au XVIIe et au XVIIIe siècles 1605-1815* (2 vols., Paris, 1931), p. 298.

4 Ibid., pp. 107-14.

5 Ibid., pp. 457-9.

6 Fielding, *Tom Jones*, ed. Sheridan Baker (New York, 1973), pp. 301-8.

7 Ibid., p. 308.

8 John Preston, 'Plot as Irony: The Reader's Role in *Tom Jones*', *ELH* xxxv (1968), 365-80, reprinted in *Tom Jones*, ed. Baker, pp. 814-5.

9 *Aristotle on the Art of Poetry*, p. 33.

10 Ibid., pp. 50-1.

11 Ibid., pp. 46-8.

12 Ibid., p. 35.

BIBLIOGRAPHY

Accarie, Maurice, 'La Structure du *Chevalier au Lion* de Chrétien de Troyes', *Le Moyen Age*, lxxiv (1978), 13-34.

Adler, Alfred, 'Sovereignty in Chrétien's *Yvain*', *PMLA* xlii (1947), 281-305.

Aebischer, Paul, 'Paléozoologie de l'*Equus clavileñus, Cervant.*', *Études et Lettres*, ii (1962), 93-130.

Allen, John J., *Don Quixote: Hero or Fool?* (Gainesville, Florida, 1969).

Don Quixote: Hero or Fool? Part Two (Gainesville, Florida, 1979).

Alonso, Dámaso, 'El hidalgo Camilote y el hidalgo Don Quijote', *RFE* xx (1933), 391-7.

'Sancho-Quijote, Sancho-Sancho', *Homenaje a Cervantes*, ii (Valencia, 1950), 55-63.

Amezcua, José, 'La oposición de Montalvo al mundo del *Amadís de Gaula*', *NRFH* xxi (1968), 320-37.

Amezúa y Mayo, Agustín G. de, *Cervantes creador de la novela corta española* (2 vols., Madrid, 1956-8).

Ariosto, Ludovico, *Orlando Furioso*, trans. Guido Waldman (Oxford, 1974).

Aristotle, *Aristotle on the Art of Poetry*, trans. Ingram Bywater (Oxford, 1920).

Atkinson, W. C., 'Cervantes, El Pinciano, and the *Novelas ejemplares*', *HR* xvi (1948), 189-208.

Auden, W. H., 'The Ironic Hero: Some Reflections on Don Quixote' in *Cervantes: A Collection of Critical Essays*, ed. Lowry Nelson, Jr. (Englewood Cliffs, NJ, 1969), 73-81.

Auerbach, Erich, *Mimesis: The Representation of Reality in Western Literature*, trans. Willard R. Trask (Princeton, NJ, 1953).

Avalle-Arce, J. B., 'El Arco de los Leales Amadores en el *Amadís*', *NRFH* vi (1952), 149-56.

Deslindes cervantinos (Madrid, 1961).

Don Quijote como forma de vida, (Valencia, 1976).

Nuevos deslindes cervantinos (Barcelona, 1975).

Avalle-Arce, J. B., and Riley, E. C., *Suma cervantina* (London, 1973).

Avellaneda, Alonso Fernández de, *Don Quijote de la Mancha*, ed. Martín de Riquer (3 vols., Madrid, 1972).

Ayala, Francisco, *Cervantes y Quevedo* (Barcelona, 1974).

'La invención del *Quijote* como problema técnico-literario', *Realidad*, ii (1947), 183-200.

'Nota sobre la creación del *Quijote*', *Cuadernos americanos*, xxv (1947), 194-206.

Azaña, Manuel, *La invención del Quijote y otros ensayos* (Madrid, 1934).

Bandera, Cesáreo, *Mimesis conflictiva. Ficción literaria y violencia en Cervantes y Calderón* (Madrid, 1975).

Bardon, Maurice, *'Don Quichotte' en France au XVIIe et au XVIIIe siècles 1605-1815* (2 vols., Paris, 1931).

Barthes, Roland, *Le Degré zéro de l'écriture* (Paris, 1953).

Le Plaisir du texte (Paris, 1973).

Bataillon, Marcel, 'L'Erasmisme de Cervantes' in *Erasme et l'Espagne* (Paris, 1937), 819-49.

'Exégesis esotérica y análisis de intenciones del *Quijote*' in *Cervantes-Sonderheft* (Berlin, 1967), 22-6.

Bayrav, Suheyda, *Symbolisme médiéval* (Paris, Istanbul, 1957).

Bednar, John, *La Spiritualité et le symbolisme dans les œuvres de Chrétien de Troyes* (Paris, 1974).

Beer, Gillian, *The Romance*, The Critical Idiom (London, 1970).

Beichner, Paul E., C.S.C., 'The Allegorical Interpretation of Medieval Literature', *PMLA* lxxxii (1967), 33-8.

Bell, Aubrey F. G., *Cervantes* (Norman, Oklahoma, 1947).

Bell, Michael, 'The Structure of *Don Quixote*', *Essays in Criticism*, xviii (1968), 241-57.

Benton, John F., 'The Court of Champagne as a Literary Center', *Speculum*, xxxvi (1961), 551-91.

Béroul, *The Romance of Tristan*, trans. Alan S. Frederick (Penguin, Harmondsworth, 1970).

Bezzola, Reto R., *Les Origines et la formation de la littérature courtoise en Occident (500-1200)* (5 vols., Paris, 1944-63).

Le Sens de l'aventure et de l'amour (Chrétien de Troyes) (Paris, 1947).

Black, Max, 'Metaphor' in *Philosophy Looks at the Arts: Contemporary Readings in Aesthetics*, ed. Joseph Margolis (New York, 1962), 216-35.

Blanco Aguinaga, Carlos, 'Cervantes y la picaresca: Notas sobre dos tipos de realismo', *NRFH* xi (1957), 313-42.

Bloch, Marc, *Feudal Society*, trans. L. A. Manyon, 2nd edn. (London, 1962).

Bloch, R. Howard, 'The Death of King Arthur and the Waning of the Feudal Age', *Orbis Litterarum*, xxix (1974), 291-305.

'From Grail Quest to Inquest: the Death of King Arthur and the Birth of France', *MLR* lxix (1974), 40-55.

Medieval French Literature and Law (Berkeley and Los Angeles, 1977).

Bloomfield, Morton W., 'Symbolism in Medieval Literature', *MPh* lvi (1958), 73-81.

Boccaccio, *The Decameron*, trans. G. H. McWilliam (Penguin, Harmondsworth, 1972).

Bogdanow, Fanni, *The Romance of the Grail* (Manchester, 1966).

Bohigas Balaguer, P., 'La novela caballeresca, sentimental y de aventuras' in *Historia general de las literaturas hispánicas*, ii (Barcelona, 1951).

Booth, Wayne C., *The Rhetoric of Fiction* (Chicago, 1961).

A Rhetoric of Irony (Chicago, 1974).

'The Self-Conscious Narrator in Comic Fiction Before *Tristram Shandy*', *PMLA* lxvii (1952), 163-85.

Borges, J. L., 'Análisis del último capítulo del *Quijote*', *Revista de la Universidad de Buenos Aires*, i (1956), 28-36.

'Magias parciales del *Quijote*' in *Otras inquisiciones* (Buenos Aires, 1960), 65-9.

Brand, C. P., *Ariosto: A Preface to the 'Orlando Furioso'* (Edinburgh, 1974).

Torquato Tasso (Cambridge, 1965).

Brenan, Gerald, 'Cervantes' in *Cervantes: A Collection of Critical Essays*, ed. Lowry Nelson, Jr. (Englewood Cliffs, NJ, 1969), 22-6.

Brody, Robert, 'Don Quijote's Emotive Adventures: Fulling Hammers and Lions', *Neophilologus*, lix (1975), 372-81.

Brooks, Cleanth, 'Irony and "Ironic" Poetry', *College English*, ix (1948), 231-7.

Brooks, Cleanth, and Warren, R. P., *Understanding Fiction* (New York, 1943).

Calderwood, James L. and Toliver, Harold E., edd., *Perspectives on Fiction* (OUP, New York, London and Toronto, 1968).

Camón Aznar, J., 'Don Quijote en la teoría de los estilos', *RFE* xxxii (1948), 429-65.

Canavaggio, Jean François, 'Alonso López Pinciano y la estética literaria de Cervantes en el *Quijote*', *AC* vii (1958), 13-107.

'Cervantes en primera persona', *JHP* ii (1977), 35-45.

Capellanus, Andreas, *The Art of Courtly Love*, trans. J. J. Parry (New York, 1941).

Carasso-Bulow, Lucienne, *The Merveilleux in Chrétien de Troyes' Romances* (Geneva, 1976).

Casalduero, Joaquín, *Sentido y forma de las 'Novelas ejemplares'* (Buenos Aires, 1943).

Sentido y forma del 'Quijote' (Madrid, 1949).

Castro, Américo, *Cervantes y los casticismos españoles* (Madrid, Barcelona, 1966, 1974).

Hacia Cervantes, 3rd rev. edn. (Madrid, 1967).

El pensamiento de Cervantes (Madrid, 1925).

Cervantes Saavedra, Miguel de, *Comedias y entremeses; Poesías sueltas*, ed. R. Schevill and A. Bonilla (6 vols., Madrid, 1915-22). *Don Quijote de la Mancha*, ed. Martín de Riquer (Juventud, Barcelona, 1968).

Don Quixote, trans. J. M. Cohen (Penguin, Harmondsworth, 1950).

Don Quixote de la Mancha, ed. R. Schevill and A. Bonilla (4 vols. Madrid, 1928-41).

El ingenioso hidalgo Don Quijote de la Mancha, ed. Diego Clemencín (8 vols., Madrid, 1894).

El Ingenioso Hidalgo Don Quijote de la Mancha, ed. John Jay Allen (2 vols., Madrid, 1977).

La Galatea, ed. J. B. Avalle-Arce, (2 vols., Madrid, 1961).

Novelas ejemplares, ed. F. Rodríguez Marín (2 vols., Madrid, 1914, 1917).

Los trabajos de Persiles y Sigismunda, ed. J. B. Avalle-Arce (Madrid, 1969).

Persiles y Sigismunda, ed. R. Schevill and A. Bonilla (2 vols., Madrid, 1914).

Viage del Parnaso, ed. R. Schevill and A. Bonilla (Madrid, 1922).

Chambers, Leland H., 'Irony in the Final Chapter of the *Quijote*', *RR* lxi (1970), 14-22.

'Structure and the Search for Truth in the *Quijote*', *HR* xxxv (1967), 309-26.

Charity, A. C., *Events and their After-Life* (Cambridge, 1966).

Chenu, M.-D., O.P., *Nature, Man and Society in the Twelfth Century*, ed. and trans. Jerome Taylor and Lester K. Little (Chicago, 1968).

Chevalier, Haakon, *The Ironic Temper: Anatole France and his Time* (New York, 1932).

Chevalier, Maxime, *L'Arioste en Espagne* (Bordeaux, 1966).

Sur le public du roman de chevalerie (Bordeaux, 1968).

Clements, Robert J., and Gibaldi, Joseph, *Anatomy of the Novella: The European Tale Collection from Boccaccio and Chaucer to Cervantes* (New York, 1977).

Clifford, Gay, *The Transformations of Allegory* (London, 1974).

Close, A. J. 'Don Quijote and the "Intentionalist Fallacy"', *BJAe* xii (1972), 19-39.

'Don Quixote as a Burlesque Hero: A Reconstructed Eighteenth-Century View', *FMLS* x (1974), 365-78.

'Don Quixote's Love for Dulcinea: A Study of Cervantine Irony', *BHS* l (1973), 237-55.

'Don Quixote's Sophistry and Wisdom', *BHS* lv (1978), 103-13.

The Romantic Approach to 'Don Quixote' (Cambridge, 1978).
'Sancho Panza: Wise Fool', *MLR* lxviii (1973), 344-57.
Collas, J. P., 'The Romantic Hero of the Twelfth Century' in *Medieval Miscellany Presented to Eugène Vinaver* (Manchester, 1965), 80-96.
Combellack, C. R. B., 'The Entrapment of Yvain', *Medieval Studies*, xxxvii (1975), 524-30.
'Yvain's Guilt', *SP* lxviii (1971), 10-25.
Cook, Robert G., 'The Ointment in Chrétien's *Yvain*', *Medieval Studies*, xxxi (1969), 338-42.
'The Structure of Romance in Chrétien's *Erec* and *Yvain*', *MPh* lxxi (1973-4), 128-43.
Copleston, F. C., *Aquinas* (Penguin, Harmondsworth, 1955).
Crane, R. S., 'The Plot of *Tom Jones*', *The Journal of General Education*, iv (1950), 112-30.
Criado de Val, Manuel, '*Don Quijote* como diálogo', *AC* v (1955-6), 183-208.
Culler, Jonathan, *Structuralist Poetics* (London, 1975).
Curtius, Ernst R., *European Literature and the Latin Middle Ages*, trans. Willard R. Trask (London, 1953).

The Death of King Arthur, trans. James Cable (Penguin, Harmondsworth, 1971).
De Chasca, Edmund, 'Algunos aspectos del ritmo y del movimiento narrativo del *Quijote*', *RFE* xlvii (1964), 287-307.
De Lollis, C., *Cervantes reazionario* (Florence, 1947).
Descouzis, Paul, *Cervantes a nueva luz*: vol. i, *El 'Quijote' y el Concilio de Trento* (Frankfurt, 1966); vol. ii, *Con la iglesia hemos dado, Sancho* (Madrid, 1973).
Deyermond, A. D., 'The Lost Genre of Medieval Spanish Literature', *HR* xliii (1975), 231-59.
Díaz-Plaja, Guillermo, *En torno a Cervantes* (Pamplona, 1977).
Dipple, Elizabeth, *Plot*, The Critical Idiom (London, 1970).
Dunlap, Rhodes, 'The Allegorical Interpretation of Renaissance Literature', *PMLA* lxxxii (1967), 39-43.
Dunn, Peter N., 'Two Classical Myths in *Don Quijote*', *Renaissance and Reformation*, ix (1972), 3-4.
Durán, Armando, 'La "amplificatio" en la literatura caballeresca española', *MLN* lxxxvi (1971), 123-35.
Estructura y técnicas de la novela sentimental y caballeresca (Madrid, 1973).
Durán, Manuel, *La ambigüedad en el Quijote* (Xalapa, Mexico, 1960).
Cervantes, Twayne World Authors Series (New York, 1974).
Durling, Robert, M., *The Figure of the Poet in Renaissance Epic* (Cambridge, Mass., 1965).

Efron, Arthur, *Don Quixote and the Dulcineated World* (Austin, Texas, 1971).

Ehrlich, Victor, *Russian Formalism: History-Doctrine* (The Hague, 1955).

Eisenberg, Daniel, *Romances of Chivalry in the Spanish Golden Age,* Juan de la Cueva Hispanic Monographs (Newark, Delaware, 1982).

El Saffar, Ruth, *'El casamiento engañoso' and 'El coloquio de los perros'*, Critical Guides to Spanish Texts, 17 (London, 1976).

'Development and Reorientation in the Works of Cervantes', *MLN* lxxxviii (1973), 203-14.

'The Function of the Fictional Narrator in *Don Quijote*', *MLN* lxxxiii (1968), 164-77.

'Montesinos' Cave and the *Casamiento engañoso* in the Development of Cervantes' Prose Fiction', *KRQ* xx (1973), 451-67.

Novel to Romance: A Study of Cervantes' 'Novelas ejemplares' (Baltimore and London, 1974).

Empson, William, 'Tom Jones', *The Kenyon Review*, xx (1958), 217-49.

Entwistle, W. J., *The Arthurian Legend in the Literature of the Spanish Peninsula* (London, 1925).

Cervantes (Oxford, 1965).

Fielding, Henry, *Joseph Andrews* and *Shamela*, ed. Martin Battestin (London, 1965).

Tom Jones, A Norton Critical Edition, ed. Sheridan Baker (New York, 1973).

Fitzmaurice-Kelly, James, *Miguel de Cervantes Saavedra: A Memoir* (Oxford, 1913).

Flores, A. and Benardete, M. J., edd., *Cervantes across the Centuries* (New York, 1947).

Flores, R. M., 'Cervantes At Work: The Writing of *Don Quixote*, Part I', *JHP* iii (1979), 135-60.

The Compositors of the First and Second Madrid Editions of 'Don Quijote' Part One (London, MHRA, 1975).

'The Printers of the Second Madrid Edition of *Don Quixote*, Part I, and the Consequences of the Division of Labour', *BHS* xlviii (1971), 193-217.

'Sancho's Fabrications: A Mirror of the Development of his Imagination', *HR* xxxviii (1970), 174-82.

Forcione, Alban K., *Cervantes, Aristotle and the 'Persiles'* (Princeton, NJ, 1970).

Cervantes' Christian Romance: A Study of 'Persiles y Sigismunda' (Princeton, NJ, 1972).

Forster, E. M., *Aspects of the Novel* (London, 1927).

Foucault, Michel, *The Order of Things: An Archaeology of the Human Sciences* (London, 1970).

Fourquet, Jean, 'Le Rapport entre l'œuvre et la source chez Chrétien de Troyes et le problème des sources bretonnes', *RPh* ix (1955-6), 298-312.

France, Marie de, *Lais*, ed. Alfred Ewert (Oxford, 1944).

Frappier, Jean, *Chrétien de Troyes: l'Homme et l'œuvre* (Paris, 1957).

Étude sur Yvain ou Le Chevalier au Lion de Chrétien de Troyes (Paris, 1969).

'The Vulgate Cycle' in *Arthurian Literature in the Middle Ages*, ed. R. S. Loomis (Oxford, 1959), 295-318.

Friedman, Norman, 'Point of View in Fiction', *PMLA* lxx (1955), 1160-84.

Frye, Northrop, *Anatomy of Criticism: Four Essays* (Princeton, NJ, 1957).

The Secular Scripture (Cambridge, Mass., and London, 1976).

Gaos, Vicente, 'El *Quijote* y las novelas interpoladas' in *Temas y problemas de literatura española* (Madrid, 1959), 107-18.

Gautier, Léon, *Chivalry*, ed. J. Levron, trans. D. C. Dunning (London, 1965).

Geoffrey of Monmouth, *History of the Kings of Britain*, trans. Lewis Thorpe (Penguin, Harmondsworth, 1966).

Gerhardt, Mia I., *Don Quijote: la vie et les livres* (Amsterdam, 1955).

Giammati, A. Bartlett, *The Earthly Paradise and the Renaissance Epic* (Princeton, NJ, 1966).

Gili Gaya, Samuel, '*Las sergas de Esplandián* como crítica de la caballería bretona', *BBMP* xxiii (1947), 103-11.

Giménez, Helio, *Artificios y motivos en los libros de caballerías* (Montevideo, 1973).

Girard, René, *Mensonge romantique et vérité romanesque* (Paris, 1961).

Glaser, Edward, 'Nuevos datos sobre la crítica de los libros de caballerías en los siglos XVI y XVII', *Anuario de estudios medievales*, iii (1966), 393-410.

Glicksberg, C. I., *The Ironic Vision in Modern Literature* (The Hague, 1969).

Goldmann, Lucien, *Pour une sociologie du roman* (Paris, 1964).

Gonthier, Denis A., *El drama psicológico del Quijote* (Madrid, 1962).

González, Eloy R. and Roberts, Jennifer T., 'Montalvo's recantation revisited', *BHS* lv (1978), 203-10.

Grant, Damian, *Realism*, The Critical Idiom (London, 1970).

Green, D. H., 'Irony and Medieval Romance' in *Arthurian Romance: Seven Essays*, ed. D. D. R. Owen (Edinburgh and London, 1970), 49-64.

Green, Otis H., 'El Ingenioso Hidalgo' in *The Literary Mind of Medieval and Renaissance Spain* (Lexington, 1970), 171-84.

Griffin, Nathanael, 'The Definition of Romance', *PMLA* xxxviii (1923), 50-70.

Guiette, Robert, 'Symbolisme et sénéfiance au Moyen Âge', pp. 33-51, and 'Lecteur de roman, lecteur de symbole', pp. 51-60, in 'Questions de littérature', *Romanica Gandensia*, viii (Ghent, 1960).

Haidu, Peter, *Aesthetic Distance in Chrétien de Troyes: Irony and Comedy in 'Cligès and Perceval'* (Geneva, 1968).

Lion-Queue-Coupée: l'écart symbolique chez Chrétien de Troyes (Geneva, 1972).

Haley, George, 'The Narrator in *Don Quijote*: Maese Pedro's Puppet Show', *MLN* lxxx (1965), 145-65.

Hamilton, G. L. 'Storm-Making Springs, Rings of Invisibility and Protection: Studies on the Sources of the *Yvain* of Chrétien de Troyes', *RR* ii (1911), 355-75.

Hanning, Robert W., *The Individual in Twelfth-Century Romance* (New Haven, Conn., 1970).

Harris, Julian, 'The Rôle of the Lion in Chrétien de Troyes' *Yvain'*, *PMLA* lxiv (1949), 1143-63.

Hatzfield, Helmut, *El Quijote como obra de arte del lenguaje*, 2nd edn. (Madrid, 1966).

Haydn, Hiram, *The Counter-Renaissance* (New York, 1950).

Hazard, Paul, *'Don Quichotte' de Cervantès: Étude et analyse* (Paris, 1949).

Heers, Jacques, *Fêtes, jeux et joûtes dans les sociétés d'Occident à la fin du Moyen Âge*, Conférence Albert-le-Grand 1970; Publications de l'Institut d'Études Médiévales (Montreal, 1971).

Hendrix, W. S., 'Sancho Panza and the Comic Types of the Sixteenth Century' in *Homenaje a Menéndez Pidal*, ii (Madrid, 1925), 485-94.

Herrero, Javier, 'Arcadia's Inferno: Cervantes' Attack on Pastoral', *BHS* lv (1978), 289-99.

Hirsch, E. D., Jr., *Validity in Interpretation* (Yale, 1967).

Homer, *The Iliad*, trans. E. V. Rieu (Penguin, Harmondsworth, 1950).

The Odyssey, trans. E. V. Rieu (Penguin, Harmondsworth, 1946).

Horace, *Satires, Epistles and 'Ars Poetica'*, trans. H. R. Fairclough (London, 1926).

Hughes, Gethin, 'The Cave of Montesinos: Don Quixote's Interpretation and Dulcinea's Disenchantment', *BHS* liv (1977), 107-13.

Huizinga, Johan, *The Waning of the Middle Ages: A Study of the Forms of*

Life, Thought and Art in France and the Netherlands in the XIVth and XVth centuries, trans. F. Hopman (Penguin, Harmondsworth, 1955).

Hutchens, Eleanor N., 'The Identification of Irony', *ELH* xxvii (1960), 352-63.

Immerwahr, Raymond, 'Structural Symmetry in the Episodic Narratives of *Don Quijote*, Part One', *CL* x (1958), 121-35.

Irwin, Michael, *Henry Fielding: The Tentative Realist* (Oxford, 1967).

Iventosch, Herman, 'Cervantes and Courtly Love: The Grisóstomo–Marcela Episode', *PMLA* lxxxix (1974), 64-76.

James, Henry, *The Art of the Novel: Critical Prefaces* (New York, 1934).

The House of Fiction: Essays On The Novel, ed. Leon Edel (London, 1957).

Jankélévitch, Victor, *L'Ironie, ou La Bonne Conscience*, 2nd rev. edn. (Paris, 1950).

Josipovici, Gabriel, *The World and the Book* (London, 1971).

Kaiser, Walter, *Praisers of Folly* (Cambridge, Mass., 1963).

Kelly, F. Douglas, *'Sens et Conjointure' in the Chevalier de la Charrette* (Mouton, The Hague, 1966).

Ker, W. P., *Epic and Romance* (London, 1931).

Knowles, David, *The Evolution of Medieval Thought* (London, 1962).

Knox, Norman, *The Word IRONY and Its Context, 1500-1755* (Durham, N. C., 1961).

Kristeller, Paul Oskar, *Renaissance Thought* (New York, 1961).

Lacy, Norris J., *The Craft of Chrétien de Troyes*, Davis Medieval Texts and Studies (Leiden, 1980).

'Organic Structure of Yvain's Expiation', *RR* lxi (1970), 79-84.

'Yvain's Evolution and the Rôle of the Lion', *RN* xii (1970-1), 198-202.

Lancelot: Roman en prose du XIIIème siècle, ed. Alexandre Micha, (3 vols., Paris, 1978, 1979).

Laurie, Helen C.R., *Two Studies in Chrétien de Troyes* (Geneva, 1972).

Le Goff, Jacques, *La Civilisation de l'occident médiévale* (Paris, 1967).

Lewis, C. S, *The Allegory of Love* (Oxford, 1936).

Levin, Harry, 'The Example of Cervantes' in *Contexts of Criticism* (Cambridge, Mass., 1957), 79-96.

Lida de Malkiel, María Rosa, 'Arthurian Literature in Spain and Portugal' in *Arthurian Literature in the Middle Ages*, ed. R. S. Loomis (Oxford, 1959), 406-18.

'"De cuyo nombre no quiero acordarme . . . "', *RFE* i (1939), 167-71.

'El desenlace del *Amadís* primitivo', *RPh* vi (1953), 283-9.

'Dos huellas del *Esplandián* en el *Quijote* y el *Persiles*', *RPh* ix (1955), 156-62.

Llorens, Vicente, 'Historia y ficción en el Quijote', *Papeles de Son Armadans*, xxxviii (1963), 235-58.

Lodge, David, *The Language of Fiction* (London and New York, 1966).

Loomis, R. S., ed., *Arthurian Literature in the Middle Ages* (Oxford, 1959).

Loomis, R. S., *Arthurian Tradition and Chrétien de Troyes* (New York, 1949).

The Development of Arthurian Romance (New York, 1970).

López Pinciano, Alonso, *Philosophía antigua poética*, ed. A. Carballo Picazo (3 vols., Madrid, 1953).

Lot, Ferdinand, *Étude sur le Lancelot en Prose* (Paris, 1918, 1954).

Lotman, Juri, 'Different cultures, different codes', *TLS* 12 Oct. 1973, 1213-15.

Lubbock, Percy, *The Craft of Fiction* (London, 1921).

Lukács, Georg, *The Theory of the Novel*, trans. A. Bostock (London, 1971).

Luria, Maxwell S., 'The Storm-making Spring and the Meaning of Chrétien's *Yvain*', *SP* lxiv (1967), 564-85.

Lyons, Faith, '*Entencion* in Chrétien's *Lancelot*', *SP* li (1954), 425-30.

The Mabinogion, trans. Jeffrey Gantz (Penguin, Harmondsworth, 1976).

Macherey, Pierre, *Pour une théorie de la production littéraire* (Paris, 1966).

Mackey, Mary, 'Rhetoric and Characterization in *Don Quijote*', *HR* xlii (1974), 51-66.

Madariaga, Salvador de, *Guía del lector del 'Quijote'*, 3rd edn. (Buenos Aires, 1947).

Don Quixote: An Introductory Essay in Psychology (Oxford, 1935; in paperback, 1961).

Maldonado de Guevara, F., 'Apuntes para la fijación de las estructuras esenciales en el *Quijote*', *AC* i (1951), 133-231.

'Del *Ingenium* de Cervantes al de Gracián', *AC* vi (1957), 97-111.

Mancing, Howard, 'Cervantes and the Tradition of Chivalric Poetry', *FMLS* xi (1975), 177-91.

The Chivalric World of 'Don Quijote': Style, Structure, and Narrative Technique (Columbia, Missouri, and London, 1982).

Mandel, Oscar, 'The Function of the Norm in *Don Quixote*', *MPh* lv (1957), 154-63.

Mann, Thomas, 'Voyage with Don Quixote' in *Cervantes: A Collection of Critical Essays*, ed. Lowry Nelson, Jr. (Englewood Cliffs, NJ, 1969), 49-72.

Maravall, J.A., *Utopía y contrautopía en el Quijote* (Santiago de Compostela, 1976).

Marías, Julián, 'La pertinencia del *Curioso impertinente*', *Obras completas*, iii (Madrid, 1953), 306-11.

Márquez Villanueva, Francisco, *Fuentes literarias cervantinas* (Madrid, 1973).

'La locura emblemática en la segunda parte del *Quijote*' in *Cervantes and the Renaissance*, ed. Michael D. McGaha, Juan de la Cuesta Hispanic Monographs (Easton, Pennsylvania, 1980), 87-112.

Personajes y temas del Quijote (Madrid, 1975).

'Sobre la génesis literaria de Sancho Panza', *AC* vii (1958), 123-55.

Martorell, Joanot, *Tirante el Blanco* in *Libros de caballerías españoles*, ed. F. Buendía (Madrid, 1954).

McGaha, Michael D., ed., *Cervantes and the Renaissance*, Juan de la Cuesta Hispanic Monographs (Easton, Pennsylvania, 1980).

Menéndez Pidal, R., 'Un aspecto en la elaboración del Quijote' in *De Cervantes y Lope de Vega* (Buenos Aires, 1948), 9-60.

Menéndez y Pelayo, M., 'Cultura literaria de Miguel de Cervantes y elaboración del *Quijote*' [1905] in *Discursos* (Madrid, 1956).

Orígenes de la novela (4 vols. Madrid, 1962).

Michels, R. J., 'Deux traces du *Chevalier de la Charrette* observées dans l'*Amadís de Gaula*', *BHisp* xxxvii (1935), 478-80.

Misrahi, Jean, 'Symbolism and Allegory in Arthurian Romance', *RPh* xvii (1963-64), 555-69.

Molho, Maurice, *Cervantes: raíces folklóricas* (Madrid, 1976).

Moore, John A., 'The Idealism of Sancho Panza', *Hispania*, xli (1958), 73-6.

Moraes, Francisco de, *Palmerín de Inglaterra*, ed. Adolfo Bonilla y San Martín, *Nueva Biblioteca de Autores Españoles*, xii (Madrid, 1908).

Moreno Báez, Enrique, 'Arquitectura del *Quijote*', *RFE* xxxii (1948), 269-85.

Reflexiones sobre el Quijote (Madrid, 1968).

Morgan, Louise B., 'The Source of the Fountain Story in the *Yvain*', *MPh* vi (1908-9), 1-11.

Muecke, D. C., *The Compass of Irony* (London, 1969).

Irony, The Critical Idiom (London, 1970).

Muir, Edwin, *The Structure of the Novel* (London, 1929).

Mumford, Lewis, *Technics and Civilization* (London, 1934).

Murillo, L.A., *The Golden Dial: Temporal Configuration in Don Quijote* (Dolphin Book Co., Oxford, 1975).

Murtaugh, Daniel M., '*Oïr et entandre*: Figuralism and Narrative Structure in Chrétien's *Yvain*', *RR* lxiv (1973), 161-74.

Nelson, William, *Fact or Fiction: The Dilemma of the Renaissance Storyteller* (Cambridge, Mass., 1973).

Neuschäfer, H. G., *Der Sinn der Parodie im Don Quijote* (Heidelberg, 1963).

Nitze, W.A., 'The Fountain Defended', *MPh* vii (1909-10), 145-64.

' "*Sans* et *matière*"dans Chrétien de Troyes', *Romania*, xliv (1915-17), 14-36.

'*Yvain* and the Myth of the Fountain', *Speculum*, xxx (1955), 170-9.

Nolan, E. Peter, 'Mythopoetic Evolution: Chrétien de Troyes' *Erec et Enide, Cligès,* and *Yvain*', *Symposium*, xxv (1971), 139-61.

Oelschläger, Victor, 'Sancho's Zest for the Quest', *Hispania*, xxxv (1952), 18-24.

O'Kane, Eleanor S., *Refranes y frases proverbiales españoles de la Edad Media,* Anejo II, *BRAE* (Madrid, 1959).

Olmedo, F. G., S. J., *El Amadís y el Quijote* (Madrid, 1947).

Ong, Walter J., S.J., *The Barbarian Within* (New York, 1962).

Ortega y Gasset, José, *Ideas sobre la novela* (Madrid, 1925).

Meditaciones del Quijote [1914], 5th edn. (Madrid, 1958).

Osterc, Ludovik, *El pensamiento social y político del Quijote* (Mexico, 1963).

Painter, Sidney, *French Chivalry: Chivalric Ideas and Practices in Mediaeval France* (Ithaca, New York, 1957; Cornell Paperbacks, 1964).

Parker, A. A., 'El concepto de la verdad en *Don Quijote*', *RFE* xxxii (1948), 287-304.

'Fielding and the Structure of *Don Quixote*', *BHS* xxxiii (1956), 1-16.

The Humour of Spanish Proverbs, Canning House 9th Annual Lecture, Diamante Series, xiii (London, 1963).

Pensom, Roger, 'Rapports du symbole et de la narration dans *Yvain* et dans *La Mort Artu*', *Romania*, xciv (1973), 398-407.

Pépin, Jean, *Dante et la tradition de l'allégorie,* Conférence Albert-le-Grand 1969; Publications de l'Institut d'Études Médiévales (Montreal, 1970).

Percas de Ponseti, Helena, *Cervantes y su concepto del Arte* (2 vols., Madrid, 1975).

Pickens, Rupert T., '*Estoire, Lai* and Romance: Chrétien's *Erec et Enide* and *Cligès*', *RR* lxvi (1975), 247-62.

Pierce, Frank, *Amadís de Gaula,* Twayne World Authors Series (Boston, 1976).

Place, E. B., 'El *Amadís* de Montalvo como manual de cortesanía en Francia', *RFE* xxxviii (1954), 151-69.

'Amadís of Gaul, *Wales* or What?', *HR* xxiii (1955), 99-107.

'The *Amadís* Question', *Speculum*, xxv (1950), 356-66.
'Fictional Evolution: The Old French Romances and the Primitive "Amadís" Reworked by Montalvo', *PMLA* lxxi (1956), 521-9.
'¿Montalvo, autor o refundidor del *Amadís* IV y V?' in *Homenaje a A. Rodríguez-Moñino*, ii (Madrid, 1966), 77-80.
'Montalvo's Outrageous Recantation', *HR* xxxvii (1969), 192-8.
Plato, *Five Dialogues of Plato, Bearing on Poetic Inspiration (Ion, Symposium, Meno, Phaedo, Phaedrus)*, trans. Percy Bysshe Shelley and others (London, 1910).
Plato's Republic, trans. A. D. Lindsay (London, 1935, 1969).
Predmore, R. L., *El mundo del 'Quijote'* (Madrid, 1958).
'El problema de la realidad en el *Quijote*', *NRFH* vii (1953), 489- 98.
Prestage, Edgar, ed., *Chivalry* (London, 1928).
Preston, John, 'Plot as Irony: The Reader's Role in *Tom Jones*', *ELH* xxxv (1968), 365-80.
Prieto, Antonio, *Morfología de la novela* (Barcelona, 1975).

The Quest of the Holy Grail, trans. Pauline Matarasso (Penguin, Harmondsworth, 1969).

Read, Malcolm K., 'Language Adrift: A Re-appraisal of the Theme of Linguistic Perspectivism in *Don Quijote*', *FMLS* xvii (1981), 271-87.
Reason, Joseph, H., *An Inquiry into the Structural Style and Originality of Chrestien's 'Yvain'*, Catholic University of America Studies in Romance Languages and Literatures, No. 57 (Washington, D. C., 1958).
Redondo, Agustín, 'Tradición carnavalesca y creación literaria: Del personaje de Sancho Panza al episodio de la ínsula Barataria en el "Quijote"', *BHisp* lxxx (1978), 39-70.
Richards, I.A., *Practical Criticism* (London, 1929).
Principles of Literary Criticism (London, 1924).
Riley, E. C., '"El alba bella que las perlas cría": Dawn Description in the Novels of Cervantes', *BHS* xxxiii (1956), 125-37.
'Anticipaciones en el *Quijote* del estilo indirecto libre' in *III Congreso de la Asociación Internacional de Hispanistas* (Salamanca, 1971).
'Aspectos del concepto de *Admiratio* en la teoría literaria del Siglo de Oro', *Homenaje a Dámaso Alonso*, iii (Madrid, 1963), 173-82.
Cervantes's Theory of the Novel (Oxford, 1962).
'Don Quixote and the Imitation of Models', *BHS* xxxi (1954), 3-16.
'Episodio, novela y aventura en *Don Quijote*', *AC* v (1955-56), 209-30.
'Metamorphosis, Myth and Dream in the Cave of Montesinos' in *Essays on Narrative Fiction in the Iberian Peninsula in Honour of Frank Pierce* (Dolphin Book Co., Oxford, 1982), 105-19.

'Symbolism in *Don Quixote*, Part II, Chapter 73', *JHP* iii (1979), 161-74.

'Three Versions of *Don Quixote*', *MLR* lxviii (1973), 807-19.

'Who's Who in *Don Quixote*? Or an Approach to the Problem of Identity', *MLN* lxxxi (1961), 113-30.

Río, Angel del, 'El equívoco del *Quijote*', *HR* xxvii (1959), 200-21.

Riquer, Martín de, *Aproximación al Quijote*, 2nd rev. edn. (Barcelona, 1967).

Robert, Marthe, *L'Ancien et le nouveau: de 'Don Quichotte' à Kafka* (Paris, 1963).

Robertson, D. W., Jr., 'Some Medieval Terminology, with Special Reference to Chrétien de Troyes', *SP* xlviii (1951), 669-92.

Rodríguez de Montalvo, Garci, *Amadís de Gaula*, ed. E. B. Place (4 vols., Madrid, 1959-71).

Amadis of Gaul, trans. Edwin B. Place, and Herbert C. Behm (2 vols., Lexington, Kentucky, 1974).

Las sergas del muy esforzado caballero Esplandián, ed. Pascual de Gayangos, *BAE* xl (Madrid, 1857).

Rodríguez-Moñino, A., 'El primer manuscrito del *Amadís de Gaula*', *BRAE* xxxvi (1956), 199-216.

Romero Flores, H. R., *Biografía de Sancho Panza, filósofo de la sensatez* (Barcelona, 1952).

Rosales, Luis, *Cervantes y la Libertad* (2 vols. Madrid, 1960).

Rosenblat, Angel, *La lengua de Cervantes* (Madrid, 1971).

Ruiz de Conde, Justina, *El amor y el matrimonio secreto en los libros de caballerías* (Madrid, 1948).

Russell, Bertrand, *History of Western Philosophy*, 2nd edn. (London, 1961).

Russell, P. E., '*Don Quixote* as a Funny Book', *MLR* lxiv (1969), 312-26.

Ryding, W. W., 'Narrative Structure, Free Association, and Chrétien's Lion', *Symposium*, xxiii (1969), 160-3.

Sainz, Fernando, 'Don Quijote educador de Sancho', *Hispania*, xxxiv (1951), 363-5.

Scholes, Robert, and Kellogg, Robert, *The Nature of Narrative* (OUP, New York, 1966).

Scruton, Roger, *Art and Imagination* (London, 1974).

Sedgewick, G. G., *Of Irony, Especially in Drama*, 2nd edn. (Toronto, 1948).

Sharrer, Harvey L., *A Critical Biography of Hispanic Arthurian Material I* (London, 1977).

Shirt, David J., '"Le Chevalier de la Charrette": A World Upside-Down?', *MLR* lxxvi (1981), 811-22.

'*Cligés*—A Twelfth-Century Matrimonial Case-Book?', *FMLS* xviii (1982), 75-89.

Singleton, Mack, 'The *Persiles* Mystery' in *Cervantes Across the Centuries*, edd. A. Flores and M. J. Benardete (New York, 1947).

Sir Gawain and the Green Knight, trans. Brian Stone (Penguin, Harmondsworth, 1959).

Sir Lancelot of the Lake: A French Prose Romance of the Thirteenth Century, trans. Lucy Allen Paton (London, 1929).

The Song of Roland: The Oxford Text, trans. D. D. R. Owen (London, 1972).

Southern, R. W., *The Making of the Middle Ages* (London, 1953).

Spitzer, Leo, 'On the Significance of *Don Quijote*' in *Cervantes: A Collection of Critical Essays*, ed. Lowry Nelson, Jr. (Englewood Cliffs, NJ, 1969), 82-97.

'Perspectivismo lingüístico en el "Quijote"' in *Lingüística e historia literaria* (Madrid, 1955), 161-225.

Stagg, Geoffrey, 'Revision in *Don Quijote* Part I' in *Hispanic Studies in Honour of I. González Llubera* (Oxford, 1959), 347-66.

'El Sabio Cid Hamete Venengeli', *BHS* xxxiii (1956), 218-25.

Stevens, John, *Medieval Romance* (London, 1973).

Tasso, Torquato, *Discorsi dell'arte poetica e del poema eroico*, ed. L. Poma (Bari, 1964).

Prose, ed. E. Mazzali (Milan, 1959).

Tharpe, Dorothy, 'The "Education" of Sancho Seen in his Personal References', *MLJ* xlv (1961), 244-8.

Thirlwall, Connop 'On the Irony of Sophocles' in *The Philological Museum*, ii (1833).

Thomas, Sir Henry, *Spanish and Portuguese Romances of Chivalry* (Cambridge, 1920).

Thompson, A. R., *The Dry Mock: A Study of Irony in Drama* (Berkeley, 1948).

Thompson, Albert Wilder, 'Additions to Chrétien's *Perceval*—Prologues and Continuations' in *Arthurian Literature in the Middle Ages*, ed. R. S. Loomis (Oxford, 1959), 206-17.

Thompson, J. A. K., *Irony: An Historical Introduction* (London, 1926).

Thompson, Raymond H., 'The Prison of the Senses: *Fin' Amor* as a Confining Force in the Arthurian Romances of Chrétien de Troyes', *FMLS* xv (1979), 238-49.

Togeby, Knud, *La Composition du roman 'Don Quijote'* (Copenhagen, 1957), translated into Spanish by Antonio Rodríguez Almodóvar as *La estructura del Quijote* (Seville, 1977).

Topsfield, L. T., *Chrétien de Troyes: A Study of the Arthurian Romances* (Cambridge, 1981).

Torrente Ballester, Gonzalo, *El "Quijote" como juego* (Madrid, 1975).

Troyes, Chrétien de, *Arthurian Romances*, trans. W. W. Comfort (London, New York, 1941, 1975).

Cligès, ed. from the Guiot copy by Alexandre Micha (Paris, 1957).

Cligès, trans. into modern French by Alexandre Micha (Paris, 1969).

Erec et Enide, ed. from the Guiot copy by Mario Roques (Paris, 1953).

Erec et Enide, trans. into modern French by René Louis (Paris, 1967).

Le Chevalier au Lion (Yvain), ed. from the Guiot copy by Mario Roques (Paris, 1960).

Le Chevalier au Lion (Yvain), trans. into modern French by Claude Buridant and Jean Trotin (Paris, 1972).

Le Chevalier de la Charrette (Lancelot), ed. from the Guiot copy by Mario Roques (Paris, 1958).

Le Chevalier de la Charrette (Lancelot), trans. into modern French by Jean Frappier (Paris, 1962).

Le Conte du Graal (Perceval), ed. from the Guiot copy by Félix Lecoy (2 vols., Paris, 1972).

Perceval, trans. into modern French by Jean Pierre Foucher and André Ortais (Paris, 1974).

Tuve, Rosemond, *Allegorical Imagery: Some Medieval Books and their Posterity* (Princeton, NJ, 1966).

Uitti, Karl D., 'Chrétien de Troyes' *Yvain*: Fiction and Sense', *RPh* xxii (1968-69), 471-83.

Unamuno, Miguel de, *Vida de Don Quijote y Sancho* [1905], 11th edn. (Madrid, 1958).

Van Doren, Mark, *Don Quixote's Profession* (New York, 1958).

Varo, Carlos, *Génesis y evolución del 'Quijote'* (Madrid, 1968).

Vilar, Jean-Pierre, 'Don Quijote arbitrista' in *Cervantes-Sonderheft* (Berlin, 1967), 124-36.

Vilar, Pierre, 'Le temps du Quichotte', *Europe*, xxxiv (1956), 3-16.

Vinaver, Eugène, 'A la recherche d'une poétique médiévale', *Cahiers de civilisation médiévale*, ii (1959), 1-16.

Form and Meaning in Medieval Romance, (Cambridge, *MHRA*, 1966).

The Rise of Romance (Oxford, 1971).

Wardropper, Bruce W., '*Don Quixote*: Story or History?', *MPh* lxiii (1965), 1-11.

'The Pertinence of *El curioso impertinente*', *PMLA* lxxii (1957), 587-600.

Watson, A. I., 'La primera salida de Don Quijote en busca de la confianza', *Clavileño*, vi (1955), 1-6.

Watt, Ian, *The Rise of the Novel* (London, 1957).

Weber de Kurlat, Frida, 'Estructura novelesca del *Amadís de Gaula*', *Revista de literaturas modernas*, v (1967), 29-54.

Weinberg, Bernard, *A History of Literary Criticism in the Italian Renaissance* (2 vols., Chicago, London, 1961).

Wellek, René, and Warren, Austin, *Theory of Literature*, 3rd edn. (Penguin, Harmondsworth, 1963).

Wetherbee, Winthrop, *Platonism and Poetry in the Twelfth Century: The Literary Influence of the School of Chartres* (Princeton, NJ, 1972).

Whitehead, F.,'Yvain's Wooing' in *Medieval Miscellany Presented to Eugène Vinaver* (Manchester, 1965), 321-36.

Williams, Grace S., 'The *Amadís* Question', *RHisp* xxi (1909), 1-167.

Williamson, Edwin, 'Romance and Realism in the Interpolated Stories of the *Quixote*', *Cervantes*, ii (1982), 43-67.

Willis, Raymond S., Jr., *The Phantom Chapters of the 'Quijote'* (New York, 1953).

'Sancho Panza: Prototype for the Modern Novel', *HR* xxxvii (1969), 207-37.

Wollheim, Richard, *Art and its Objects* (Penguin, Harmondsworth, 1970).

Woods, W. S., 'The Plot-Structure in Four Romances of Chrestien de Troyes', *SP* l (1953), 1-15.

Woodward, L. J., 'El casamiento engañoso y el coloquio de los perros', *BHS* xxxvi (1959), 80-7.

Worcester, D., *The Art of Satire* (Cambridge, Mass., 1940).

Wright, A. H., 'Irony and Fiction', *JAAC* xii (1953), 111-8.

Zaddy, Z. P., 'The Structure of Chrétien's "Yvain"', *MLR* lxv (1970), 523-40.

Zimic, Stanislav, 'El"engaño a los ojos"en las bodas de Camacho del "Quijote"', *PMLA* lv (1972), 881-6.

INDEX

145–57, 159, 160, 163, 166,
167, 168–9, 170, 173, 176, 179,
182, 201, 207, 211, 212;
negative, 27, 111, 155, 172,
217–18; positive, 16–17, 22,
23, 108, 155, 172

James, Henry, ix, 207

Kellogg, Robert, 176, 224, 225
Ker, W. P., 7

Lacy, Norris J., 216, 217
Lazarillo de Tormes, 80
Lida de Malkiel, M. R., 39, 225,
234
Lobeira, Joham de, 38
Loomis, R. S., 34
López Pinciano, Alonso, 76

Madariaga, Salvador de, 118,
170, 194, 232, 234, 237
magic, 12, 13–15, 20, 70, 90, 217
Mandel, Oscar, 234
Mann, Thomas, 189, 236
Map, Walter, 35, 36, 56
Maravall, José Antonio, 183
Marivaux, 208
Márquez Villanueva, Francisco,
239
Martorell, Joanot, 76; *Tirant lo
blanc*, 76, 81
marvellous, the, 50, 65, 70, 73,
75, 76, 90, 126, 161, 163, 180,
202, 204, 217, 230; in *Amadis*,
54–6; in Chrétien, 13–15,
16–19; 'legitimate', 75, 209; in
thirteenth-century romances,
35, 36, 222
matiere, 15
Matter of Britain, 1, 2, 6–7, 29,
32, 35, 70
Matter of France, viii, 70
Matter of Rome, viii, 220
Menéndez y Pelayo, M., 40
metaphor, 129, 131, 134, 136–8,

145, 222
Michels, R. J., 38
mimesis, 73, 74, 86–7, 229
miracles, 3, 13–15, 75, 130, 131,
213
Monmouth, Geoffrey of; *Historia
regum Britanniae*, 6, 7, 29, 34
Moreno Báez, E., 239
Muecke, D. C., 218, 228, 229
Murtaugh, D. M., 218

necessity, 47–8, 69, 74, 162, 174,
177, 180, 204, 237
Nelson, William, 224, 225
neo-Aristotelianism, 74, 75, 76,
77, 78, 81, 85, 86, 181, 204,
226, 229, 230
neo-Platonism, 3, 7
novel, the, ix, 7, 25, 182, 202,
210, 211, 230
novella, the, 78, 79, 161, 162

O'Kane, Eleanor S., 228
Oliveros de Castilla, 224
Olmedo, F. G., 225
Ortega y Gasset, J., 230, 233

Painter, Sydney, 6
Parker, A. A., 228–9, 234
parody, 18, 79, 81, 84, 85, 110,
123, 138, 141, 142, 163, 164,
165, 169, 177, 183, 184, 185,
186, 189, 192, 198, 199, 201,
208, 212, 236, 237
pastoral, 78, 94, 120, 123, 195,
208
pathos, 171, 176, 184, 198, 199,
201, 212
Patristic exegesis, 5, 131. *See also*
the *figura*
Percas de Ponseti, Helena, 234
peripeteia, 162, 213
Perspectivism, 91, 104, 109, 212,
230, 231, 233, 235
picaresque, the, 78, 79, 80
Pierce, Frank, 48, 49